SOUTHERN LAWNS

The Complete Guide to Growing Lawns in the South

CHRIS HASTINGS

LONGSTREET PRESS
Atlanta, Georgia

Published by
LONGSTREET PRESS, INC.
2140 Newmarket Parkway
Suite 122
Marietta, GA 30067

Printed in the United States of America

1st printing 2000

Library of Congress Catalog Card Number: 00-105065

ISBN: 1-56352-623-9

Cover photographs: Chris Hastings
Cover design by Burtch Bennett Hunter
Interior page layout and design by Jill Dible

DEDICATED
WITH ALL MY LOVE
TO AMY

TABLE OF CONTENTS

INTRODUCTION

A homeowner's dream is to have a green carpet of grass accentuating the beauty of the landscape and home. For those of us who have more than a few square feet of open area, it is as American as baseball and apple pie to turn it into a lawn. More money is spent on America's lawns to fulfill that dream than on any other part of the landscape. If developing a good lawn were as easy as buying a baseball ticket or making an apple pie, the amount of money we Americans spend on lawns would be less than we spend on shrubs, trees, and yearly flower beds. It isn't that easy, so we often spend more without getting the beautiful lawn we want.

Every lawn is different. The same grass may do well for you but look ratty next door despite receiving the same care. Lawns are different from one place to another because conditions may vary a great deal from yard to yard. Soils in an area are seldom homogeneous and yours may be much better than your neighbor's. The amount of sunlight reaching the grass varies with different types of trees. Your trees may give the right amount of light for your type of grass while theirs may give too much or too little. The topography may also be different, causing your neighbor to have problems like bad drainage that you do not have.

My turf professor taught us many years ago that if you lived a hundred miles south or a hundred miles north of Washington, D.C., your chances of having a good lawn were far greater than if you lived in between. South of the line you had to grow certain grasses like Bermuda Grass and Kentucky-31 Tall Fescue while north of the line you had to grow others like Kentucky Bluegrass and Creeping Bentgrass. In the middle, you didn't know what to grow.

This book is about lawns in the South because that's what the author, my son Chris, has grown up with and knows about. He's lived with my successes and failures. As a child, he romped on one of the early Centipede lawns in the South at his grandfather's home near Lovejoy, Georgia, south of Atlanta. Until he was grown and moved away to his own home, he helped me overcome old worn-out cotton soil, his and his brother's pounding feet, a whole bunch of puppies, and our neighbor's stray cows as well as our own horses loose

from nearby pastures. I freely admit that I frequently ask his advice when our grass needs attention, which it does now because we have our seventh puppy.

Few people really understand the principles of growing a lawn in the South, but Chris does. The right grasses to grow are easy to find. The general rules are set forth over and over, but failures are all too common. Chris explains the small things like the great effect soil temperature has on grass seed germination, fertilizer activity, and a whole host of other activities. He doesn't just tell you these principles; he tells you how to use them to have better success. I didn't know, until he told me, that an inexpensive meat thermometer is a great way to check my soil's temperature so I can plant grass seed at the right time and not waste my time and money because of poor seed germination.

Methods of planting are very different from the way we started a new lawn in my early days in the seed and nursery business. Now, it is as common as a hot July day to start an instant lawn from sod blocks or strips. These new planting methods give instant success but no immunity to future problems with weeds, improper fertilizing, bad watering practices, and insects and diseases. Chris has many of the answers stored in his brain and shares them freely.

I've learned a lot from reading the drafts of this book and wish I could have given it to my sister and brother-in-law many years ago when they were having little success starting a Zoysia lawn in an old section of Atlanta filled with water oaks. I threatened to stick a sign on her lawn that read, "No kin to Don Hastings." Her reply was how could they have a good lawn when she asked me, our mother who was a well-known horticulturist, and our father whose horticultural reputation was renowned, and each of us told her to do something different? So much for the sign.

Chris wrote this book for the likes of my sister, our friends, readers, and those in the South who need to know how to start and keep a beautiful lawn. I know it was also written for you and me to help us achieve the American homeowner's dream.

Don Hastings

How to Use This Book

BEFORE THE INVENTION OF THE LAWN MOWER, AND BEFORE OUR MODERN LAWN GRASSES were available, many people in the South had what was known as a "swept yard." It was a dirt area around the house that was free of vegetation and was swept routinely with a broom. The idea was to have an open space to discourage snakes and other creatures from coming near the house. Unfortunately, a swept yard would become a muddy mess in the first heavy rainstorm.

People grew tired of swept yards and started to grow grass lawns instead. A lush, green lawn is an obvious improvement to a swept yard. It prevents erosion, cuts down on dust and mud, cools the area, and is a wonderful place to enjoy a variety of outdoor activities. A well-grown lawn is also beautiful. It is an integral part of our landscapes and gardens and is one of the primary components of any good view. This may all seem self-evident, but there is one caveat that you must consider before you opt for a lawn rather than a swept yard. A lawn is a collection of grass plants. To grow one, you must dabble in horticulture.

Horticulture is defined as the art *and* science of growing plants. The art of horticulture is working a clump of soil in your hand and knowing that it could use some peat moss to improve the drainage. The science of horticulture is knowing that fescue roots grow best when the soil temperature is 50–65 degrees. This book contains a mix of the art and science of growing a lawn. I firmly believe that we need both to grow plants well. If you rely on the science and neglect the art, or rely on the art and neglect the science, it is pretty hard to succeed at growing anything, especially a lawn.

A lawn is a very specific entity. I have noticed that a person with a Bermuda Grass lawn could care less about how to grow Kentucky Bluegrass, and a person with a fescue lawn rarely enjoys a good discussion of overseeding. I have split this book into chapters that cover each specific Southern lawn grass. This way, you will know that the information you are reading is pertinent to your own lawn. As a result, items that appear in one chapter may be repeated when discussing a different grass in a later chapter. For those of you who have a Centipede lawn, you can skip the discussion of Bermuda Grass by heading directly to Chapter Three. If your next home has a fescue lawn, you can move to Chapter Six when you get there.

When it comes to growing a lawn, it is important to be on time and to be on target. The second section of this book is a month-by-month guide to growing a Southern lawn. It will tell you what to do and when to do it. Certain activities, like aerating, that appear in June might be repeated in July and August since you can aerate in those months as well.

For those of you who stray toward the scientific side of growing a lawn, I have included references to soil temperature in connection with many of the major lawn activities. I am a great believer in soil temperature as an accurate indicator of when to perform certain lawn tasks. While air temperatures fluctuate from week to week, the soil is insulated and buffered from unseasonable weather. The temperature of the soil steadily rises and falls with the seasons and is a good way to know when grass plants are growing and when weed seeds are germinating.

I have found that the easiest way to measure soil temperature is to purchase a meat thermometer from the local grocery store. They usually cost less than $10. Make sure the temperature gauge begins at 0° and does not have the words "rare/medium rare/well done." I have found these gauges to be just as accurate as soil thermometers ordered from a specialty supplier.

Using a soil thermometer is simple. Insert the probe 2–4 inches into the soil and read the gauge. I have recommended lawn activities based on the average soil temperature. A good way to approximate the average daily temperature is to take your measurement around noon in the shade. You might want to take several measurements in different areas of the lawn. You will be amazed how the temperature can vary on slopes, behind buildings, and in different exposures.

Another way to monitor soil temperature is to consult the Internet. There are numerous weather stations across the South that monitor soil temperature on a daily basis and publish their data on the web.

You can measure the soil temperature with a meat thermometer.

This topographical map of the South delineates the three growing regions referred to throughout this book:

LOWER SOUTH: The areas of the South that include the Coastal Plain from Virginia south to Georgia and west through Alabama to Texas.

MIDDLE SOUTH: The areas of the South that include the Piedmont region extending south from Virginia to Georgia and west through Alabama to Texas.

UPPER SOUTH: The area of the South that includes the western Piedmont and mountain regions from Virginia and North Carolina west through northern Tennessee and Arkansas.

A warm-season grass lawn in winter.

A warm-season grass lawn in summer.

An evergreen grass lawn in winter.

An evergreen grass lawn in summer.

Chapter One

Choosing a Southern Lawn Grass

ONE OF THE FIRST DECISIONS WHEN PLANNING A NEW LAWN IS TO DECIDE what type of grass you are going to use. There are two major types of grass used for lawns in the South: warm-season grass and evergreen grass.

The **warm-season grasses** are of tropical origin and thrive during our scorching summer heat. They are tough grasses and form a dense lawn cover that becomes thicker each year. They are not, however, green during the winter months. Their leaves turn brown in the late fall and new green leaves do not emerge until the weather warms in mid-spring. Generally speaking, a warm-season grass will be green about 55% of the year (approximately 200 days). Warm-season grasses are best suited for the lower and middle South. Zoysia and cold-tolerant cultivars of Bermuda Grass can be grown in the upper South.

The **evergreen grasses** are originally from Europe and grow best in the South during the fall and spring. They grow slowly during the winter months and struggle in the summer when temperatures soar into the 90s. Evergreen grasses grow into a beautiful lawn cover and have the unmistakable advantage of maintaining most of their green color over the winter. This is their primary selling point. People often nurse an evergreen lawn through the summer so they can enjoy its green color for the 165 days that their neighbor's warm-season grass is brown. Evergreen grasses are best suited for the upper and middle South and in most situations should not be considered as a general-purpose lawn grass for the lower South and Coastal Plain.

Warm-Season Grasses

The four major types of warm-season lawn grass have a variety of different characteristics and attributes. Make your decision based on your specific situation and preferences. You might want to consider the amount of shade in your lawn area, whether the kids and dogs play there, and the height at which you mow. If you spend a lot of time on the lawn, you might want to consider the texture of the grass—whether it is fine and soft, or coarse and rough.

Many people inherit a lawn when they buy a new house. If you are switching to a new kind of grass, try to pin down the reason that your current lawn isn't working. For instance, if your Bermuda Grass lawn is thinning underneath the trees, you might want to switch to a grass like Zoysia that will grow in moderate shade.

Bermuda Grass—Chapter Two.

Centipede—Chapter Three.

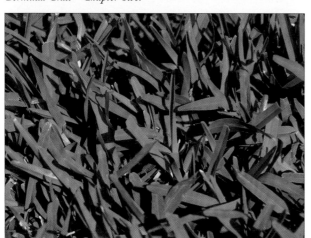

Saint Augustine—Chapter Four.

Zoysia—Chapter Five.

WARM-SEASON GRASS CHARACTERISTICS

Bermuda Grass

Texture: Common is medium/Hybrid is fine
Cold Tolerance: Good (some types more than others)
Shade Tolerance: Poor
Foot Traffic Tolerance: Good
Rate of Establishment: Medium/Fast
Regrowth When Damaged: Medium/Fast
Maintenance Level: Medium/High
Mowing Height: Low

Centipede

Texture: Medium
Cold Tolerance: Fair (damage possible below 15°)
Shade Tolerance: Fair/Good
Foot Traffic Tolerance: Fair
Rate of Establishment: Medium/Slow
Regrowth When Damaged: Medium
Maintenance Level: Low
Mowing Height: Medium

Saint Augustine Grass

Texture: Coarse
Cold Tolerance: Poor (damage possible below 20°)
Shade Tolerance: Good
Foot Traffic Tolerance: Poor
Rate of Establishment: Medium/Fast
Regrowth When Damaged: Fast
Maintenance Level: Medium
Mowing Height: High

Zoysia

Texture: Emerald is fine/Meyer is medium
Cold Tolerance: Good
Shade Tolerance: Fair
Foot Traffic Tolerance: Fair/Good
Rate of Establishment: Slow
Regrowth When Damaged: Slow
Maintenance Level: Medium/High
Mowing Height: Medium

Evergreen Grasses

Evergreen grasses are not naturally adapted to the Southern climate and you should choose one carefully. Do not merely buy the first bag of grass seed you find for sale. Stores often stock grass seed that is meant for specialty uses. In addition, large chain stores might stock seed that is more suitable for northern lawns. Some of these grasses will die promptly during a hot Southern summer.

Tall fescue (including Kentucky-31 and the Turf-types) and Kentucky Blugrass are general-purpose lawn grasses. They both have a dark green color and will form a thick turf when grown properly. They will also tolerate moderate amounts of shade. Tall Fescue is very versatile and is usually the best choice for the middle and upper South. Kentucky Bluegrass can be considered as an alternative in the mountains and western Piedmont regions of the upper South. Do not grow Tall Fescue or Kentucky Bluegrass as a general-purpose lawn grass in the lower South and Coastal Plain.

Creeping Red Fescue and Chewing Fescue are specialty grasses. They are very tolerant of shade and are sometimes sown in the shaded areas of a Tall Fescue lawn. Creeping Red and Chewing Fescue are very similar to one another and are actually varieties of the same species. They are not as durable as Tall Fescue but have a finer texture. They will need plenty of water since they usually have to compete with tree roots in shaded areas.

Tall Fescue—Chapter Six.

Kentucky Bluegrass—Chapter Seven.

Creeping Red Fescue—Chapter Six.

EVERGREEN GRASS CHARACTERISTICS

Tall Fescue

Texture: Medium/Coarse
Growth Habit: Clump Forming
Area of Adaptation: Middle South, Upper South
Shade Tolerance: Fair
Foot Traffic Tolerance: Fair
Rate of Establishment: Medium
Regrowth When Damaged: Slow/Poor
Maintenance Level: Medium
Mowing Height: High

Creeping Red/Chewing Fescue

Texture: Fine/Medium
Growth Habit: Clump Forming
Area of Adaptation: Shade of Middle South, Upper South
Shade Tolerance: Excellent
Foot Traffic Tolerance: Poor
Rate of Establishment: Medium/Slow
Regrowth When Damaged: Slow/Poor
Maintenance Level: Medium
Mowing Height: Medium

Kentucky Bluegrass

Texture: Medium
Growth Habit: Mat Forming
Area of Adaptation: Mountains and Upper South
Shade Tolerance: Good/Fair
Foot Traffic Tolerance: Fair
Rate of Establishment: Slow
Regrowth When Damaged: Medium/Fair
Maintenance Level: Medium
Mowing Height: High

*Bermuda Grass is one of the most
popular Southern lawn grasses.*

Chapter Two

Bermuda Grass
(Cynodon sp.)

BERMUDA GRASS IS *THE* LAWN GRASS OF THE SOUTH. IT WAS THE FIRST WARM-SEASON grass on the scene over a hundred years ago and continues to be the most popular Southern grass. How can you not like a beautiful hybrid Bermuda Grass lawn? It withstands traffic, adores blazing hot temperatures, and spreads quickly into a dense mass. It is even forgiving of the occasional scalped spot, mole intrusion, and errant child with a shovel.

But besides these "selling points," Bermuda Grass just feels good. It is the perfect grass for bare feet, soccer kicking, baseball throwing, and kid stomping. It is used on golf courses (greens, tees, fairways), in baseball stadiums, football fields, and parks. It also won't stain your white poodle green.

There are those detractors who will tell you that Bermuda Grass is a weed and that its seeds end up in farm fields and flower beds alike. In all honesty, common Bermuda Grass is a problem weed for farmers and some gardeners. But don't be dissuaded! Hybrid Bermuda Grass is sterile and does not produce seeds that can cause problems in a garden. The worst you will have to worry about is your lawn inching out over the driveway. And that is a small price to pay for a dense, thick, beautiful lawn.

At a Glance:

- Tough, thick, durable grass
- Light green to dark green, depending on the cultivar
- Hates shade
- Spreads well
- Can be seeded, sodded, or plugged
- Mowed at 1-2 inches when it reaches 1.5-3 inches
- Needs 4-5 lbs. of actual nitrogen per 1000 square feet per year applied in three applications

I. Maintaining an Established Bermuda Grass Lawn

While Bermuda Grass is known as a durable grass, you will need to work on it every weekend to have a lawn that thrives and is the envy of the neighborhood. In most cases, Bermuda Grass will flourish when mowed consistently at the correct height, irrigated when needed, and fertilized regularly.

MOWING

One of the first jobs of the spring season is to mow your brown Bermuda Grass lawn to remove as much dead top-growth as possible. Set your mower lower than normal at about .5–1 inch. Try to do this after the danger of hard freezes has passed, but before new grass blades emerge. This is usually in mid-March when soil temperatures are around 55° and the Bradford Pear trees are in full bloom. Do not mow below .5 inches or you may damage grass rhizomes and stolons growing near the soil surface. Bag your grass clippings as you mow to remove as much of the debris as possible and prevent thatch accumulations—do not leave the clippings sitting on the soil surface. If you live in the middle or upper South, do not mow your dormant lawn too early. The dormant blades act as insulation and prevent hard freezes from affecting shallow roots and rhizomes.

Your lawn will begin to turn green several weeks later when the soil warms to 60–65°. This is usually in mid-March to mid-April, depending on the weather.

If you wait too long before mowing, you will scalp your lawn.

Do not mow your lawn lower at this time than you will mow during the rest of the season. Wait until it reaches the recommended height.

There are generally two categories of Bermuda Grass lawns: common Bermuda Grass (like Common, Sahara, and Yuma) and hybrid Bermuda Grass (like TifGreen and Tifway). Throughout the growing season, mow common Bermuda Grass at 2 inches and mow hybrid Bermuda Grass at 1–1.5 inches. (Note: for an easy method for accurately setting the height of your mower blade, see Rotary Mower in the Glossary.)

> **Rhizome:** a modified stem that grows horizontally on, or just below, the soil surface and sends up stems or leaves from the tip.
> **Stolon:** a shoot that grows horizontally near the soil surface, rooting at the nodes to form new plants.

Once you have determined the correct mowing height for your type of Bermuda Grass, mow frequently and consistently. One of the worst things for a lawn is to allow it to grow tall before you mow again. If you remove more than one-third of a grass blade at a time, you will shock your lawn and stall its growth. During the ensuing recovery period, the lawn is more susceptible to stresses like heat, weed competition, and drought. The chart on page 9 will help you mow at the right height, at the right time.

If you allow your Bermuda Grass to grow much higher than about three inches, you will scalp your lawn by removing most of the green portion of the grass when you mow. This is not only ugly, but it is absolutely horrible for your lawn. If compounded by heat and drought, scalping during the summer can kill areas of your lawn. Avoid this at all costs.

With the rise in popularity of golf, people often wonder why their hybrid Bermuda Grass lawn does not look like a hybrid Bermuda Grass golf green. The answer is that it could look like a golf green! Unfortunately, you would need a specialized reel mower with 9–11 blades per reel that can cut at a very low height. Second, the lawn would have to be mowed

Recommended Mowing Heights (in inches)		
TYPE OF BERMUDA GRASS	MOW TO:	MOW WHEN GRASS IS:
Common Bermuda Grass	2	3
Hybrid Bermuda Grass	1–1.5	1.5–2.25

constantly so that you would not break the one-third rule. In fact, golf greens are mowed daily to maintain the grass like a lush green carpet. Even if you lowered your mowing height to a mere .5 inches, you would probably need to mow your hybrid Bermuda Grass lawn every 2–3 days.

> **The One-Third Rule:** Never reduce the height of your lawn by more than one-third when mowing.

Allow your Bermuda Grass to grow to 3 inches in the fall in preparation for cold weather. This extra height will act as insulation for roots, rhizomes, and stolons over the winter months. Plan ahead because Bermuda Grass grows slowly in late fall.

IRRIGATION

People often claim that Bermuda Grass is a drought-resistant grass. This is true, but it might give you the wrong impression. As a plant, Bermuda Grass is drought-resistant and capable of surviving extended dry periods in a semi-dormant state. As a lawn, Bermuda Grass requires

Bermuda Grass lawns lose their color and thin without rainfall or irrigation.

weekly rainfall or irrigation to remain dark green, thick, and lush. A drought-stricken Bermuda Grass lawn will turn yellow, and then tan. With consistent rain, it will green up, but it will be thinner than before and prone to weed infestations. A year after a drought hits, an un-watered Bermuda Grass lawn is usually filled with weeds.

In the South, we often have significant rainfall (on average) during the summer months but it is sporadic and undependable. It usually takes a little finesse to water only when your lawn needs it. In general, lawns will need 1 inch of water every 7–10 days if there has been no significant rainfall. Try to water deeply and infrequently. For example, apply 1 inch of water on a single day rather than .25 inches per day for four days. Deep and infrequent watering will train Bermuda Grass roots to grow deep into the soil where there is more moisture. Stop watering, however, if water begins to pool or run on the surface. Wait an hour or so until all the water is absorbed and begin again.

If you have an automatic sprinkler system, take a moment to investigate your control box and settings. Place a rain gauge or straight-sided jar on the lawn and turn on the sprinklers. Monitor how much water is applied in a given time period. Most systems will have several different types of sprinkler heads, so you might have to test each irrigation zone. I like to draw a rough diagram of the lawn and record the various sprinkler outputs for future reference. This helps me manipulate the irrigation system during the sporadic rain and drought periods of the coming season. Do not be shy about increasing the pre-set cycles during droughts or turning off the entire system after a heavy rainfall. While lack of water will affect your lawn's color and growth, excess water can kill a poorly drained Bermuda Grass lawn.

If you water your lawn with a manual sprinkler, use your gauge to make sure that you don't apply more, or less, than 1 inch at a time. Again, stop watering if water begins to run on the surface.

A dormant Bermuda Grass lawn will occasionally need to be watered during a winter dry spell to prevent rhizomes and stolons near the soil surface from drying out.

You will need to apply only .25–.5 inches of water at a time. If possible, water dormant lawns when temperatures are expected to drop below 20°. Wet soil will freeze and keep soil temperatures close to 32°, while dry soil allows damaging sub-20° air to penetrate the root zone.

> **One Step Further:** A grass plant absorbs water from the soil to replace water that evaporates from its leaf blades. The perfect way to irrigate is to supply the soil with the exact same amount of water that evaporates. Search the Internet for a weather station in your area that records "pan evaporation rate" or "evapotranspiration." Water loss from Bermuda Grass blades is roughly 75% of the pan evaporation rate.
> **Formula:** 75% x (Weekly Pan Evaporation Total) - (Weekly Rainfall Total) = Amount to irrigate that week

FERTILIZER

Fertilizing is one of the most satisfying lawn activities. Within a matter of days, a fertilized lawn will turn dark green and look healthy. This is especially true for Bermuda Grass because it responds very quickly to fertilizer. In fact, a Bermuda Grass lawn has one of the highest fertilizer requirements of any Southern lawn grass. It grows best with a steady, consistent amount of fertilizer supplied throughout the growing season (whenever the grass is green). If you apply more than the recommended amount, your lawn will not be any darker green, it will only grow faster and you will have to mow more often. The most efficient way to fertilize is to use one of the dry, granular fertilizers that are sold in 10–50 pound bags. Hose-end liquid fertilizers work, but they are difficult to use correctly and you will need to fertilize twice as often as with granular fertilizer.

> **Bermuda Grass Fertilizer Facts:**
>
> • 4–5 lbs. of actual nitrogen per 1000 sq. ft. per year
> • Three applications of 1.5 lbs. of actual nitrogen in mid-spring, mid-summer, and early fall
> • Use slow-release fertilizers whenever possible
> • Water approximately 1 inch after fertilizing

What Kind of Fertilizer to Use

Fertilizer is described by the percentages of nitrogen (N), phosphorus (P), and potassium (K) contained in the bag. All fertilizer bags are clearly labeled with these three numbers, known as the N-P-K ratio. Whenever possible, I use a slow-release lawn fertilizer with a 3-1-2 ratio. An example would be a 12-4-8 fertilizer. A bag of 12-4-8 fertilizer contains 12% nitrogen, 4% phosphorus, and 8% potassium by weight. The remaining 76% is inert material that adds bulk to the mixture and makes it easier to spread.

It is important to use slow-release fertilizers whenever possible. Most major brands of lawn fertilizer will have a combination of soluble and slow-release forms of nitrogen (indicated on the label). Soluble nitrogen is available to the grass plant immediately while slow-release nitrogen becomes available over a period of two to three months. In most situations it is best to have as much of the nitrogen in slow-release form as possible. Good brands of fertilizer will have 40–50% of the nitrogen in slow-release form. This is usually noted in a statement like "containing 6% nitrogen in slow-release form."

Be careful when using hose-end fertilizer sprayers or dry fertilizers in which all of the nitrogen is in a soluble, quick-release form. Soluble nitrogen will cause a major flush of growth for a week or two and will completely dissipate in 4–6 weeks. For most of us, it is almost impossible to fertilize with quick-release fertilizers without causing wild, fluctuating growth spurts. If you decide to use quick-release fertilizer, never apply more than 1 pound of actual nitrogen per 1000 square feet per application. You will need to fertilize every 4–6 weeks during the growing season for a total of 4 or 5 applications. Stay on schedule throughout the season so that nitrogen levels will remain fairly constant in the soil.

Up to this point, I have only mentioned three major nutrients: nitrogen, phosphorus, and potassium. These three nutrients are used by grass plants in relatively large quantities and are known as macronutrients. Grass plants use other nutrients in relatively small quantities. Those nutrients are known as micronutrients or "minor elements." Most major brands of fertilizer will contain the needed minor elements and you will not have to worry about them.

> **Common Forms of Nitrogen** *(indicated on the label)*
> **Soluble:** *Available immediately, lasts 4–6 weeks*
> Urea, ammonium nitrate, potassium nitrate, ammonium sulfate
> **Slow-Release:** *Available slowly in small amounts, generally lasts 2–3 months*
> Urea-Formaldehyde (UF), Isobutylidene diurea (IBDU), Sulfur Coated Urea (SCU), Polymer Coated Urea products (like "Polyon")

How Much Fertilizer to Apply

Most bags of fertilizer are covered from top to bottom with completely useless information that is written by the fertilizer company's marketing department. I continue to be amazed by the fact that the closest thing to directions is usually a vague phrase like "fertilizes up to 10,000 square feet." Luckily, there is a universal way to know how much fertilizer to apply, regardless of the brand or the specific N-P-K ratio. All you have to do is figure out how much "actual nitrogen" is contained in the bag. Bermuda Grass lawns generally need 4–5 pounds of actual nitrogen per 1000 square feet each year, regardless of the brand of fertilizer you purchase. If you use a fertilizer that contains a slow-release form of nitrogen, you can apply the needed nitrogen in three applications of 1.5 pounds of actual nitrogen per 1000 square feet in mid-spring, mid-summer, and early fall.

Unfortunately, the average bag of fertilizer does not tell you how much actual nitrogen it contains in the bag. It is easy to calculate, though, using two simple pieces of information: the N-P-K ratio and the weight of the bag. Multiply the percentage of nitrogen (the first number in the N-P-K ratio) by the weight of the bag and you will know the amount of actual nitrogen it contains. For instance, a 50-pound bag of 12-4-8 fertilizer has 6 pounds of actual nitrogen (12% of 50).

Determine the amount of coverage by dividing the amount of actual nitrogen in the bag by the amount of nitrogen you want to apply in a single application. With Bermuda Grass, you want to apply 1.5 pounds of actual nitrogen per 1000 square feet. Therefore, a bag that contains 6 pounds of actual nitrogen will cover 4000 square feet (6 divided by 1.5 pounds per 1000 square feet). If your lawn is less than 4000 square feet, remove the amount you do not need. Two

Fertilize in mid-spring after the danger of frost has passed.

Here is an example using a 50-pound bag of 12-4-8 slow-release fertilizer:

1. Multiply the nitrogen percentage (12%) by the net weight of the bag (50 lbs.) to determine how many pounds of actual nitrogen are in the bag (6 lbs.).
2. Next, divide the actual nitrogen in the bag (6 lbs.) by the amount you want to apply per 1000 square feet (1.5 lbs.).
3. Multiply this number (4) by 1000 to determine how many square feet the bag will cover (4000).
4. If your lawn is only 3000 square feet, you will need to apply only 75% of the 50-pound bag. Two cups of granular fertilizer weigh approximately 1 pound, so remove 25 cups.

cups of granular fertilizer weigh about 1 pound.

All of this calculating may seem like a hassle, but it really is the best way to apply the correct amount of fertilizer to your lawn. It is also a great way to compare the cost of different fertilizers so that you get a good deal. The best part is that you won't have to rely on the fertilizer company's marketing department for lawn advice.

How to Spread Fertilizer

You can apply granular fertilizer using a broadcast fertilizer spreader, a drop-type fertilizer spreader, a hand-held spreader, or by hand (wear a glove). I will be completely honest with you. Spreading fertilizer is not an exact science. The calibrated settings on even the most expensive broadcast spreader are usually inaccurate. In addition, the majority of spreaders will clog, break, and jam.

I have had great success with a very simple and effective method. Begin by measuring your lawn and calculating the amount of fertilizer that you need to spread (see "How Much Fertilizer to Apply"). If you only need 40 pounds of a 50-pound bag, remove 20 cups and set it aside. Next, turn off your fertilizer spreader and fill it. Begin moving and barely open the spreader only once you are up to speed. Try to spread as little fertilizer as possible while still broadcasting an even pattern. Continue covering the entire lawn at the same speed. If you must slow to turn around, turn off the spreader or you will drop too much in a single location and burn your grass. Work across the entire lawn until you return to your starting point and turn off the fertilizer spreader. Now, see how much of the needed fertilizer is left. If 50% remains, repeat the entire process and you will be finished. If 25% remains, repeat the entire process but move twice as fast. Remember, it is impossible to be exact. Your foremost

goal should be to spread the designated amount of fertilizer evenly over the entire lawn; avoid heavy doses in some areas and light doses in others.

When to Fertilize

When it comes to fertilizer, timing is critical. The following schedule will help you maintain a consistent level of nutrients in the soil so that your lawn will be healthy throughout the growing season.

• **Mid-Spring:** Bermuda Grass begins to green when soil temperatures reach a consistent 60–65°. The best time to apply fertilizer is after the danger of frost has passed and your lawn is at least 50% green. Depending on the particular year, this is usually in mid-March to mid-April, when the Dogwoods are in full bloom. Use a complete lawn fertilizer that contains a slow-release form of nitrogen. Apply at the rate of 1.5 pounds of actual nitrogen per 1000 square feet. This application will last 2–3 months.

Don't fertilize too early! It is hard to be patient with this first fertilizing of the season. The minute the Bermuda Grass begins to green, I have a driving impulse to run out and fertilize. Two things happen, though, if you fertilize early. First, you stimulate leaf growth at a time when the Bermuda Grass roots should be growing foremost. Second, early leaf growth is particularly vulnerable to late season freezes. Be patient!

• **Mid-Summer:** Fertilize again in mid-summer, approximately 2–3 months after your spring application. This is usually in late June/early July. I like to fertilize the weekend before the 4th of July so that my lawn will be gorgeous for the big barbeque. Use a complete lawn fertilizer containing a slow-release form of nitrogen. Apply at the rate of 1.5 pounds of actual nitrogen per 1000 square feet. This application will last 2–3 months.

• **Early Fall:** Fertilize your Bermuda Grass lawn again in late August/early September. You can use the same complete fertilizer as you have been using, or switch to a fertilizer with little or no phosphorus, but a higher rate of potassium. This might be something like 12-4-14 or 12-0-12. Either way, make sure the fertilizer contains a slow-release form of nitrogen and apply at the rate of 1.5 pounds of actual nitrogen per 1000 square feet.

Winterizing Lawns: There is a movement afoot to recommend a *late fall* application of fertilizer to "winterize" warm-season grasses like Bermuda Grass. Studies have shown benefits and detriments to these applications. In my opinion, the benefits are so short-lived that they do not justify the costs. Growing up in a family of horticulturists, one of the first phrases I remember hearing was "sounds like he's trying to sell some fertilizer." I think this could be one of those times.

• **Winter:** Do not fertilize Bermuda Grass lawns in the winter. You may stimulate your lawn to break dormancy during a winter warm spell only to be damaged in the next wave of freezing temperatures.

SOIL PH AND LIME

Liming a lawn is a way to raise the pH of the soil. Soil pH is measured on a scale of 0–14 with 7 being neutral. A soil pH below 7 is considered acidic while a soil pH above 7 is considered basic (alkaline). Bermuda Grass prefers a soil pH of 6–7. The pH of a soil is important because it affects the availability of different nutrients. Nitrogen in the soil is more available at a pH of 6 than a pH of 5, and liming would actually increase the nitrogen available to grass roots. In addition, a soil pH below 5 or above 7.5 can decrease the effectiveness of slow-release fertilizers.

The best way to determine your lawn's pH is to have the soil tested by your local Cooperative Extension Service. The soil test results will recommend the amount of lime needed to raise the pH to the optimal level.

Many Southern soils are acidic and will need approximately 50 pounds of lime per 1000 square feet. Whenever possible purchase lime in pelletized form since it is much easier to distribute. Broadcast the limestone with a fertilizer spreader, or by hand. Lime can take up to three months to affect the pH of your soil and can be applied at any time of the year. Since lime moves slowly in the soil, the best time to apply it is when planting or immediately after core aerating.

Occasionally, you may encounter an alkaline Southern soil with a pH above 7.5. In such a case, you can lower the soil pH to the 6–7 range with an elemental sulfur product. The most common form of elemental sulfur is aluminum sulfate. It is often available in 50-pound bags and should be applied at the rate recommended on the bag.

AERATING

Aerating a Bermuda Grass lawn is a great way to increase the flow of air, water, and nutrients into the root zone. Aerating each year will improve the quality, and consistency, of your lawn's growth. It can also be used to renovate areas like dry banks, poorly drained corners, and compacted dog paths.

Bermuda Grass lawns can be aerated any time during the growing season, as long as they are not suffering from drought. I prefer not to aerate dormant, brown Bermuda Grass since it will disrupt my late winter pre-emergence weed control application and open the soil to weed seed infiltration. In addition, I avoid aerating during spring green-up since it will damage tender roots and shoots at a time when the grass is low on stored energy. The best time for a once-a-year aeration is in the late spring when your lawn is completely green and soil temperatures reach 80°. This is usually in late May.

The only effective way to aerate a lawn is to use a core aerator. Core aerators are powered by an engine and remove cores of soil from the top layer of soil. Since most people do not own a core aerator, they rent one or have a lawn service aerate for them. Core aerators work best on moist soil so you will need to irrigate a day or two before you plan to aerate. A core aerator will bounce along the surface of dry soil. Run the core aerator across the lawn once or twice so that the average distance between the holes is about 4–6 inches. Afterwards, there will be cores of soil deposited all over the lawn. If the cores bother you, you can rake the lawn and most will break and drop below the level of the grass where they are not as noticeable. Otherwise, they will naturally disintegrate in a couple of weeks with the help of a few passing rainstorms. I prefer not to collect and remove the cores since they eventually return to the soil surface where they help thatch to decompose. Finally, irrigate the aerated lawn deeply to moisten exposed roots and rhizomes.

You will often see "spike aerators" of various sorts. Some roll behind a riding lawn mower; others are attached to fertilizer spreaders, and manual types look like a pitch fork that you are supposed to press into the soil with your foot. There are even special spike-clad shoes that claim to aerate while you wander around the lawn. When a spike is forced into the soil, it creates an opening but compacts the surrounding areas. Even worse, you would need to take 10,000 steps with spike-clad shoes to even come close to core aeration. In my opinion, all of these are useless and should be avoided.

DETHATCHING

Thatch is a collection of dead plant parts like stems and grass clippings that accumulate on the soil surface. Thatch is only a problem if it becomes thicker than .5 inches and grass roots begin to grow into it as if it was soil. Thatch dries very quickly in hot summer conditions and grass roots growing in it are much more susceptible to drought. When mowed at the right height and at the right time, Bermuda Grass lawns do not usually accumulate excessive amounts of thatch.

The best way to prevent thatch from accumulating is to begin the year with a clean slate. Before your Bermuda Grass begins to green in the spring, mow the entire lawn as described in the "Mowing" section to remove dead top-growth. After removing all of the debris, I usually rake the entire lawn vigorously with a metal-tined leaf rake to dredge up as much thatch as I can. This takes quite a bit of energy and requires that extra level of motivation. I have noticed that my level of motivation seems to be directly linked with the size of the lawn. On big lawns, you can skip the vigorous raking and opt for aerating in late spring. Core aerating also helps to prevent thatch from accumulating.

Occasionally, hybrid Bermuda Grass lawns will accumulate greater than .5 inches of thatch during the growing season. This is usually as a result of improper mowing or excessive fertilizing. In this case, begin by

aerating (if you have not done so already). If the problem doesn't go away in several weeks, you may want to rent a vertical mower or "dethatcher" from a tool rental store. Vertical mowing is tricky, though, and should be performed with extreme care. Do not cut too deeply or make more than one pass over the entire lawn. In addition, never vertical mow during periods of drought. After vertical mowing, rake and remove all the thatch brought to the soil surface and irrigate.

In the old days, people would burn their Bermuda Grass lawn during the winter to remove thatch and dead top-growth. This process works, but if the Bermuda Grass rhizomes and stolons are not completely dormant, you might kill large patches of your lawn. In addition, burning a lawn is extremely dangerous. I have had to fight pasture fires, and I can tell you that a grass fire burns quickly and expands exponentially. However tempting it may be, my best advice is to never burn your Bermuda Grass lawn.

TOPDRESSING

You may hear people at the golf course talking about topdressing Bermuda Grass golf greens. Topdressing is a technique used to create a smooth playing surface. A thin layer of soil or sand is distributed across the grass surface using a special topdressing machine. Bermuda Grass rhizomes and stolons grow into the topdressed soil and the grass shifts in response to the new, flatter soil surface.

Despite what many people think, topdressing is not a remedy for thinning turf or poor drainage. In fact, topdressing may compound these problems by smothering grass plants and causing the soil to form inconsistent layers. For the typical homeowner, topdressing should be limited to filling gullies and holes that make mowing difficult. A single depression should be filled layer by layer over the entire growing season, never covering the surface with more than .25 inches of soil or sand at a time. Greater amounts will smother the grass and cause more harm than good.

There are a few situations when you might consider topdressing your entire lawn. For instance, if your sod was laid poorly and the entire lawn is bumpy, you may want to hire a lawn care professional who has a topdressing machine and access to high-quality topdressing soil mixtures. Topdressing with the wrong grade of soil or sand can cause the soil to "layer," which obstructs drainage and causes growth problems.

Topdressing is not the remedy for a thinning or poorly drained lawn.

BLOWING AND EDGING

Many people own their own blower these days. Blowers are wonderful tools that take a lot of the backache out of lawn work. A blower can be used to clean debris from driveways, walks, and porches. It is also an invaluable tool in October when falling ieaves are getting the best of us. I also use a blower to disperse grass clippings if they accumulate in lines along the surface of my lawn.

There are three types of blowers: electric blowers, backpack blowers, and rolling street blowers. If you are going to be doing yard work for many years to come, I would definitely invest in a gas-powered blower. Electric blowers are inexpensive, but the inevitable tangled power cord is a complete hassle. Backpack blowers are great if you need a versatile machine that can reach various nooks and crannies. Rolling street blowers are the best for blowing leaves, but they are expensive and difficult to maneuver if your property has hills or steps.

Lawn maintenance companies regularly edge lawns and flower beds with a special machine that has vertically rotating blades. Most homeowners can accom-

plish the same effect by rotating their string trimmer and letting the string dig into the soil. Edging is largely a matter of aesthetics, although it does keep Bermuda Grass from creeping out across your driveway. Remember this, though. Edging opens the soil surface and will disrupt the chemical barrier of your pre-emergence weed control. It is common to see weeds sprouting between a lawn and a driveway after it was edged in early March. If needed, it is safer to edge during June, July, and August.

WEED CONTROL

While it may be hard to believe, most weeds blow into your lawn as seeds and sprout the minute they find enough bare soil, moisture, and light to grow. This is true for both annual weeds and perennial weeds. Annual weeds sprout, grow, flower, seed, and die within one year. Perennial weeds sprout from a seed as well, but the weed plant continues to grow and spread for more than one season (even though the top may die back in the winter).

Winter weeds are very noticeable in a dormant Bermuda Grass lawn.

Weeds enter a lawn for one reason: your lawn is not growing well. In fact, two of the most common reasons for weeds in a Bermuda Grass lawn are drought and shade. It is not that drought and shade increase the number of weeds or weed seeds trying to creep into your turf. Instead, drought and shade cause Bermuda Grass to thin, thus offering weed seeds an open space to germinate and grow. Your trouble may be different. Compacted soil, cold damage, insect/disease damage, flooding, steep slopes (causing dry soil), lack of fertilizer, and irregular pH can cause Bermuda Grass to thin. The underlying point is that a thick, well-grown stand of Bermuda Grass is the first step toward "closing the door" and stopping weeds. Even then, most of us will have to employ various weed control measures to keep our lawns weed-free.

> ☛ **TIP:** Neighboring lawns, woods, and adjacent untended areas produce enormous numbers of weed seeds that blow into your lawn. If possible, mow or "weed-eat" them to prevent seed formation.

Types of Weed Control

There are two ways to control weeds in a lawn: as the weed seeds germinate (pre-emergence weed control) and after the weeds have already sprouted and are growing (post-emergence weed control). When using weed control products, always make sure the product is approved for use on Bermuda Grass and follow the labeled directions. Do not apply more than the recommended rate; it will not give you better results and may injure your lawn.

Pre-emergence weed controls kill immature weeds immediately after they germinate and before they emerge from the soil surface. Since annual weeds like annual bluegrass and henbit die and return from seed each year, a pre-emergence weed control will eradicate them from your Bermuda lawn over several seasons. At the same time, it will prevent annual and perennial weed seeds that blow into your lawn from emerging. Most pre-emergence products are sold in a granular form (with or without fertilizer) that you spread using a fertilizer spreader. It is important to spread the chemical "wall to wall" at the recommended rate. Areas that are not covered by the chemical will not be protected. After spreading the product, irrigate your lawn with at least .5 inches of water to activate the chemical (unless otherwise stated on the bag). Once activated, pre-emergence weed controls create a chemical barrier in the upper inches of your lawn that will prevent weed seeds from germinating. Do not cultivate, aerate, or disturb the soil after treating your lawn or you will disrupt the chemical barrier and open the soil to weed seed infiltration. Pre-emergence weed controls are usually effective for 2–3 months, depending on the temperature and amount of rainfall.

> **Pre-Emergence Weed Control:** Usually sold as a dry, granular product in a 10–30 pound bag. May be labeled as "crabgrass control" although it will stop other weeds as well.
> **Post-Emergence Weed Control:** Usually sold as a liquid that you spray from a pressurized sprayer or a hose-end sprayer. May be labeled as "broadleaf weed killer" or "grassy weed killer."

Post-emergence weed controls kill weeds that are already growing in your lawn. These products are referred to as "selective" since they are targeted at specific annual and perennial weeds listed on the label. Usually, controls will either treat grassy weeds like crabgrass (monocotyledons) or broadleaf weeds like chickweed (dicotyledons). Choose the weed control spray that best fits your needs. You may need to purchase a spray for each category of weeds. In most cases, post-emergence products are designed to disrupt one of the weed's critical metabolic processes and should be sprayed when the weed is actively growing. If the weed is dormant because of cold weather or drought (i.e., not using the metabolic process), it may not die. Post-emergence products are most often sold as a liquid spray. The liquid sprays are very effective when weeds are young and actively growing. Spray on a still day when air temperatures are between 60 and 80° and the grass is dry. Avoid spraying during the 4–6 weeks in the spring when your Bermuda Grass is greening up. Post-emergence weed controls are sometimes sold in a granular form that is spread with a fertilizer spreader when the grass is wet. The dry particles need the moisture to adhere to weed leaves.

> ☛ **WARNING:** Weed controls can have dramatic and damaging effects on ornamental trees, shrubs, and plants growing in or near your lawn. This is true for pre-emergence and post-emergence weed controls. For instance, some post-emergence sprays are absorbed by tree roots and can cause the leaves to burn or defoliate. Read the product label carefully for directions and never spray underneath shallow-rooted trees and shrubs like Dogwoods and Boxwoods.

Another group of post-emergence weed controls are the non-selective sprays like Round-Up. The term "non-selective" means they will kill all vegetation including your Bermuda Grass. The trick is that non-selective weed sprays are absorbed through plant leaves. During the winter months when your Bermuda Grass is brown, you can carefully spray green weeds without affecting the dormant Bermuda Grass. WATCH OUT! Be very cautious and make sure that your lawn's leaves and stolons have not emerged during a winter warm spell. Even then, spray only the weed and expect some Bermuda Grass in the vicinity to be killed as well.

When to Apply Weed Controls

When it comes to weed control, timing is critical. Pre-emergence weed controls have to be applied before weed seeds germinate or they are useless. Post-emergence weed control sprays and granules have to be applied when the weeds are young, tender, and actively growing. I have found that when it comes to weed control, it is always better to be a little early rather than a little late.

Under normal conditions, a thick, lush Bermuda Grass lawn will remain weed-free with two applications of granular pre-emergence weed control (late winter and early fall) and spot treatments of problem weeds with a post-emergence weed control spray in mid-winter and early summer. I have included two "optional" pre-emergence weed control applications for people trying to renovate a very weedy lawn and people that live near a major source of weeds like an old pasture.

• **Late Winter:** Apply a pre-emergence weed control when the soil temperature reaches a consistent 50°. This is usually February/early March, when the Forsythia is in bloom. This application will control annual weeds and perennial weeds that germinate in the spring. Make sure the product is approved for use on Bermuda Grass and apply at the rate recommended on the bag. Do not aerate for 3 months after you apply pre-emergence weed control because it will affect the chemical barrier. Irrigate after applying unless otherwise stated on the bag. Do not use a pre-emergence weed control that contains fertilizer. If you fertilize now, you might stimulate your lawn to break dormancy during a warm spell, only to be damaged by freezing temperatures.

• **Late Spring and Summer:** Apply pre-emergence weed control without fertilizer around June 1 to control annual and perennial weeds that continue to germinate into the summer (optional application). If your lawn is mostly weed-free, and weeds do not usually blow in from surrounding areas, you can skip this application. Use a product approved for use on Bermuda Grass and apply at the rate recommended on the bag. Remember not to aerate for 3 months after you apply pre-emergence weed control because it may affect the chemical barrier. Irrigate after applying unless otherwise stated on the bag.

Once your Bermuda Grass lawn is completely green and soil temperatures reach 75–80° (usually in May), begin treating weed outbreaks with a post-emergence weed control spray approved for use on Bermuda Grass. Do not spray weed control during March/April when your Bermuda Grass is turning green since it can harm your lawn. Most sprays should be used when the air temperature is 60–80° (check the product label) and weeds are young and tender. If you wait another month or two, weeds will be older, tougher, and require repeated applications to kill them.

If your lawn is still overrun with weeds in mid-summer, consider using a combination fertilizer/ post-emergence weed control (granular form) when you fertilize around July 1. Follow the labeled instructions and make sure your lawn is wet when you broadcast the product.

• **Early Fall:** Wait until soil temperatures drop to 70° to apply pre-emergence weed control (without fertilizer) to your Bermuda Grass lawn. This is usually September 15 in the upper South and October 15 in the lower South. If you think you will forget, you can apply pre-emergence weed control when you fertilize in early September but you will be sacrificing some effectiveness. This application will control weeds like Annual Bluegrass and Henbit that germinate in the fall and winter.

Either way, make sure the pre-emergence product is approved for use on Bermuda Grass and apply at the rate recommended on the bag. Irrigate after applying unless otherwise stated on the bag. This application will last 2–3 months.

• **Winter:** Apply a pre-emergence weed control without fertilizer 2–3 months after your fall application (optional application). This is usually in late November/early December. If your lawn is mostly weed-free, and weeds do not usually blow in from surrounding areas, you can skip this application. Use a product approved for use on Bermuda Grass and apply at the rate recommended on the bag. Remember not to aerate for 3 months after you apply pre-emergence weed control because it may affect the chemical barrier. Irrigate after applying unless otherwise stated on the bag.

During the winter, treat winter weed outbreaks as soon as you see them (young weeds will die quickly) with a post-emergence weed control spray approved for use on Bermuda Grass. This is usually in January and February. Most of your problems this time of year will be from annual weeds like Annual Bluegrass and Henbit. Spray on a warm afternoon (air temperature is at least 60°) when the weeds are young and actively growing. It may take two applications to kill them. You can also spray during the winter with a non-selective weed control like Round-Up. Make sure your Bermuda Grass is completely brown and spray only the leaves of the weeds. Be very careful because Bermuda Grass stolons and leaves can emerge very prematurely during a winter warm spell. With both types of sprays, read the product label for specific instructions.

INSECTS AND PESTS

Crickets, beetles, grasshoppers, worms, and a variety of other insects will take up residence in a nice, thick Bermuda Grass lawn. Some feed on grass blades, some feed on grass roots, and some feed on each other. Luckily, Bermuda Grass usually grows faster than the average insect can eat and we don't have to worry. In fact, a certain level of insect feeding can actually stimulate grass growth. There are, however, a few classes of insects that can increase in populations large enough to harm your lawn. These can be treated fairly easily with a soil insecticide or with natural products like BT and Milky Spore. The best time for a once-a-year insect treatment is in late July or early August.

Insect damage usually appears as an irregularly shaped patch of discolored or brown grass in a lawn. Driving around town in the summer, I usually pass a thousand lawns that could fit that definition. The problem is this. Only about ten of those thousand lawns are likely to have an insect problem. Lawns are finicky, and irregular patches of brown grass pop up for different reasons. One of the most common is drought. You might think your lawn is evenly watered but even a slight rise or a different soil texture can alter the amount of water that penetrates the soil. When you think you have an insect problem, look for another cause first. Then, wait to see if the troubled lawn area expands. Only then should you worry about treating with a soil insecticide. Following is a list of insects that may trouble a Bermuda Grass lawn. Don't panic! You may never see any of these bugs.

The most common and problematic insects on Bermuda Grass lawns in the South are white grubs. White grubs are the larval, soil-inhabiting form of several different types of beetles. The most notorious beetle in the South is the Japanese Beetle, known for its voracious feeding on Crape Myrtle, grapes, ornamental cherry trees, and almost anything green. Japanese Beetles lay their eggs in lawns and grassy areas beginning in July. The eggs hatch as white grubs in late July and begin a two-month feeding frenzy on grass roots. As soil temperatures cool in October, the white grubs tunnel down 4–8 inches into the soil where they pass the winter. As the soil warms in the spring white grubs move to the surface, feed briefly in April/May, and then pupate into beetles. Of all insects, white grubs are the most pervasive lawn problem in areas where you commonly see Japanese Beetles. White grubs can be controlled with a granular soil insecticide applied in early August according to the labeled directions. Milky spore is a natural product that contains spores of *Bacillus popilliae*, a disease that kills white grubs. Milky spore will not kill every white grub, but spores will remain active in your lawn for many years.

While white grubs feed on Bermuda Grass roots, there are several types of larval worms that feed on Bermuda Grass leaf blades. They include cutworms and sod webworms. Unlike white grubs, larval worms can have several life cycles during a given growing season and are less predictable in their arrival. In addition, they are night-feeders and hide in tunnels beneath your lawn during the day. Sod webworms leave behind a silken spider web on the surface of your lawn that you see first thing in the morning. Larval worm damage usually appears as areas of brown or unevenly clipped grass. They can be controlled with a soil insecticide approved for use on Bermuda Grass. BT (*Bacillus thuringiensis*) is an effective natural product.

Armyworms are another type of larval worm that feed in masses throughout the day and night. They move quickly and can literally devour a lawn. Keep a lookout beginning in the late spring and through the growing season. Young larvae eat the edges of grass blades while the mature larvae eat the entire blade. Armyworms usually affect an entire subdivision/area at a time, so listen to your neighbors and state agencies for "armyworm alerts." The worst outbreaks of large populations usually occur from July to October. If found, apply a soil insecticide approved for use on Bermuda Grass. BT (*Bacillus thuringiensis*) is an effective natural product. Damaged lawns can usually be revived with careful irrigation.

Billbugs are black, hard-shelled beetles with a curved snout like a short elephant trunk. You may see them in the spring as they prepare to lay their eggs. The eggs hatch into legless white grubs that feed on Bermuda Grass roots during the late spring and summer. Damaged lawns usually have circular areas of brown or yellowing grass. If you tug on the discolored turf, it will easily pull from the soil. Billbugs can be controlled with a soil insecticide approved for use on Bermuda Grass.

Mole crickets are a major concern in the lower South in sandy soils. These horrendous burrowing crickets tunnel through the soil at night, loosening the sandy soil and disrupting grass roots. Mole crickets are active throughout the growing season but are most common when night air temperatures remain above 60°. Damage usually appears as if someone cultivated areas of your lawn. They can be controlled with a soil insecticide labeled for control of mole crickets and approved for use on Bermuda Grass.

Chinch bugs can be a problem on Bermuda Grass, although they are most destructive on Saint Augustine and Centipede grass lawns. Infested lawns usually have irregular patches of yellowing or wilted grass in sunny areas. Chinch bug problems are most common in July through September. To confirm their presence, cut the top and bottom from a coffee can and pound it several inches into the yellow grass. Fill the inside of the can with several inches of water and maintain the water level for five minutes. The chinch bugs will float to the surface. Once you have located them, treat the area with a soil insecticide labeled for control of chinch bugs and approved for use on Bermuda Grass.

Fire ants drive me nuts. I have tried chemical control and home remedies and none of them seem to work that well. Every time I treat a mound, a new fire ant hill seems to pop up ten feet away. There are numerous entomologists working on the problem, so hopefully they will find a better cure soon.

If moles are tunneling through your lawn, they are probably after white grubs. Treat for white grubs in late July/early August and hope that the moles will go away also.

There is always another insect or pest that *might* plague your lawn. You might hear or read about ground pearls, nematodes, mites, viruses, and a long list of other potential problems. In general, don't worry. Just keep an eye on things and treat problems when you find them. Your lawn is tougher than you think.

DISEASES

Bermuda Grass is susceptible to a variety of fungal diseases including brownpatch, dollar spot, leaf spot, pythium, fairy rings, and spring dead spot. While individual diseases appear at different times of the year (depending on the weather), it is almost impossible to predict when your lawn will be afflicted. In many cases, a disease will

Diseases like Helminthosporium leaf spot may come and go without you knowing it.

come and go without your ever knowing it. Since fungal diseases are very difficult to identify, it is important to keep a sharp watch for anything abnormal.

In general, fungal diseases appear as brown or damaged patches of grass with smooth outlines. If you find a patch that fits this description, don't run out and spray the entire lawn with fungicide. Wait to see if the patch of damaged grass expands over the next day or two. It is likely that the fungal disease has already run its course. An "active" patch of diseased turf will grow and expand concentrically over a couple of days. Grass plants along the outline of the damaged patch will have the most telling signs: wilted plants, shriveled leaves, or discolored leaf blades. Once you have located one of these areas, spray with a lawn fungicide approved for use on Bermuda Grass.

If your lawn has a history of fungal problems, you may want to renovate the dead areas and then spray preventatively with a lawn fungicide the following year so that the disease does not recur. Follow the directions on the product label explicitly.

Many fungal diseases are exacerbated by water. This is especially true with fungal diseases that are prevalent in the spring and fall when daytime air temperatures are 60–80° and nighttime air temperatures are around 60°. During these critical times, do not irrigate unless it is necessary. When needed, water on a sunny day when moisture will evaporate quickly from grass leaves. If there is a daytime watering ban in effect for your area, irrigate immediately before dawn.

OVERSEEDING

If a tan, dormant lawn in the winter is more than you can bear, you might want to consider overseeding your Bermuda Grass lawn with a cool-season grass. The cool-season grass will germinate in the fall and begin to grow as your Bermuda Grass is going dormant. As spring arrives, your Bermuda Grass will begin to green as normal. During this "spring transition," the over-seeded grass and Bermuda Grass will both be alive and will be competing with one another. As the heat of summer arrives, though, the overseeded grass will die and leave the Bermuda Grass to prosper for the rest of the summer.

Bermuda Grass can be overseeded with a variety of cool-season grasses. The key is to choose one that will not last too long into summer, thus competing with your Bermuda Grass. Annual Rye (a.k.a. Italian Rye) is a good, generic choice for the South. It cannot tolerate hot weather and will die quickly as heat approaches. Perennial Rye can be used in the lower South although it lingers too long into summer in areas where fescue grows well. Creeping Bentgrass is another choice, but it is expensive and is seldom available. Do not overseed Bermuda Grass with Tall Fescue or Kentucky Bluegrass since they will last well into summer and compete with your Bermuda Grass.

Bermuda Grass can be overseeded with Annual Ryegrass for a green winter cover.

Steps in Overseeding

1. Do not apply pre-emergence weed control in the three months prior to overseeding.

2. Overseed Bermuda Grass lawns when the soil temperature drops to 70°. This is usually around September 15 in the upper South and October 15 in the lower South.

3. Prepare the lawn before seeding by mowing your Bermuda Grass to about 1 inch and by raking the lawn vigorously with a metal-tined rake.

4. Sow 6–8 pounds of Annual Rye per 1000 square feet and broadcast a complete lawn fertilizer than contains a slow-release form of nitrogen, if you have not done so already. Apply at the rate of 1.5 pounds of actual nitrogen per 1000 square feet.

5. Keep the soil surface moist for 7–10 days to ensure even germination. After that, water weekly if there has been no significant rainfall.

6. Begin mowing as soon as the Annual Rye reaches 2.5 inches. This is a good time to install a new mower blade, or sharpen the old one. A dull blade will rip seedlings from the lawn.

7. Continue to mow throughout the winter at 2 inches, whenever the grass reaches 3 inches.

8. Fertilize lightly every 4–6 weeks throughout the winter whenever the Annual Rye is light green. Use a fertilizer like 10-10-10 that contains a soluble form of nitrogen, not a slow-release form of nitrogen. Slow-release forms of nitrogen are not effective during winter cold. Apply at the rate of .5 pound of actual nitrogen per 1000 square feet. If using 10-10-10, this equals 5 pounds per 1000 square feet. Stop fertilizing in February, however, to slow its growth so it will not compete with your Bermuda Grass during the spring green-up.

9. In March, mow your lawn below 1 inch as described in the "mowing" section. This will shock the Annual Rye and give the Bermuda Grass a chance to emerge. The remaining Annual Rye will die once warm weather arrives.

II. Renovating a Bermuda Grass Lawn

There are those times that you walk out of the house and realize that your lawn is in horrible shape. Worse yet, a gloating neighbor points it out as he invites you for a tour of his immaculate turf. Regardless of the source of your motivation, a large percentage of "troubled" Bermuda Grass lawns can be renovated without extreme effort. The general rule is that if you can find two healthy Bermuda Grass clumps in a given square foot of lawn, you can renovate. Otherwise, grab your wallet and head for the section entitled "Starting a New Bermuda Grass Lawn."

The first step in renovating a Bermuda Grass lawn is to admit that there is a problem. There are two categories of problems that will ruin a Bermuda Grass lawn: maintenance problems and fundamental problems. Unfortunately, the results of both often appear the same. For instance, a thinning lawn can be the result of improper mowing or shade. Think about your lawn's history and work your way toward the logical cause.

CORRECTING MAINTENANCE PROBLEMS

As we know from golf, your game will not improve by buying a new set of clubs. You have to address the underlying problem with your swing. Read through the maintenance section above and determine if you are skipping any critical steps. Are you fertilizing, mowing at the right height, mowing consistently, aerating, irrigating, and applying pre-emergence weed control? Do you have an insect or disease problem? Address these problems accurately to stimulate your grass to grow denser, fill voids, and darken in color. Below are two "recipes" for Bermuda Grass lawn renovation. They cover approximately eight months of the year. Avoid renovation attempts in the two months when lawns are greening in the spring and the two months when lawns are going dormant in the fall.

CORRECTING FUNDAMENTAL PROBLEMS

There are times when all the maintenance in the world cannot cure a lawn's woes. In such times we have to remember that a lawn is not a cure-all. Bermuda Grass is not a plant that will grow where all other plants have failed. In fact, in certain situations there may be hundreds of plants more suitable for a particular area. See "Ground Cover" in the glossary for some suggestions. Remember this as you read the remedies below. The most efficient and inexpensive approach might be to reconfigure or abandon areas that are not suitable for a lawn.
• **Shade.** Bermuda Grass hates shade. Shaded lawns will become thin and weak. The only answer is to switch to a more shade-tolerant grass (like Zoysia), cut down a few trees, or reduce the size of your lawn to avoid the shade. Raising the mowing height in the shaded areas may alleviate some of the problem but

---

Recipe for Growing-Season Renovation *(May through August)*

1. Kill Weeds. Spray weedy areas with a post-emergence weed control as soon as possible. Young weeds die faster than mature weeds (see "Weed Control").

2. Rake. Rake the entire lawn vigorously with a metal-tined rake to remove leaves, dead weeds, grass clippings, rocks, etc.

3. Mow. Check your mowing height and mow frequently.

4. Irrigate. Water deeply once every week or so if there has been no rain. Don't drop the ball! Even short periods of drought can cause discoloration.

5. Fertilize. Fertilize immediately (if you have not done so) and again in late August/early September.

6. Aerate. Consider core-aerating to stimulate grass to grow and spread.

7. Do not topdress unless you are trying to smooth your lawn surface. It will not stimulate growth.

8. Control Future Weeds. Apply pre-emergence weed control ON TIME in the fall (see "Weed Control").

Recipe for Dormant-Season Renovation *(November through February)*

1. Kill Weeds. Spray weedy areas with a post-emergence weed control as soon as possible, on a warm day. Young weeds die faster than mature weeds (see "Weed Control"). Hand-pull problem weeds like bunches of fescue.

2. Control future weeds. Apply pre-emergence weed control ON TIME in late winter (see "Weed Control").

3. Scalp and rake. Be ready to scalp your lawn and rake it vigorously in late February/early March (see "Mowing").

4. Wait until late April **to fertilize** and late May **to core aerate**.

---

is often impractical. My favorite fix is to end the lawn at the edge of the tree canopy and grow a ground cover under the tree instead.

• **Compacted soil.** Compacted soil is low in oxygen and causes Bermuda Grass to thin and die. Consider aerating once or twice during the summer when soil temperatures are 75–80°. Also, evaluate the cause of the compaction and correct continuing problems by creating walkways for people and pets.

• **Poor drainage.** Bermuda Grass will thin and die in wet, soggy soils. These are also some of most difficult and expensive problems to correct. Before you begin, determine the source of the water and where it is trying to flow. Occasionally, you can correct poor drainage by diverting a water source (like a gutter outlet) or removing an obstruction (a clogged ditch). Other solutions include re-grading, French drains, and surface drains. Once the soil dries, core-aerate to help renovate the root zone.

• **Improper pH.** At the wrong soil pH, Bermuda Grass will grow slowly, lose density, and be light green/yellow *despite* your best maintenance practices. Always consider your maintenance routine before you blame soil pH. If you suspect soil pH, take a soil sample to your local Cooperative Extension Service testing. They will recommend the needed lime or elemental sulfur to correct the problem.

Many new lawns suffer because the soil was compacted during home construction.

III. Planting a New Bermuda Grass Lawn

There are three methods used to create a new Bermuda Grass lawn: sod, plugs, or seed. The most common method is to lay sod blocks so that they cover the entire new lawn surface "wall to wall." Plugging is a variation of sodding in which you plant pieces of sod about one foot apart. The lawn will develop over several months as the plugs grow to fill the gaps. Seeding is least common and least expensive. The hybrid Bermuda Grass cultivars are sterile, so your only option is to seed common Bermuda Grass or one of the new common Bermuda Grass cultivars.

A Sampling of Hybrid Bermuda Grass Cultivars:

• **Tifway (419):** Dark green, fine texture, dense
• **Tifway II:** Dark green, fine texture, dense, tolerates colder temperatures
• **Tifgreen (328):** Medium green, fine texture, very dense
• **Midway:** Dark green, medium texture, dense, tolerates colder temperatures

A Sampling of Common Bermuda Grass Selections:

• **Yuma:** Dark green, medium texture, dense
• **Sahara:** Dark green, medium/fine texture, dense
• **Mohawk:** Dark green, medium/fine texture, tolerates colder temperatures

---

Whether you are sodding, plugging, or seeding your new lawn, the best time of year to begin is in the late spring once the danger of frost has passed and the sod is green. The optimal soil temperature for establishing a new lawn is 75–80°. This usually occurs in May. With proper care, new Bermuda Grass lawns can be started throughout June and July. Try not to plant after August 1 because your new lawn will not have enough warm weather to become established.

☛ **TIP:** Soil-related problems are the number-one killer of new and established Bermuda Grass lawns. This is your only chance to fix soil problems! Kill weeds, cultivate the soil deeply, and amend with humus before you plant.

READING SEED LABELS

Common Bermuda Grass lawns can be grown from seed and will usually germinate in 1 or 2 weeks. Since seeding Bermuda Grass is not as common as growing it from sod, the seed you find at the nursery may have been there a while. It is very important to read the special seed label attached or printed on the bag for several pieces of information. First, make sure the germination test date is within the last year. Old seed will not germinate as well as new seed. Second, make sure the bag contains only Bermuda Grass seed. Do not buy a seed bag that contains a mixture of Bermuda Grass and other grasses like Bahiagrass or Carpetgrass. Despite what the package says, these other grasses will only look like weeds in your Bermuda Grass lawn.

Common Bermuda Grass Net. Wt. 5 lbs.	Lot: XXX-1234-XXX Origin: Arizona
98% Pure Seed 1% inert matter 1% weed seed Test Date: 2-1-20XX 98% Bermuda Grass	Germ: 85%

STEPS IN PLANTING A NEW BERMUDA GRASS LAWN

Planting a new Bermuda Grass lawn is not a one-weekend project. Laying a sod lawn is back-breaking labor and is especially difficult if you've been rototilling all morning. Imagine how it feels when it's 95°. The best thing to do is to spread the various steps over two weekends. For instance, I would strongly suggest cultivating one weekend and planting the next.

STEP 1. Spray existing weeds. The first step in planting a new Bermuda Grass lawn is to eliminate all weeds from the lawn area. Use a non-selective weed control like Round-Up. Plan ahead since you will need to wait approximately two weeks (check the product label) after spraying before you seed, sod, or sprig. Do not apply a pre-emergence weed control any time within three months of seeding a Bermuda Grass lawn.

STEP 2. Establish the grade. One of the best ways to guarantee a beautiful lawn is to establish the proper grade before you begin. This may be more than most of us can afford, but consider it nonetheless. The proper slope has the potential to prevent both drought and poor drainage. It also makes mowing easier. In general, a 2–6% grade is optimal.

STEP 3. Cultivate the soil as deeply as possible. Whether you use sod, plugs, or seed, grass roots will need to grow into the existing soil surface. The deeper you can cultivate the soil, the more quickly your lawn will establish and thrive. Remember to wait the allotted time after spraying your herbicide before cultivating. Begin by raking and removing debris like dead weeds, leaves, and rocks from the area. Next, cultivate the soil with a rear-tine rototiller. If you don't have a roto-tiller, consider renting one from a tool rental store. Rototill the entire area lengthwise, then again crosswise. Try to work at least 4–6 inches of soil into a nice pulverized soil mix. If you prefer not to rototill, cultivate as much of the area as you can with a hoe, garden rake, or shovel. Again, the deeper you work the soil, the better.

STEP 4. Amend the soil. Most soils will need to be amended with humus before you plant. In almost all cases, it is better to spend time amending the current soil with humus rather than hauling in new "topsoil." Humus is a general term for the organic material that naturally occurs in the top layer of soil. Unfortunately, most lawn areas are graded during home construction and the top layer of soil is buried or removed. Adding humus will renovate these soils by improving drainage in clay soils and improving water retention in sandy soil. Peat moss, composted bark products, and compost are all good choices. I prefer adding at least two 3.8 cubic foot bales of sphagnum peat moss per 1000 square feet. Work the peat moss into the top 4–6 inches of soil as you rototill.

STEP 5. Lime and fertilizer. A lawn is a big investment and it does not hurt to have the soil pH determined by your County Extension Service. Bermuda Grass prefers a soil pH 6–7, and your soil test results will recommend the specific amount of lime to add if the pH needs to be raised. Many Southern soils are acidic and will need approximately 50 pounds of pelletized limestone per 1000 square feet. Spread the limestone with a fertilizer spreader or by hand, and work it into the top layer of soil using a garden rake. At the same time, apply a complete lawn fertilizer that contains a slow-release form of nitrogen. I prefer to start lawns with a 3-1-2 ratio fertilizer like 12-4-8. Fertilizers labeled as "starter fertilizer" are helpful, but not critical. Apply at the rate of 1.5 pounds of actual nitrogen per 1000 square feet. Work the fertilizer into the top layer of cultivated soil using a garden rake.

STEP 6. Seeding. If you are seeding a Bermuda Grass lawn, plan on using 1 pound of hulled Bermuda Grass seed per 1000 square feet. Do not buy unhulled Bermuda Grass seed and do not a buy a mix that contains other types of grass. If you are unsure, check the seed label for the exact percentage of each ingredient. Also, make sure the seed is fresh by checking that the germination test date is within the last year.

Begin by raking the area to create as smooth a soil surface as possible. I like to use a leaf rake because it creates tiny furrows and ridges on the soil surface that "capture" the seed. Bermuda Grass seed is minute and should be mixed with an equal amount of dry sand before sowing. In short, if you have a 5-pound bag of seed, mix it in a bucket with 5 pounds of dry sand. The seed/sand mix can be placed in a spreader (a fertilizer spreader works fine) or broadcast by hand. When using a spreader, distribute half the allotted mix lengthwise and the second half crosswise to avoid any skips. Since Bermuda Grass seed is small, rake the area very carefully to cover the seeds with a fine layer of soil. Do not bury them under more than .25 inches of soil. Next, cover the lawn with a layer of wheat straw to prevent washing and erosion while the seed is germinating. You will need one bale per 1000 square feet. Finally, water the entire area to work the seed into the soil but do not water so much that the seed begins to wash. Bermuda Grass seed will usually germinate in 7–14 days.

STEP 7. Sodding. Before you lay sod, cultivate the soil as described in step 3. Do not skip this step! Bermuda Grass laid on uncultivated soil will be susceptible to a wide range of growth problems and will be very susceptible to drought.

Unless you are planting a small lawn, it is almost always cheaper and more efficient to order pallets of sod from your local nursery to be delivered to your house. Most people prefer to order enough sod to cover the entire lawn area "wall to wall." It is hard to measure an irregular lawn area, so you might want to order a little extra sod. Plan on laying the sod soon after it arrives on pallets. Stacked sod should not sit for more than a day or two. It is usually a good idea to cultivate and amend the soil one weekend, and lime/fertilize and lay sod the next.

Begin by raking the entire cultivated area to prepare as smooth a surface as possible. Be careful because the sod will mimic the soil surface below, not compensate for it. It is best for the soil to be moist at the time of sodding, but not wet. Start at the top of the lawn and lay the sod lengthwise, so that the long side of each piece of sod is running perpendicular to a hill or rise. As you place each piece of sod, work it tight against the surrounding pieces to prevent the edges from browning and ruts from forming. Sod is often cut on a slant so that the edges will overlap. Make sure the edges slant appropriately so that they interlock. Pound each block of sod with your palm to press it into the soil below and remove any air pockets. Stagger the second row of sod so that the perpendicular edges do not line up. The

result should look like a brick wall, not a checkerboard. If you are placing sod along steep gradients, pin them in place with stakes or metal pins (available from sod distributors) so they do not shift. Irrigate deeply once all the sod is placed.

STEP 8. Plugging. A plug is essentially a four-square-inch piece of sod. Plugs can either be purchased or you can create your own by cutting sod into smaller pieces. The idea behind plugging is to set each individual piece about a foot apart and allow the grass to grow together over the coming months to form a solid grass surface. Unlike sodding, individual plug roots must be worked 1–2 inches into the top layer of soil to cover the roots and provide support. Once all the plugs are set, the lawn should be irrigated. Plugging is less expensive than sodding because you purchase less grass. It usually takes about the same time to plug as it does to lay sod.

STEP 9. Irrigation during establishment. Whether you begin with seed, sod, or plugs, tend your lawn diligently over the coming 4–6 weeks. Begin by watering lightly every day. After a week or so, decrease the frequency of irrigation but increase the amount of water you apply. By six weeks, you should be applying an inch of water per week, in one application, if there has been no significant rainfall. If you have seeded your lawn, follow these same guidelines but rely on your instinct. If the soil surface is eroding or remains damp, skip a watering. If the soil surface dries rapidly, irrigate more frequently.

STEP 10. Mowing during establishment. Newly seeded common Bermuda Grass should be mowed as soon as it reaches about two inches. Use a mower with a sharp blade and cut frequently. Mowing will encourage the grass blades to toughen and spread. Sodded/plugged lawns should be mowed at 1.5–2 inches from the start.

STEP 11. Fertilizing during establishment. Fertilize six weeks after planting with a complete lawn fertilizer that contains a slow-release form of nitrogen. Apply at the rate of 1 pound of actual nitrogen per 1000 square feet. This application will last until you fertilize again in early fall (see "Fertilizer").

STEP 12. Weed control during establishment. Weeds are especially troublesome with seeded and plugged Bermuda Grass lawns. With sod and plugs, begin spraying weeds as soon as they appear with a post-emergence weed control approved for use on Bermuda Grass. Spray only the weeds since the spray may slow your lawn's growth. With seeded lawns, wait until you have mowed 2–3 times before you begin spraying with post-emergence weed controls. Check the product label for specific instructions. In all cases, do not use pre-emergence weed control products when you plant since it will prevent Bermuda Grass seed germination and hamper plug and sod root growth. Wait until the following fall to begin applying pre-emergence weed control.

Amend the soil with humus before you plant.

Work fertilizer into the top layer of soil with a garden rake.

Plugs are sometimes available in trays.

Individual plugs must be planted in the soil to cover the roots.

Plant Bermuda Grass plugs one foot apart in staggered rows.

Water thoroughly once all the plugs are planted.

*Centipede is a low-maintenance grass
that spreads by runners.*

CHAPTER THREE

Centipede
(Eremochloa ophiuroides)

MY GRANDFATHER HAD A CENTIPEDE LAWN AT HIS HOME NEAR LOVEJOY, GEORGIA, THAT he never mowed. It was at the end of the house under high pines and near a beautiful Flowering Dogwood tree. I still remember it as a magical place with dappled shade and pine needles poking up at angles from the dense Centipede. The grass seemed to be in a delightful equilibrium—never fertilized, never mowed. I think he had happened on one of those golden moments in gardening when everything comes together and a plant grows with little help from us.

Most of us will not be quite as lucky as my grandfather was with his Centipede. But then again, a Centipede lawn is well worth the occasional mowing and fertilizing. It is a resilient grass that spreads quickly by runners to form a thick stand of grass. It is soft and has a finer texture than Saint Augustine, its main lawn grass rival. It will grow in light shade and has few problems with pests.

I seldom run through these attributes, though, when thinking of a new Centipede lawn. Instead, I always choose it for those areas at the end of the house where the kids won't be pounding back and forth playing soccer and the dog won't be digging holes—those quiet areas meant for strolling in the dappled shade.

> **At a Glance:**
>
> - Tough, spreading, low-maintenance grass
> - Light green color
> - Prefers sun; will grow in light shade
> - Can be sodded, plugged, or seeded
> - Mow at 1.5–2 inches when it reaches 2.25–3 inches
> - Water approximately 1 inch of water per week during the growing season
> - Fertilize twice a year

I. Maintaining an Established Centipede Lawn

Of all Southern lawn grasses, Centipede is most often referred to as a low-maintenance grass. It is even called "lazy man's grass." It has grown in popularity because of its low fertilizer needs and spreading growth habit. These two factors also reduce the frequency of your mowing. Centipede does, however, have several critical maintenance issues. In fact, while the amount of lawn maintenance is small, the need to understand your Centipede lawn is great.

MOWING

At the end of the winter, a Centipede lawn will have a certain amount of dead top growth. Unlike other warm-season grasses, do not mow your Centipede closely before the growing season begins. Centipede spreads by stolons that grow along the surface of the soil. New grass leaves will grow from these stolons and it is best not to disrupt them when they are low on stored energy at the end of the winter. It is a good idea, however, to mow at 1–1.5 inches around the time the Bradford Pears are in bloom (mid-March). Rake and remove as many of the grass clippings and as much leftover thatch as possible.

Your lawn will begin to turn green several weeks later when soil temperatures reach a consistent 60–65°. This is usually in mid-March to mid-April, depending on the weather. Do not mow lower at this time than you will during the rest of the season. Wait until it reaches the recommended height.

Centipede lawns should be mowed consistently at 1.5–2 inches throughout the growing season. Most of a Centipede lawn's growth is horizontal, so you will not have to mow as frequently as with other types of lawn grass. Don't neglect to mow, however. Consistent mowing will train the grass to spread and form a dense turf. (For an easy method for accurately adjusting your mower blade to the correct height, see **Rotary Mower** in the Glossary.)

Centipede lawns are often grown in areas with partial shade. In these situations, Centipede grass plants elongate in much the same way a houseplant stretches toward light from a window. You can still have a beau-

tiful, thick lawn, but it helps to raise your mowing height to about 2.5 inches. This will prevent you from removing too much leaf material at a given time. The chart below will help you mow at the right height, at the right time.

Be careful not to allow your Centipede to grow higher than these recommendations. In some cases, you can scalp a Centipede lawn if it has grown too high. Scalping occurs when you remove most of the green portion of the grass.

Allow your Centipede lawn to grow to 3 inches in the fall in preparation for cold weather. This extra height will act as insulation for roots, rhizomes, and stolons over the winter months. Plan ahead because Centipede grows slowly in late fall.

Recommended Mowing Heights (in inches)

EXPOSURE	MOW TO:	MOW WHEN GRASS IS:
Full Sun	1.5	2.25
Full Sun, Light Shade	2	3

A consistently mowed Centipede lawn will be thick and healthy.

> **The One-Third Rule:** Never reduce the height of your lawn by more than one-third when mowing.

IRRIGATION

Centipede lawns will need to be watered during the growing season. They are not as drought-resistant as Bermuda Grass or Saint Augustine lawns (due to their relatively shallow root system) and will thin and become infested with weeds if not irrigated. This is not to say, however, that a Centipede lawn will wilt and die in modestly dry weather. Just be careful and keep your lawn watered with about an inch per week if there has been no significant rainfall.

The best way to water a Centipede lawn is deeply and infrequently. For example, apply an inch of water on a single day rather than .25 inches a day for four days. Deep and infrequent watering will encourage Centipede roots to grow deep into the soil where there is more moisture. Stop watering, however, if water begins to pool or run on the surface. Wait about an hour until all the water is absorbed and begin again.

If you have an automatic sprinkler system, take a moment to investigate your control box and settings. Place a rain gauge or straight-sided jar on the lawn and turn on the sprinklers. Monitor how much water is applied in a given period. Most systems will have several different types of sprinkler heads, so you might have to test each irrigation zone. I like to draw a rough diagram of the lawn and record the various sprinkler outputs for future reference. This will help you to manipulate your irrigation system during the sporadic rain and drought periods of the coming season. Do not be shy about increasing the pre-set cycles during droughts or turning off the entire system after a heavy rainfall. While lack of water will affect your lawn's color and growth, excess water can kill a poorly drained Centipede lawn.

If you water your lawn with a manual sprinkler, use your gauge to make sure that you don't apply more, or less, than an inch at a time.

Centipede lawns do not enter a deep dormancy during the winter months. In areas of the lower South, they might not even lose all of their color. Be aware of winter dry spells and apply .25–.5 inches of water to prevent stolons near the soil surface from drying out. In addition, water dormant Centipede lawns when

Centipede beyond the reach of a sprinkler often turns brown and is weed-infested.

temperatures are expected to drop below 20°. Wet soil will freeze and keep soil temperatures close to 32°, while dry soil allows damaging sub-20° air to penetrate the root zone.

> **One Step Further:** Grass roots absorb water from the soil to replace water that evaporates from its leaf blades. The perfect way to irrigate is to supply the soil with the exact same amount of water that evaporates. Search the Internet for a weather station in your area that records "pan evaporation rate" or evapotranspiration. Water loss from Centipede grass blades is roughly 75% of the pan evaporation rate.
> **Formula:** (75% x Weekly Pan Evaporation Total) – Weekly Rainfall Total = Amount to irrigate that week.

FERTILIZER

Fertilizing a lawn is satisfying, but can be one of those spring chores you would rather ignore. It is always a hassle to lug bags of fertilizer, haul the spreader out of the garage, and realize that you should have washed it better last season to prevent rust. Luckily, Centipede lawns have the lowest fertilizer requirement of any Southern lawn and only need to be fertilized twice. It is very important to understand that Centipede is not just *tolerant* of low levels of fertilizer, it *requires* low levels of fertilizer. In fact, it is more common for a Centipede lawn to suffer from excess fertilizer than lack of fertilizer. Don't get carried away!

Centipede Fertilizer Facts:

• 1–2 pounds of actual nitrogen per 1000 square feet each year

• Use a fertilizer labeled "Centipede Fertilizer"

• Two applications: mid-spring and mid-summer

• Water approximately 1 inch after fertilizing

What Kind of Fertilizer to Use

Fertilizer is described by the percentages of nitrogen (N), phosphorus (P), and potassium (K) contained in the bag. All fertilizer bags are clearly labeled with these three numbers, known as the N-P-K ratio. Whenever possible, I use a slow-release fertilizer specifically designed for Centipede lawns with an N-P-K ratio of 1-0-1. An example would be 15-0-15. A bag of 15-0-15 fertilizer contains 15% nitrogen, 0% phosphorus, and 15% potassium by net weight. The remaining 70% is inert material that adds bulk to the mixture and makes it easier to spread.

It is important to use slow-release fertilizers whenever possible. Most major brands of lawn fertilizer will have a combination of soluble and slow-release forms of nitrogen (indicated on the label). Soluble nitrogen is available to the grass plant immediately while slow-release nitrogen becomes available over a period of two to three months. In most situations it is best to have as much of the nitrogen in slow-release form as possible. Good brands of fertilizer will have 40–50% of the nitrogen in slow-release form. This is usually noted in a statement like "containing 6% nitrogen in slow-release form."

I do not recommend fertilizing Centipede lawns with hose-end fertilizer sprayers or dry fertilizers in which all of the nitrogen is in a soluble, quick-release form. Soluble nitrogen will cause a major flush of growth for a week or two and will completely dissipate in 4–6 weeks. Centipede does not grow well in situations where the level of soil nutrients fluctuates dramatically.

Up to this point, I have only mentioned three major nutrients: nitrogen, phosphorus, and potassium. These three nutrients are used by grass plants in relatively large quantities and are known as macronutrients. Grass plants use other nutrients in relatively small quantities. Those nutrients are known as micronutrients or "minor elements." Most good brands of Centipede fertilizer will already contain the needed minor elements and you will not have to worry about them.

Common Forms of Nitrogen *(indicated on the label)*
Soluble: *Available immediately, lasts 4–6 weeks*
Urea, ammonium nitrate, potassium nitrate, ammonium sulfate
Slow-Release: *Available slowly in small amounts, generally lasts 2–3 months*
Urea-Formaldehyde (UF), Isobutylidene diurea (IBDU), Sulfur Coated Urea (SCU), Polymer Coated Urea products (like "Polyon")

How Much Fertilizer to Apply

Most bags of fertilizer are covered from top to bottom with completely useless information that is written by the fertilizer company's marketing department. I continue to be amazed by the fact that the closest thing to directions is usually a vague phrase like "fertilizes *up* to 10,000 square feet." Luckily, there is a universal way to know how much fertilizer to apply, regardless of the brand or the specific N-P-K ratio. All you have to do is figure out how much "actual nitrogen" is contained in the bag. Centipede lawns grow best with 1–2 pounds of actual nitrogen per 1000 square feet each year, regardless of the brand of fertilizer you purchase. If you use a fertilizer that contains a slow-release form of nitrogen, you can apply the needed nitrogen in two applications of .75 pounds of actual nitrogen per 1000 square feet in mid-spring and mid-summer.

Unfortunately, the average bag of fertilizer does not tell you how much actual nitrogen it contains in the bag. It is easy to calculate, though, using two simple pieces of information: the N-P-K ratio and the weight of the bag. Multiply the percentage of nitrogen (the first number in the N-P-K ratio) by the weight of the bag and you will know the amount of actual nitrogen it contains. For instance, a 50-pound bag of 15-0-15 fertilizer has 7.5 pounds of actual nitrogen (15% of 50).

Determine the amount of coverage by dividing the amount of actual nitrogen in the bag by the amount of

Fertilize in mid-spring when the danger of frost has passed.

nitrogen you want to apply in a single application. With Centipede, you want to apply .75 pounds of actual nitrogen per 1000 square feet. Therefore, a bag that contains 7.5 pounds of actual nitrogen will cover 10,000 square feet (6 divided by 1.5 pounds per 1000 square feet). If your lawn is less than 10,000 square feet, remove the amount you do not need. Two cups of granular fertilizer weigh about 1 pound.

All of this calculating may seem like a hassle, but it really is the best way to apply the correct amount of fer-

tilizer to your lawn. It is also a great way to compare the cost of different fertilizers so that you get a good deal. This best part is that you won't have to rely on the fertilizer company's marketing department for lawn advice.

How to Spread Fertilizer

You can broadcast granular fertilizer using a rolling fertilizer spreader, a hand-held spreader, or by hand (wear a glove). I will be completely honest with you.

Here is an example using a 50-pound bag of 15-0-15 slow-release fertilizer:

1. Multiply the nitrogen percentage (15%) by the net weight of the bag (50 lbs.) to determine how many pounds of actual nitrogen are in the bag (7.5 lbs.).

2. Next, divide the actual nitrogen in the bag (7.5 lbs.) by the amount you want to apply per 1000 square feet (.75 lbs.).

3. Multiply this number (10) by 1000 to determine how many square feet the bag will cover (10,000).

4. If your lawn is only 3000 square feet, you will need to apply 30% of the 50-pound bag. Two cups of granular fertilizer weigh approximately 1 pound so use only 30 cups.

Spreading fertilizer is not an exact science. The calibrated settings on even the most expensive broadcast spreader are usually completely inaccurate. In addition, the majority of spreaders will clog, break, and jam.

I have had great success with a very simple and effective method. Begin by measuring your lawn and calculating the amount of fertilizer that you need to spread (see "How Much Fertilizer to Apply"). If you only need a third of a 50-pound bag, remove two-thirds and set it aside. Next, shut off your fertilizer spreader and fill it. Begin moving and barely open the spreader only once you are up to speed. Try to spread as little fertilizer as possible while still broadcasting an even pattern. Continue covering the entire lawn at the same speed. If you must slow to turn around, shut off the spreader or you will drop too much fertilizer in a single location and burn your grass. Work across the entire lawn until you return to your starting point and shut off the fertilizer spreader. Now, see how much of the needed fertilizer is left. If 50% remains, repeat the entire process and you will be finished. If 25% remains, repeat the entire process but move twice as fast. Remember, it is impossible to be exact. Your foremost goal should be to spread the designated amount of fertilizer evenly over the entire lawn; avoid heavy doses in some areas and light doses in others.

When to Fertilize

It is very important to fertilize Centipede moderately and at the right time. The following schedule will help you be on time and on target.

> ***Don't fertilize too early!*** The minute the first Centipede leaf emerges, most of us have a driving impulse to run out and fertilize. Hold off! Centipede is never truly dormant and fertilizer will stimulate it to begin growing immediately. This tender, leafy growth is particularly vulnerable to that inevitable late-season frost.

• **Mid-Spring:** Centipede lawns begin to green when soil temperatures reach a consistent 60–65°. Depending on the particular year, this is usually between mid-March and mid-April. The best time to apply fertilizer is after the danger of frost has passed and when your Centipede lawn is mostly green. This is

usually in mid-April. Use a fertilizer specifically labeled for use on Centipede that contains a slow-release form of nitrogen. A common formula is 15-0-15. Apply at the rate of .75 pounds of actual nitrogen per 1000 square feet.

• **Mid-Summer:** Fertilize your Centipede lawn again in early July, using the same kind of fertilizer and same procedure as in mid-Spring. This is your second and final fertilizer application of the season. Remember that Centipede prefers low levels of nutrients. Do not apply more than the recommended rate.

Light green or yellow Centipede is caused by an iron deficiency, not a lack of nitrogen (see "Lime, Soil pH, and Iron Deficiencies"). Centipede can be "greened up" with an application of liquid iron. Better yet, correct the underlying pH problem by applying an elemental sulfur product like aluminum sulfate. Apply both iron and aluminum sulfate at the rate recommended on the bottle/bag.

> ***Winterizing Lawns:*** You will hear a lot these days about winterizing lawns with a *late fall* application of fertilizer. This is not meant for Centipede grass. If someone suggests you fertilize your Centipede in late fall, he is surely trying to sell you a bag of fertilizer.

LIME, SOIL pH, AND IRON DEFICIENCIES

Soil can have a dramatic effect on the color, growth rate, and overall health of your lawn. One particular soil measurement, soil pH, is especially important in dealing with Centipede lawns. Soil pH is measured on a scale of 0–14 with 7 being neutral. A soil pH below 7 is considered acidic while a soil pH above 7 is considered basic (alkaline). Centipede lawns prefer a soil pH between 4.5 and 5.5, which is lower than other lawn grasses. We can manipulate soil pH by applying lime to raise the pH and elemental sulfur to lower the pH. Since most soils in the South are naturally acidic, we can often grow Centipede without having to change the soil pH. As a rule, your soil pH will not be too acid for a Centipede lawn and you should never apply lime.

The best way to determine the exact pH of your soil is to have the soil tested by your local Cooperative Extension Service. If your soil pH is above the preferred range for Centipede, the soil test results will recommend the amount of elemental sulfur needed to lower the pH to the acceptable range. Again, you can safely assume that your soil will never be too acidic for a Centipede lawn. *Do not add lime.*

Problems with Light Green or Yellow Grass

Centipede lawns are naturally light green and will never achieve the dark green hue of a Zoysia or fescue lawn. All too often we look at a Centipede lawn and think it needs to be fertilized when it is actually growing at its optimal color. This is especially dangerous since excess nitrogen applications can cause Centipede growth problems.

Centipede lawns can, however, become an abnormal yellow-green. This may be caused by one of several reasons. First, it could be chinch bugs. Pound a coffee can in the yellow turf as described in the "Insects and Pests" section on page 42. If you do not find chinch bugs, the problem is probably chlorosis. Centipede chlorosis is usually caused by an iron deficiency in soils with high pH (6 and above). You can correct an iron deficiency in one of two ways. First, you can spray with liquid iron for a short-term cure. Iron will help the Centipede to return to its natural green within a week or so. The darker color will last, however, for only about four weeks. Better yet, you can correct the iron deficiencies by lowering the soil pH to the 4.5–5.5 range with an elemental sulfur product. As you lower the pH, iron that is already in the soil will become available to the grass. The most common form of elemental sulfur is aluminum sulfate. It is usually available in 50-pound bags and should be applied at the rate recommended on the bag.

Centipede grass turns yellow in soils with a high pH.

Occasionally, Centipede lawns develop iron chlorosis because they are growing in compacted or soggy soil that is low in oxygen. You may see this problem in a low spot of the lawn near a surface drain. In these situations, grass roots have trouble absorbing iron from the soil. The best way to fix the problem is to correct your irrigation and add extra drainage if necessary. Compacted soils should be core aerated.

The same problem can occur in the spring if grass blades begin to emerge while soil temperatures are still cold. In these situations, the problem is short-lived and will correct itself within several weeks as the soil warms.

AERATING

Aerating is a great way to increase the flow of air, water, and nutrients into the grass root zone. Aerating each year will improve the quality and consistency of your lawn's growth. It can also be used to renovate areas like dry banks, poorly drained corners, and compacted dog paths.

Centipede lawns can be aerated any time during the growing season, as long as they are not suffering from drought. I prefer not to aerate in the spring before the grass begins to green, since it will disrupt my late winter pre-emergence weed control application and open the soil to weed seed infiltration. In addition, I avoid aerating during spring green-up since it will damage tender roots and shoots at a time when the grass is low on stored energy. The best time for a once-a-year aeration is in the late spring when your lawn is completely green and the soil temperature is near 80°. This usually occurs in late May.

The only effective way to aerate a lawn is to use a core aerator. Core aerators are powered by an engine and remove cores of soil from the top layer of soil. Since most people do not own a core aerator, they rent one or have a lawn service aerate for them. Core aerators work best on moist soil so you will need to irrigate deeply several days before you plan to aerate. A core aerator will bounce along the surface of dry soil. Make one or two passes across the entire lawn so that there is a hole every 4–6 inches. Afterwards, there will be cores of soil deposited all over the lawn. If the cores bother you, you can rake the lawn and most will break and drop below the level of the grass where they are not as visible. Otherwise, they will naturally disintegrate in a couple of weeks with the help of a few passing rainstorms. I

Core aeration increases the flow of air and water into the soil by removing plugs of earth.

prefer not to collect and remove the cores since they eventually return to the soil surface where they help thatch to decompose. Finally, irrigate the aerated lawn deeply to moisten exposed roots and rhizomes.

You will often see various kinds of "spike aerators." Some roll behind a riding lawn mower, others are attached to fertilizer spreaders, and manual types are like a pitch fork that you are supposed to press into the soil with your foot. There are even special spike-clad shoes that claim to aerate while you wander around the lawn. When a spike is forced into the soil, it creates an opening but compacts the surrounding areas. Even worse, you would need to take at least 10,000 steps with spike-clad shoes to even come close to core aeration. In my opinion, all of these products are useless and should be avoided.

DETHATCHING

Thatch is a collection of dead plant parts like stems and grass clippings that accumulate on the soil surface.

Centipede lawns seldom have a thatch problem since they grow slowly and grass clippings have plenty of time to decompose. Thatch can become a problem, however, if it becomes thicker than .5 inches and grass roots begin to grow into the thatch as if it was soil. This may happen to a Centipede lawn in very specific situations like when a lawn is over-fertilized. Thatch is dangerous because it dries very quickly in hot summer conditions and grass roots growing in it are more susceptible to drought.

In most cases, you don't need to worry about thatch. Begin the year by mowing your Centipede lawn to 1–1.5 inches in the early spring before it greens and bagging your grass clippings (see "Mowing"). If possible, rake your lawn at the same time with a metal-tined leaf rake. This won't do much good if your lawn is thick and forms a mat of intertwining grass stolons. It is helpful, though, in areas that are thinning where you can dredge up quite a bit of thatch from the soil surface. Collect and remove as much of the debris as possible. Aerating in late spring will also help to prevent thatch problems.

I prefer not to mechanically dethatch a Centipede lawn unless I have discovered a major, sustained thatch problem (.5 inches or more) and want to renovate the lawn. Even then I will do my best with a core aerator and raking before I rent a vertical mower, or "dethatcher," from the local tool rental store. Vertical mowing is tricky and should be performed with extreme care since it will ravage grass stolons. Do not cut too deeply or make more than one pass over the entire lawn. In addition, never vertical mow during periods of drought. After vertical mowing, rake and remove all thatch from the lawn surface.

Though you may have heard it's a good idea, do not burn your Centipede lawn during the winter in an attempt to remove thatch and dead top-growth. Centipede Grass stolons are not completely dormant in the winter and fire will injure them and kill large patches of your lawn.

TOPDRESSING

Topdressing is a process by which a thin layer of soil or sand is distributed across the grass surface using a special topdressing machine. You may have heard the term because it is a common practice on golf greens where it is used to create a smooth playing surface. The idea is that grass roots and rhizomes grow into the topdressed soil and the grass shifts in response to the new, flatter soil surface.

Despite what many people may tell you, topdressing is not the answer to thinning turf or poor drainage. In fact, topdressing may compound these problems by smothering grass or creating impermeable layers in the soil profile. For the typical homeowner, topdressing should be limited to filling gullies and holes that make mowing difficult. A single depression should be filled layer by layer over the entire growing season, never covering the surface with more than .25 inches of soil or sand at a time. Greater amounts will smother the grass and cause more harm than good.

There are only a few circumstances when you might consider topdressing your entire Centipede lawn—for instance, if your sod was laid poorly and the entire lawn is bumpy. In that case, you may want to hire a lawn care professional who has a topdressing machine and access to high-quality topdressing soil mixtures.

Topdressing with the wrong grade of soil or sand can cause the soil to "layer," which obstructs drainage and causes growth problems.

BLOWING AND EDGING

Many people own their own blower these days. Blowers are wonderful tools that take a lot of the backache out of lawn work. A blower can be used to clean debris from driveways, walks, and porches. It is also an invaluable tool in October when falling leaves are getting the best of us. I also use a blower to disperse grass clippings if they accumulate in lines along the surface of my lawn.

There are three types of blowers: electric blowers, backpack blowers, and rolling street blowers. If you are going to be doing yard work for many years to come, I would definitely invest in a gas-powered blower. Electric blowers are inexpensive, but the inevitable tangled power cord is a complete hassle. Backpack blowers are great if you need a versatile machine that can reach various nooks and crannies. Rolling street blowers are the best for blowing leaves, but they are expensive and difficult to maneuver if your property has hills or steps.

Lawn maintenance companies regularly edge lawns and flower beds with a special machine that has a vertically rotating blade. You can achieve the same effect by rotating your string trimmer and letting the string dig into the soil. Edging is largely a matter of aesthetics, although it does keep Centipede from creeping out across your driveway. Remember this, though. If you edge a lawn during winter and spring, it will disrupt the chemical barrier of your pre-emergence weed control and expose soil in which weed seeds will germinate. It is common to see winter weeds sprouting in the edged groove between a lawn and a driveway. You can avoid this by edging your lawn in June, July, and August.

WEED CONTROL

Have you ever wondered how all those weeds manage to pop up in the middle of your lawn? While it may be hard to believe, most weeds blow into your lawn as seeds and sprout the minute they find enough bare soil, moisture, and light to grow. This is true for both annual weeds and perennial weeds. Annual weeds sprout, grow, flower, seed, and die within one

Weeds quickly overwhelm a thinning Centipede lawn.

year. Perennial weeds sprout from a seed as well, but the weed plant continues to grow and spread for more than one season (even though the top may die back in the winter).

☛ **TIP:** Nearby woods, meadows, and untended areas produce enormous numbers of weed seeds that blow into your lawn. If possible, mow or "weed-eat" them to prevent seed formation.

Weeds invade a Centipede lawn for one reason: your lawn is not growing well. In fact, two of the most common reasons for weeds in a Centipede lawn are drought and dense shade. It is not that drought and shade increase the number of weeds or weed seeds trying to creep into your turf. Instead, drought and dense shade cause your Centipede to thin, thus offering weed seeds an open space to germinate and grow. Your particular trouble may be different. Soil compaction, cold

damage, insect/disease damage, flooding, steep slopes (causing dry soil), lack of fertilizer, and irregular pH can cause Centipede to thin. The underlying point is that a thick, well-grown stand of Centipede grass is the first step in preventing weeds. It's not always that easy, though. Weeds are a formidable enemy and most of us will have to include weed control as part of our lawn maintenance routine.

Types of Weed Control

There are two ways to control weeds in a lawn: as the weed seeds germinate (pre-emergence weed control) and after the weeds have already sprouted and are growing (post-emergence weed control). When using weed control products, always make sure the product you are using is approved for use on Centipede. Some herbicides will be approved for use on Bermuda and Zoysia, but *not Centipede*. Follow the labeled directions. Do not apply more than the recommended rate; it will not give you better results and may injure your lawn. Be very careful around ornamental plantings as well because certain weed controls can damage them.

Pre-Emergence Weed Control: Usually sold as a dry, granular product in a 10–30 pound bag. May be labeled as "crabgrass control" although it will stop other weeds as well.

Post-Emergence Weed Control: Usually sold as a liquid concentrate you spray from a pressurized sprayer or a hose-end sprayer. May be labeled as "broadleaf weed killer" or "grassy weed killer."

Pre-emergence weed controls kill immature weeds immediately after they germinate and before they emerge from the soil surface. Since annual weeds like annual bluegrass and henbit die and return from seed each year, a pre-emergence weed control will eradicate them from your Centipede lawn over several seasons. At the same time, it will prevent annual and perennial weed seeds that blow into your lawn from neighboring areas from emerging. Most pre-emergence products are sold in a granular form (with or without fertilizer) that you spread using a fertilizer spreader. It is important to spread the chemical "wall to wall" at the recommended rate. Areas that are not covered by the chemical will not be protected. After spreading the product, irrigate your lawn with at least .5 inches of water to activate the chemical (unless otherwise stated on the bag). Once activated, pre-emergence weed controls create a chemical barrier in the upper inches of your lawn that will prevent weed seeds from germinating. Do not cultivate, aerate, or disturb the soil after treating your lawn or you will disrupt the chemical barrier and open the soil to weed seed infiltration. Pre-emergence weed controls are usually effective for 2–3 months, depending on the temperature and amount of rainfall.

Post-emergence weed controls kill weeds that are already growing in your lawn. These products are referred to as "selective" since they are targeted at specific annual and perennial weeds listed on the label. Usually, controls will either treat grassy weeds like crabgrass (monocotyledons) or broadleaf weeds like chickweed (dicotyledons). Choose the weed control spray that best fits your needs. You may need to purchase a spray for each category of weeds. In most cases, post-emergence products are designed to disrupt one of the weed's critical

metabolic processes and should be sprayed when the weed is actively growing. If the weed is dormant because of cold weather or drought (i.e., not using the metabolic process), it may not die. Post-emergence products are most often sold as a liquid spray. The liquid sprays are very effective when weeds are young and actively growing. Spray on a still day when air temperatures are between 60–80° and the grass is dry. Avoid spraying during the 4–6 weeks in the spring when your Centipede is greening up because they can harm tender, emerging grass blades. Post-emergence weed controls are sometimes sold in a granular form that should be spread with a fertilizer spreader when the grass is wet. The dry particles need moisture to adhere to weed leaves.

☛ **Warning:** Weed controls can have dramatic and damaging effects on ornamental trees, shrubs, and plants growing in or near your lawn. This is true for pre-emergence and post-emergence weed controls. For instance, some post-emergence sprays are absorbed by tree roots and can cause the leaves to burn or defoliate. Read the product label carefully for directions and never spray underneath shallow-rooted trees and shrubs like Dogwoods and Boxwoods.

There are other post-emergence weed controls like Round-Up that are non-selective. The term "non-selective" means they will kill all vegetation including your Centipede lawn. During the winter months, it is tempting to spray green weeds with Round-Up since your Centipede is brown. WATCH OUT! Centipede lawns never become truly dormant during the winter months. Be very cautious and spray only the leaves of the weeds. Even then, expect some Centipede in the vicinity to be killed as well.

When to Apply Weed Controls

The timing of your weed control applications is critical. Pre-emergence weed controls have to be applied before weed seeds germinate or they are useless. Post-emergence weed control sprays and granules have to be applied when the weeds are young, tender, and actively growing. I have found that when it comes to weed control, it is always better to be a little early rather than a little late.

Under normal conditions, a dense Centipede lawn will remain weed-free with two applications of granular pre-emergence weed control (late winter and early fall) and spot treatments of problem weeds with post-emergence weed control spray in mid-winter and early summer. I have included two "optional" pre-emergence weed control applications for people trying to renovate a very weedy lawn and people that live near a major source of weeds like an old pasture.

• **Late Winter:** Apply a pre-emergence weed control without fertilizer when the soil temperature reaches a consistent 50°. This is usually February/early March, when the Forsythia is in bloom. This application will control annual weeds and perennial weeds that germinate in the spring. Make sure the product is approved for use on Centipede and apply at the rate recommended on the bag. Do not aerate for 3 months after you apply pre-emergence weed control because it will affect the chemical barrier. Irrigate after applying unless otherwise stated on the bag. Again, do not use a pre-emergence weed control that contains fertilizer. If you fertilize now, you might stimulate your lawn to break dormancy during a warm spell, only to be damaged by freezing temperatures.

• **Late Spring and Summer:** Apply pre-emergence weed control without fertilizer around June 1 to control annual and perennial weeds that continue to germinate into the summer (optional application). If your lawn is mostly weed-free, and weeds do not usually blow in from surrounding areas, you can skip this application. Use a product approved for use on Centipede lawns and apply at the rate recommended on the bag. Remember not to aerate for 3 months after you apply pre-emergence weed control because it may affect the chemical barrier. Irrigate after applying unless otherwise stated on the bag.

Once your Centipede lawn is completely green and soil temperatures reach 75–80° (usually in May), begin treating weed outbreaks with a **post-emergence weed control** spray approved for use on Centipede. Do not spray weeds during March/April when your Centipede is turning green because it may harm emerging grass blades. Most sprays should be used when the air temperature is 60–80° (check the product label) and weeds are young and tender. If you wait another month or two, weeds will be older, tougher, and require repeated applications to kill them.

• **Early Fall:** Wait until soil temperatures drop to 70° to apply pre-emergence weed control (without fertilizer) to your Centipede lawn. This is usually October 15 in the lower South and September 15 in the upper South. This application will control weeds like annual bluegrass and henbit that germinate in the fall and winter.

Either way, make sure the pre-emergence product is approved for use on Centipede and apply at the rate recommended on the bag. Irrigate after applying unless otherwise stated on the bag. This application will last 2–3 months.

• **Winter:** Apply a **pre-emergence weed control** without fertilizer 2–3 months after your fall application (optional application). This is usually in late November/early December. If your lawn is mostly weed-free, and weeds do not usually blow in from surrounding areas, you can skip this application. Use a product approved for use on Centipede and apply at the rate recommended on the bag. Irrigate after applying unless otherwise stated on the bag.

During the winter, treat winter weed outbreaks as soon as you see them with a **post-emergence weed control** spray approved for use on Centipede. This is usually in January and February. Most of your problems this time of year will be from annual weeds like annual bluegrass and henbit. Spray on a warm afternoon (air temperature is at least 60°) when the weeds are young and actively growing. It may take two applications to kill them.

INSECTS AND PESTS

It would be impossible to keep track of all the insects that live in a well-grown Centipede lawn. The most common inhabitants are usually crickets, beetles, grasshoppers, millipedes, and worms. Some of these insects feed on grass blades, some feed on grass roots, and some feed on each other. In most cases, your Centipede will grow faster than the average insect can eat and you don't have to worry. There are, however, a few classes of insects that can increase in populations large enough to harm your lawn. These can be treated fairly easily with soil insecticides and natural products like BT. The best time for a once-a-year insect treatment is in late July or early August.

Insect damage is often defined as an irregularly

Chinch bugs cause irregular patches of yellow or brown turf.

shaped patch of discolored or brown grass in a lawn. If you take a drive around town, you will probably pass a thousand lawns that could fit that definition. The problem is, only about ten of those thousand lawns are likely to have an insect problem. Lawns are finicky and irregular patches of brown grass pop up for different reasons. One of the most common is drought. You might think your lawn is evenly watered but even a slight rise or a different soil texture can alter the amount of water that penetrates the soil. When you think you have an insect problem, look for another cause first. Then, wait to see if the troubled lawn area expands. Only then should you worry about treating with a soil insecticide. Following is a list of insects that might cause problems in a Centipede lawn. Don't panic! You may never see any of these bugs.

White grubs are one of the most common insect pests on Centipede lawns. White grubs are the larval, soil-inhabiting form of several different types of beetles. The most notorious beetle in the South is the Japanese Beetle, known for its voracious feeding on Crape Myrtle, grapes, ornamental cherry trees, and almost anything green. Japanese Beetles lay their eggs in lawns and grassy areas beginning in July. The eggs hatch as white grubs in late July and begin a two-month feeding frenzy on grass roots. As soil temperatures cool in October, the white grubs tunnel down 4–8 inches into the soil where they pass the winter. As the soil warms in the spring, white grubs move to the surface, feed briefly in April/May, and then pupate. White grubs can be controlled with a granular soil insecticide applied in late July/early August according to the labeled directions. Milky Spore is a natural product that contains spores of *Bacillus popilliae*, a disease that kills white grubs. Milky spore will not kill every last white grub, but spores will remain active in your lawn for many years.

There are several types of **larval worms** that feed on Centipede leaf blades. They include cutworms and sod webworms. Unlike white grubs, larval worms can have several life cycles during a given growing season and are less predictable in their arrival. In addition, they are night-feeders and hide in tunnels beneath your lawn during the day. Sod webworms leave a spidery web on grass blades that you notice early in the morning. Insect damage appears as areas of brown or unevenly clipped grass. Larval worms can be controlled with a soil insecticide approved for use on Centipede. BT (*Bacillus thuringiensis*) is an effective natural product.

Armyworms feed in masses on Centipede leaf blades and are visible throughout the day and night. They move quickly and can literally devour a lawn. Keep a lookout beginning in the late spring and through the growing season. Young larvae eat the edges of grass blades while the mature larvae eat the entire blade. Armyworms usually affect an entire subdivision/area at a time, so listen to your neighbors and state agencies for "armyworm alerts." The worst outbreaks of large populations usually occur from July to October. They can be controlled with soil insecticide approved for use on Centipede lawns. BT (*Bacillus thuringiensis*) is an effective natural product.

A notorious insect problem in the lower South is the **chinch bug**. These disgusting little creatures can have numerous generations per growing season in the lower South. Their damage usually appears as irregular patches of yellowing or wilted grass and is most common in July through September. There is a fairly simple way to find out if they are there. Cut the top and bottom from a coffee can and pound it several inches into the yellow grass. Fill the inside of the can with several inches of water and maintain the water level for five minutes. The chinch bugs will float to the surface. If you find any, apply a soil insecticide labeled for control of chinch bugs and approved for use on Centipede.

Mole crickets are a major concern in the lower South in sandy soils. These horrendous burrowing crickets tunnel through the soil at night, loosening the sandy soil and disrupting shallow Centipede grass roots. Mole crickets are active throughout the growing season but are most commonly seen in the spring when night air temperatures remain above 60°. Damage usually appears as if someone cultivated areas of your lawn. Mole crickets can be controlled with a soil insecticide labeled for control of mole crickets and approved for use on Centipede.

I loathe **fire ants**. I have tried almost every chemical available, and a number of home remedies, and have had only average results killing them. Every time I treat

a mound it seems to pop up in another location. Sometimes the mounds seem to multiply. There are numerous entomologists working on the problem, so hopefully they will find a good cure soon.

If **moles** are tunneling through your lawn, they are probably after white grubs. Treat for white grubs in late July/early August and the moles will probably go away.

There is always another insect or pest that *might* plague your lawn. You might hear or read about ground pearls, billbugs, nematodes, mites, viruses, and a long list of other potential problems. In general, don't worry. Just keep an eye on things and treat problems when you find them. Your lawn is tougher than you think.

DISEASES

Under certain environmental conditions, Centipede lawns are susceptible to a variety of fungal diseases including brownpatch, pythium blight, dollar spot, and spring dead spot. These diseases are most prevalent in the spring and fall when daytime air temperatures are 60–80°, nighttime air temperatures are around 60°, and there is plenty of moisture on the grass. During these critical times, do not irrigate unless it is absolutely necessary. If needed, water on a sunny day when moisture will evaporate quickly from grass leaves.

Since fungal diseases are very difficult to identify, it is important to keep a sharp watch for anything abnormal. In general, fungal diseases appear as brown or damaged patches of grass with smooth outlines. If you find a patch that fits this description, don't run out and spray the entire lawn with fungicide. Wait to see if the patch of damaged grass expands over the next day or two. It is quite possible that the fungal disease has already run its course. An "active" patch of diseased turf will grow and expand concentrically over a couple of days. Grass plants along the outline of the damaged patch will have the most telling signs: wilted plants, shriveled leaves, or discolored leaf blades. Once you have located a fungal disease, spray immediately with a lawn fungicide approved for use on Centipede.

If your lawn has a history of fungal problems, you may want to renovate the dead areas and then spray preventatively with a lawn fungicide the following year so that the disease does not recur. Follow the directions on the product label explicitly. You will probably need to spray several times over a 2–4 week period.

In general, good maintenance practices like weekly

mowing at the right height and limited fertilizer applications will go a long way toward preventing disease problems on Centipede lawns.

OVERSEEDING

Centipede lawns can be overseeded in the fall with a cool-season grass to create a temporary, green lawn over the winter months. This is especially common in the lower South. An overseeded Centipede lawn will not be as thick and green as an overseeded Bermuda Grass lawn, but it is worth the try nonetheless. Here's how it works. The cool-season grass germinates in the fall and begins to grow as your Centipede is going dormant. As spring arrives, the Centipede permanent lawn will begin to green as normal. During this "spring transition," the cool-season grass and Centipede lawn will both be green and will be competing with one another. As the heat of summer arrives, though, the cool-season grass will die and leave the Centipede to prosper for the rest of the summer.

Centipede can be overseeded with a variety of cool-season grasses. The key is to choose one that will not linger too long into summer, thus allowing your Centipede lawn to recover fully. Annual Rye (a.k.a. Italian Rye) is a good, generic choice for the South. It cannot tolerate hot weather and will die quickly as heat approaches. Perennial Rye can be used in the lower South although it will remain too long into the summer in areas where fescue grows well. Creeping Bentgrass is a good choice, but it is expensive and seldom available. Do not overseed Centipede with Tall Fescue or Kentucky Bluegrass since they will last well into summer and compete with your Centipede.

Steps in Overseeding

1. Do not apply pre-emergence weed control in the three months prior to overseeding.

2. Overseed Centipede lawns when the soil temperature drops to 70°. This is usually around September 15 in the upper South and around October 15 in the lower South.

3. Prepare the lawn before seeding by mowing your Centipede to about 1 inch and raking the lawn vigorously with a metal-tined rake.

4. Sow 6–8 pounds of Annual Rye per 1000 square feet and broadcast a complete lawn fertilizer than contains a slow-release form of nitrogen, if you have not done so already. Apply at the rate of 1 pound of actual nitrogen per 1000 square feet.

5. Keep the soil surface moist for 7–10 days to ensure even germination. After that, water weekly if there has been no significant rainfall.

6. Begin mowing as soon as the Annual Rye reaches 2.5 inches. This is a good time to install a new mower blade, or sharpen the old one. A dull blade will rip seedlings from the lawn.

7. Continue to mow throughout the winter at 2 inches, whenever the grass reaches 3 inches.

8. Fertilize lightly every 4–6 weeks throughout the winter whenever the Annual Rye is light green. Use a fertilizer like 10-10-10 that contains a soluble form of nitrogen, not a slow-release form of nitrogen. Slow-release forms of nitrogen are not effective during cold weather. Apply at the rate of .5 pounds of actual nitrogen per 1000 square feet. If using 10-10-10, this equals 5 pounds per 1000 square feet. Stop fertilizing in February, however, to slow its growth so it will not compete with your Centipede during the spring green-up.

9. In March, mow your Centipede to 1 inch (see "Mowing" on page 29). This will shock the Annual Rye and give the Centipede a chance to emerge. Continue to mow frequently and consistently at 1.5–2 inches while your Centipede grass is turning green. The remaining Annual Rye will die once warm weather arrives.

II. Renovating a Centipede Lawn

There are few things as demoralizing as discovering that your Centipede lawn is more weed than Centipede. Worse yet, a gloating neighbor points it out as he invites you for a tour of his immaculate turf. Regardless of the source of your motivation, most "troubled" Centipede lawns can be renovated without extreme effort. The general rule is that if you can find two healthy Centipede grass clumps in a given square foot of lawn, you can renovate. Otherwise, grab your wallet and head for the section entitled "Planting a New Centipede Lawn."

The first step in renovating a Centipede lawn is to admit that there is a problem. There are two categories of problems that will ruin a lawn: maintenance problems and fundamental problems. Unfortunately, the results of both often appear the same. For instance, a thinning lawn may be the result of improper mowing or poor drainage. Think about your lawn's history and work your way toward the logical cause.

CORRECTING MAINTENANCE PROBLEMS

Although Centipede is "lazy man's grass," a healthy lawn has distinct requirements. This means that you should care for your lawn enough, but not too much. Read through the maintenance section on page 29 and determine if you are skipping, or overdoing, any critical steps. Are you fertilizing moderately, mowing at the right height, mowing consistently, aerating, irrigating, and applying pre-emergence weed control? Do you have an insect or disease problem? Address these problems accurately to stimulate your grass to grow denser, fill voids, and darken in color. Below are two "recipes" for Centipede lawn renovation. They cover approximately eight months of the year. Do not renovate your lawn during the two months when lawns are greening in the spring and the two months when your lawn is going dormant in the fall.

CORRECTING FUNDAMENTAL PROBLEMS

There are times when a Centipede lawn will not grow well despite your best efforts. In these frustrating situations, it's wise to remember that Centipede will not necessarily grow where all other plants have failed. In fact, in certain situations there may be hundreds of plants that are better suited for a particular area. Remember this as you read the remedies below. The most efficient and inexpensive approach might be to reconfigure or abandon areas that are not suitable for a lawn.

Recipe for Growing-Season Renovation *(May through August)*

1. Kill Weeds. Spray weedy areas with a post-emergence weed control as soon as possible. Young weeds die faster than mature weeds (see "Weed Control").

2. Rake. Rake the entire lawn vigorously with a metal-tined rake to remove leaves, dead weeds, grass clippings, rocks, etc.

3. Mow: Check your mowing height and mow frequently.

4. Irrigate. Water deeply once every week if there has been no rain. Don't drop the ball! Even short periods of drought can cause discoloration.

5. Fertilize. Fertilize moderately if you have not done so this year (see "Fertilizing").

6. Aerate. Core aerate to stimulate grass to grow and spread.

7. Correct the pH. Consider having a soil test performed by your local Cooperative Extension Service (see "Lime, Soil pH, and Iron Deficiencies").

8. Control Future Weeds. Apply pre-emergence weed control ON TIME in the fall (see "Weed Control").

Recipe for Dormant-Season Renovation *(November through February)*

1. Kill Weeds. Spray weedy areas with a post-emergence weed control as soon as possible, on a warm day. Young weeds die faster than mature weeds (see "Weed Control"). Hand-pull problem weeds like bunches of fescue.

2. Control Future Weeds. Apply pre-emergence weed control ON TIME in late winter (see "Weed Control").

3. Rake. Mow your lawn to one inch in late February/early March. Rake and remove all of the debris (see "Mowing").

4. Wait until late April **to fertilize** and late May **to core aerate.**

• **Shade.** While a Centipede lawn will grow in a moderate amount of shade, it will become thin and weak in dense shade. You may be forced to remove a few tree limbs or reduce the size of your lawn to avoid the shade. Raising the mowing height in the shaded areas may alleviate some of the problem but is often impractical. Also consider this: Areas of dense shade often have a high density of tree roots. Increase your irrigation in the shaded areas temporarily to see if the problem is actually drought.

• **Compacted soil.** Centipede will thin and die in compacted soil that is low in oxygen. Consider aerating once or twice during the growing season when soil temperatures are 75–80°. Also, evaluate the cause of the compaction and correct continuing problems by creating walkways for people and pets.

• **Poor drainage.** Centipede lawns need well-drained soil to grow well. There are few things worse for a Centipede lawn than wet, soggy soil. These are also some of most difficult and expensive problems to correct. Before you begin, determine the source of the water and where it is trying to flow. Occasionally, you can correct poor drainage by diverting a water source (like a gutter outlet) or removing an obstruction (a clogged ditch). Other solutions include re-grading, French drains, and surface drains. Once the soil dries, core-aerate to help renovate the root zone.

• **Improper pH.** Centipede grows best at a low soil pH between 4.5 and 5.5. If your soil is naturally alkaline, or if you have recently limed the area, your lawn will grow slowly, lose density, and turn light green/yellow *despite* your best maintenance practices. Always consider your maintenance before you blame soil pH. If you suspect soil pH, take a soil sample to your local Cooperative Extension Service testing. They will recommend the amount of elemental sulfur needed to correct the problem.

Drainage problems will kill Centipede grass plants and allow weeds to enter your lawn.

III. Planting a New Centipede Lawn

A new Centipede lawn can be started from sod, plugs, or seed. The most common method is to lay sod blocks so that they cover the entire new lawn surface "wall to wall." Plugging is a variation of sodding in which you plant pieces of sod about one foot apart. The lawn will develop over several months as the plugs grow to fill the gaps. Seeding is the least common and the least expensive way to start a new Centipede lawn. Centipede seed is very small and requires special attention.

> ☛ **TIP:** Soil-related problems can devastate new Centipede lawns and established Centipede lawns. This is your only chance to fix soil problems! Kill weeds, cultivate the soil deeply, and amend with humus before you plant.

Whether you are sodding, plugging, or seeding your new lawn, the best time of year to begin is in the late spring once the danger of frost has passed and the sod is green. A new Centipede lawn will establish quickly and thrive when planted after the soil temperature rises to 75–80°. This usually occurs in May. With good irrigation, a Centipede lawn can be started throughout June and July. Try not to plant after August 1, however, because your new lawn will not have enough warm weather to become established.

READING SEED LABELS

Centipede lawns are sometimes grown from seed. Centipede seed may take 2–3 weeks to germinate and may need a full growing season to become a nice stand of grass. Since seeding Centipede grass is not very common, the seed you find at the nursery may have been there a while. It is very important to read the special seed label attached or printed on the bag for several pieces of information. First, make sure the germination test date is within the last year. The newer the seed, the better. Second, make sure the bag contains only Centipede grass seed. Do not buy a seed bag that contains a mixture of Centipede and other grasses like Bahiagrass or Carpetgrass. Despite what the package says, these other grasses will only look like weeds in your Centipede lawn.

Centipede Grass	Lot: XXX-1234-XXX
Net. Wt. 5 lbs.	Origin: Georgia
98% Pure Seed	
1% inert matter	
1% weed seed	
Test Date: 2-1-20XX	
98% Centipede Grass	Germ: 85%

STEPS IN PLANTING A NEW CENTIPEDE LAWN

Planting a Centipede lawn is not a one-weekend project. This is especially true if you are planning to lay sod. There is nothing worse than spending a Saturday on your hands and knees in blazing 95° weather. Now imagine beginning at noon, after a morning of rototilling and cultivating. The best thing to do is to spread the various steps over two weekends. For instance, I would strongly suggest cultivating one weekend and planting the next.

STEP 1. Spray existing weeds. The first step in planting a new Centipede lawn is to eliminate all weeds from the lawn area. Use a non-selective weed control like Round-Up. Plan ahead since you will need to wait 1–2 weeks (check the product label) after spraying before you seed, sod, or sprig. Remember not to apply a pre-emergence weed control any time within three months of seeding a Centipede lawn.

STEP 2. Establish the grade. One of the best ways to guarantee a beautiful lawn is to establish the proper grade before you begin. This may be more than most of us can afford, but consider it nonetheless. The proper slope has the potential to prevent both drought and poor drainage. It also makes mowing easier. In general, a 2–6% grade is optimal.

STEP 3. Cultivate the soil as deeply as possible. Whether you use sod, plug, or seed, Centipede roots will need to grow into the existing soil surface. The deeper you can cultivate the soil, the more quickly your lawn will become established and prosper. Remember to wait the allotted time after spraying your herbicide before cultivating. Begin by raking and removing debris like dead weeds, leaves, and rocks from the area. Next, cultivate the soil with a rear-tine rototiller. If you don't have a rototiller, consider renting one from a tool rental store. Rototill the entire area lengthwise, then again crosswise. Try to work at least 4–6 inches of soil into a nice pulverized soil mix. If you prefer not to rototill, cultivate as much of the area as you can with a hoe, garden rake, or shovel. Again, the deeper you work the soil, the better.

STEP 4. Amend the soil. During home construction, most of the natural humus in the top layer of soil is usually scraped away or buried. The remaining soil will probably be low in organic matter and will be greatly improved if you add humus. It is almost always better to amend the existing soil than to order a load of top-soil. Adding humus will improve drainage in clay soils and improve water retention in sandy soils. Peat moss, composted bark products, and compost are all good choices. Be careful, however, if you use a soil amendment that contains a gel-like substance to retain water. These products can cause strange drainage problems. I prefer adding two 3.8 cubic foot bales of sphagnum peat moss per 1000 square feet. Work the peat moss into the top 4–6 inches of soil as you rototill.

STEP 5. Fertilizer and soil pH. After cultivating, apply a complete lawn fertilizer that contains a slow-release form of nitrogen. I prefer to start a Centipede lawn with a 3-1-2 ratio fertilizer like 12-4-8. Apply at the rate of 1.5 pounds of actual nitrogen per 1000 square feet. Work the fertilizer into the top layer of cultivated soil using a garden rake.

A lawn is a big investment and it does not hurt to have the soil pH determined by your County Extension Service. Centipede prefers a soil pH of 4.5–5.5 and your soil test results will recommend the specific amount of elemental sulfur to add if your soil pH needs to be lowered. Elemental sulfur products should be raked into the top inch of the soil using a garden rake. Many Southern soils are naturally acidic and will not need elemental sulfur. It would be extremely rare for your soil pH to be so low that it would need to be raised with lime. In the absence of a soil test to prove me wrong, **do not add lime**.

STEP 6. Seeding. If you are seeding a Centipede lawn, plan on using about .5 pounds of seed per 1000 square feet. Centipede seed should germinate in 2–3 weeks. Remember not to buy a mix that contains other types of grass besides Centipede and make sure the seed is fresh by checking that the germination test date is within the last year.

Begin by raking the area to create as smooth a soil surface as possible. I like to use a metal-tined leaf rake because it creates tiny furrows and ridges on the soil surface that "capture" the seed. Centipede seed is minute and should be mixed with about twice as much dry sand before sowing. In short, 1 pound of seed should be mixed in a bucket with 2 pounds of dry sand. The seed/sand mix can be placed in a spreader (a fertilizer spreader works fine) or broadcast by hand. When using a spreader, distribute half the allotted mix lengthwise and the second half crosswise to avoid any skips. Since Centipede seed is so small, rake the area very carefully to cover the seeds with a fine layer of soil. Do not bury them under more than .25 inches of soil. Next, water the entire area to work the seed into the soil. Finally, cover the lawn with a layer of wheat straw to prevent washing and erosion while the seed is germinating. You will need about 1 bale of wheat straw per 1000 square feet.

STEP 7. Sodding. Before you lay sod, cultivate the soil as described in step 3. Do not skip this step! Centipede laid on uncultivated soil will be susceptible to a wide range of growth problems and will be very susceptible to drought.

Unless you are planting a small lawn, it is almost always cheaper and more efficient to order pallets of sod from your local nursery to be delivered to your house. Most people prefer to order enough sod to cover the entire lawn area "wall to wall." Plan on laying the sod soon after it arrives on pallets. Stacked sod should not sit for more than a day or two. It is usually a good idea to cultivate and amend the soil one weekend, and fertilize/sod the next.

Begin by raking the entire cultivated area to prepare as smooth a surface as possible. Be careful because the sod will mimic the soil surface below, not compensate for it. It is best for the soil to be moist at the time of sodding, but not wet. Start at the top of the lawn and lay the sod lengthwise so that the long side of each piece of sod is running perpendicular to a hill or rise. As you place each piece of sod, work it tight against the surrounding pieces to prevent the edges from browning and ruts from forming. Sod is often cut on a slant so that the edges will overlap. Make sure the edges slant appropriately so that they interlock. Pound each block of sod with your palm to press it into the soil below and remove any air pockets. Stagger the second row of sod so that the perpendicular edges do not line up. The result should look like a brick wall, not a checkerboard. If you are placing sod along steep gradients, pin them

in place with stakes or metal pins (available from sod distributors). Irrigate deeply once all the sod is placed.

STEP 8. Plugging. A plug is essentially a four-square-inch piece of sod. Plugs can either be purchased or you can create your own by cutting sod into smaller pieces. The idea behind plugging is to plant each individual piece about a foot apart and allow the grass to grow together over the coming months to form a solid grass surface. Unlike sodding, individual plugs must be planted so that the roots are surrounded by soil and the grass runners are flush with the soil surface. Once all the plugs are set, the lawn should be irrigated. Plugging is less expensive than sodding because you purchase less grass. It usually takes about the same time to plug as it does to lay sod.

STEP 9. Irrigation during establishment. Whether you begin with seed, sod, or plugs, tend your Centipede lawn diligently over the coming 4–6 weeks. Begin by watering lightly every day. After a week or so, decrease the frequency of irrigation but increase the amount of water you apply. By six weeks, you should be applying an inch of water per week, in one application, if there has been no significant rainfall. If you have seeded your lawn, follow these same guidelines but rely on your instinct. If the soil surface is eroding or remains damp, skip a watering. If the soil surface dries rapidly, irrigate more frequently.

STEP 10. Mowing during establishment. A newly seeded Centipede lawn should be mowed as soon as it reaches about 1.5 inches. This will take a relatively long time because of Centipede's horizontal growth habit. Sodded and plugged lawns should be mowed at 1.5–2 inches from the start. It is always a good idea to use a mower with a sharp blade and cut frequently. Mowing will encourage the grass blades to toughen and spread.

STEP 11. Fertilizing during establishment. Centipede lawns prefer low levels of soil nutrients. The slow-release fertilizer you applied at planting should be enough for the coming summer. Your next application will be the normal early September application (see "Fertilizer").

STEP 12. Weed control during establishment. Weeds are especially troublesome with seeded and plugged

Centipede lawns. There is plenty of bare earth, moisture, and fertilizer to help weed seeds germinate. With sod and plugs, begin spraying weeds with a post-emergence weed control (labeled for use on Centipede) as soon as they appear. With seeded lawns, wait until you have mowed two or three times before you begin spraying with post-emergence weed controls. Check the product label for specific instructions. In all cases, wait until early fall to begin applying pre-emergence weed control.

Loosen and pulverize the soil with a rototiller before you plant.

Amend the soil with sphagnum peat moss before you plant.

Broadcast fertilizer. Do not add lime.

Work fertilizer into the top layer of soil with a garden rake.

Place sod so that the overhanging (right) and underhanging (left) edges interlock.

Stagger the rows so that the perpendicular edges do not line up.

*Saint Augustine lawns are most suitable
for the lower South and Coastal Plain.*

Chapter Four

Saint Augustine Grass
(*Stenotaphrum secundatum*)

SAINT AUGUSTINE, OR "CHARLESTON GRASS," MAY BE COARSER THAN SOME OF THE OTHER Southern lawn grasses, but it can be your best friend in the lower South and Coastal Plain. It is tough, aggressive, dense, and loves blazing hot temperatures. In some situations, it would probably be substituted for Centipede grass in the middle South if it were not for its poor cold tolerance. Saint Augustine grass should be considered a Zone 8 plant and should not be planted in areas of the South where temperatures regularly drop below 20° in the winter. If you want to push the envelope a little, you can try 'Raleigh' Saint Augustine Grass, which is more tolerant of cold weather.

When you watch a Saint Augustine lawn kick into gear in May and stretch its runners to cover bare areas overnight, it is easy to love this grass. It is one of those plants that you feel is truly working with you. It is aggressive but controllable, and shade-tolerant but not invasive. It also grows more horizontally than vertically. As a result, its vigorous growth does not mean that you have to mow every time you turn around.

A Saint Augustine lawn is also welcoming. It is soft underfoot and the intertwining runners make you feel like you are walking on a spider web. It may not be the best grass for soccer or baseball (it doesn't like heavy traffic), but it is certainly a welcome addition in the heat of the lower South.

Saint Augustine lawns have one nemesis—insects. The worst offender is the chinch bug, a tiny hideous creature that sucks the juice from grass stems. Chinch bugs are such a widespread problem that cultivars like 'Floratam' and 'Floralawn' have been developed specifically for their chinch-bug resistance. Consider using one of these cultivars so that you won't have to rely heavily on lawn insecticides.

> **At a Glance:**
>
> - Tough, coarse, mat-forming grass
> - Tolerates moderate shade
> - Spreads quickly and vigorously by runners ("stolons")
> - Can be sodded or plugged
> - Mowed at approximately 3 inches when it reaches 4.5 inches
> - Fertilized 2–3 times a year
> - Needs approximately one inch of water per week during the growing season

I. Maintaining an Established Saint Augustine Lawn

Saint Augustine lawns are tough and grow vigorously during a hot Southern summer. Horizontal runners called stolons grow quickly over the soil surface and intertwine to form a dense mat. In general, a thick and healthy Saint Augustine lawn is not very hard to maintain if you mow consistently, irrigate when needed, and fertilize on time. In turn, the dense layer of turf will prevent weeds from sprouting and your lawn will be self-perpetuating. Keep a constant watch, however, for the nemesis of Saint Augustine lawns, the dreaded chinch bug.

MOWING

By the end of the winter season, a Saint Augustine lawn will have a fair amount of dead top growth. This

Saint Augustine Mowing Heights (in inches)

EXPOSURE	MOW TO:	MOW WHEN GRASS IS:
Full Sun	2.5	3.75
Full Sun, Light Shade	3	4.5
Partial Shade	3.5	5.25

top growth can be removed by mowing your lawn when it is still dormant and brown. Do not, however, mow as low as you would with a Bermuda Grass or Zoysia lawn. Saint Augustine runners, or stolons, are exposed and vulnerable above the soil surface. New grass leaves will grow from these stolons, and it is best not to disrupt them when they are low on stored energy at the end of the winter. It is safe to mow at about 2 inches in late February/early March. This is usually around the time the Bradford Pear trees bloom. Rake and remove as many of the grass clippings and as much leftover thatch as possible. This can be frustrating or impossible if the grass stolons crisscross like a spider web. Do your best.

Stolon: a shoot that grows horizontally near the soil surface, rooting at the nodes to form new plants.

A couple of weeks later, your Saint Augustine lawn will begin to turn green as soil temperatures rise to a consistent 60–65°. This is usually in mid-March to early April, depending on the particular season. Do not mow lower at this time than you will mow during the rest of the season. Wait until your lawn reaches the recommended height.

Saint Augustine lawns should be mowed consistently at 2.5–3 inches throughout the growing season. The semi-dwarf cultivars like 'Jade' and 'Seville' can be mowed at 2 inches. At these heights, a healthy lawn will probably need to be mowed about once a week. Since Saint Augustine grass grows horizontally and vertically, it is tempting to skip a week of mowing and allow the grass to grow to taller heights. Do not do this. Consistent mowing at the recommended height will train the grass to spread and form a dense turf. (For instructions on accurately setting your mower blade to the correct height, see **Rotary Mower** in the Glossary.)

Saint Augustine grass is often grown in partial shade. In these situations, the Saint Augustine grass plants elongate in much the same way a houseplant stretches toward light from a window. You can still grow a thick turf, but it is helpful to raise your mowing height to 3.5 inches. This will prevent you from removing too much leaf material at a given mowing. The chart above will help you mow at the right height, at the right time.

The One-Third Rule: Never reduce the height of your lawn by more than one-third when mowing.

Be careful not to allow your Saint Augustine to grow higher than these recommendations. In some cases, you can scalp a Saint Augustine lawn if it has grown too high. Scalping occurs when you remove most of the green portion of the grass and leave the bare, exposed stolons. Scalping is not only horrible for your lawn, it is ugly.

Allow your Saint Augustine lawn to grow to 4 inches in the fall in preparation for cold weather. This extra height will act as insulation for roots and stolons over the winter months. Plan ahead because Saint Augustine does not grow as vigorously in late fall.

If you mow below the recommended height, you will scalp your lawn.

Irrigation

There is usually plenty of rainfall in the South during a given year, but it seldom falls on a regular schedule. Even along the coast, a Saint Augustine lawn will need to be watered during the growing season to encourage healthy growth and a good, rich color. Saint Augustine lawns can survive brief periods of drought or little rainfall, but they will become thin and off-color. As a general rule, your lawn should be watered with about an inch per week if there has been no significant rainfall.

The best way to water a Saint Augustine lawn is deeply and infrequently. For example, apply an inch of water on a single day rather than .25 inches a day for four days. Deep and infrequent watering will encourage grass roots to grow deep into the soil where there is more moisture. Be careful, though, not to overwater. Saint Augustine grass prefers well-drained soil. Stop watering if you notice water pooling or if the soil is constantly saturated.

If you have an automatic sprinkler system, take a moment to investigate your control box and settings. Place a rain gauge or straight-sided jar on the lawn and turn on the sprinklers. Monitor how much water is applied in a given period. Most systems will have several different types of sprinkler heads, so you might have to test each irrigation zone. I like to draw a rough diagram of the lawn and record the various sprinkler outputs for future reference. This will help you to manipulate your irrigation system during the sporadic rain and drought periods of the coming season. Do not be shy about increasing the preset cycles during droughts or turning off the entire system after a heavy rainfall. While lack of water will affect your lawn's color and growth, excess water can kill a poorly drained Saint Augustine lawn.

If you water your lawn with a manual sprinkler, use your gauge to make sure that you don't apply more, or less, than an inch at a time.

Saint Augustine lawns do not enter a deep dormancy during the winter months. In areas of the lower South, they might even remain slightly green. Be aware of winter dry spells and water if the top .5 inches of soil is dry to the touch. This will prevent stolons near the soil surface from drying out. Most of the time, you will need to apply only .25–.5 inches of water. In addition, water dormant Saint Augustine lawns when temperatures are expected to drop below 20°. Wet soil will freeze and keep soil temperatures close to 32°, while dry soil allows damaging sub-20° air to penetrate the root zone.

> **One Step Further:** A grass plant absorbs water from the soil to replace water that evaporates from its leaf blades. The perfect way to irrigate is to supply the soil with the exact amount of water that evaporates. Search the Internet for a weather station in your area that records "pan evaporation rate" or "evapotranspiration." Water loss from Saint Augustine grass blades is roughly 75% of the pan evaporation rate.
>
> **Formula:** (75% x Weekly Pan Evaporation Total) − Weekly Rainfall Total = Amount to irrigate that week

Fertilizer

Fertilizing is one of the most satisfying lawn activities. Within a matter of days, a fertilized lawn will turn dark green and look healthy. This is especially true for Saint Augustine Grass in mid-spring because it is usually light green. A Saint Augustine lawn will also need a moderate amount of fertilizer throughout the growing season. A fertilized Saint Augustine lawn will turn a dark green and grow quickly. The only worry is that this fast, succulent growth is very attractive to insects and diseases. Most of the time, you can avoid problems by using a granular fertilizer that contains a slow-release form of nitrogen. Hose-end liquid fertilizers work, but they are difficult to use correctly and you will need to fertilize twice as often as with granular fertilizer.

> **Saint Augustine Fertilizer Facts:**
>
> • 4 pounds of actual nitrogen per 1000 square feet each year
>
> • Use a fertilizer that contains a slow-release form of nitrogen
>
> • Three applications: mid-spring, mid-summer, and early fall
>
> • Water approximately one inch after fertilizing

Saint Augustine lawns remain thick and healthy if fertilized properly.

What Kind of Fertilizer to Use

Fertilizer is described by the percentages of nitrogen (N), phosphorus (P), and potassium (K) contained in the bag. All fertilizer bags are clearly labeled with these three numbers, known as the N-P-K ratio. Whenever possible, I use a slow-release lawn fertilizer with a 3-1-2 ratio. An example would be a 12-4-8 fertilizer. A bag of 12-4-8 fertilizer contains 12% nitrogen, 4% phosphorus, and 8% potassium by weight. The remaining 76% is inert material that adds bulk to the mixture and makes it easier to spread.

It is important to use slow-release fertilizers whenever possible. Most major brands of lawn fertilizer will have a combination of soluble and slow-release forms of nitrogen (indicated on the label). Soluble nitrogen is available to the grass plant immediately while slow-release nitrogen becomes available over a period of two to three months. In most situations it is best to have as much of the nitrogen in slow-release form as possible. Good brands of fertilizer will have 40–50% of the nitrogen in slow-release form. This is usually noted in a statement like "containing 6% nitrogen in slow-release form."

Be careful when using hose-end fertilizer sprayers or dry fertilizers in which all of the nitrogen is in a soluble, quick-release form. Soluble nitrogen will cause a major flush of growth for a week or two and will completely dissipate in 4–6 weeks. For most of us, it is almost impossible to fertilize with quick-release fertilizers without causing wild, fluctuating growth spurts. If you decide to use quick-release fertilizer, never apply more than 1 pound of actual nitrogen per 1000 square feet per application. You will need to fertilizer every 4–6 weeks during the growing season for a total of 4 applications. Stay on schedule throughout the season so that nitrogen levels will remain fairly constant in the soil.

Common Forms of Nitrogen *(indicated on the label)*
Soluble: *Available immediately, lasts 4–6 weeks*
Ammonium nitrate, potassium nitrate, ammonium sulfate
Slow-Release: *Available slowly in small amounts, generally lasts 2–3 months*
Urea-Formaldehyde (UF), Isobutylidene diurea (IBDU), Sulfur Coated Urea (SCU), Polymer Coated Urea products (like "Polyon")

Up to this point, I have only mentioned three major nutrients: nitrogen, phosphorus, and potassium. These three nutrients are used by grass plants in relatively large quantities and are known as macronutrients. Grass plants use other nutrients in relatively small quantities. Those nutrients are known as micronutrients or "minor elements." Most major brands of fertilizer contain the needed minor nutrients and you do not need to worry about them.

How Much Fertilizer to Apply

Most bags of fertilizer are covered from top to bottom with completely useless information that is written by the fertilizer company's marketing department. I continue to be amazed by the fact that the closest thing to directions is usually a vague phrase like "fertilizes *up* to 10,000 square feet." Luckily, there is a universal way to know how much fertilizer to apply, regardless of the brand or the specific N-P-K ratio. All you have to do is figure out how much "actual nitrogen" is contained in the bag. Saint Augustine Grass lawns grow best with 4 pounds of actual nitrogen per 1000 square feet applied each year, regardless of the brand of fertilizer you purchase. If you use a fertilizer that contains a slow-release form of nitrogen, you can apply the needed nitrogen in two applications of 1.5 pounds of actual nitrogen per 1000 square feet in mid-spring and early fall. Apply 1 pound of actual nitrogen per 1000 square feet in mid-summer.

Unfortunately, the average bag of fertilizer does not tell you how much actual nitrogen it contains in the bag. It is easy to calculate, though, using two simple pieces of information: the N-P-K ratio and the weight of the bag. Multiply the percentage of nitrogen (the first number in the N-P-K ratio) by the weight of the

bag and you will know the amount of actual nitrogen it contains. For instance, a 50-pound bag of 12-4-8 fertilizer has 6 pounds of actual nitrogen (12% of 50).

Determine the amount of coverage by dividing the amount of actual nitrogen in the bag by the amount of nitrogen you want to apply in a single application. With Saint Augustine Grass, your first application will be 1.5 pounds of actual nitrogen per 1000 square feet. Therefore, a bag that contains 6 pounds of actual nitrogen will cover 4000 square feet (6 divided by 1.5 pounds per 1000 square feet). If your lawn is less than 4000 square feet, remove the amount you do not need. Two cups of granular fertilizer weigh about 1 pound.

All of this calculating may seem like a hassle, but it really is the best way to apply the correct amount of fertilizer to your lawn. It is also a great way to compare the cost of different fertilizers so that you get a good deal. This best part is that you won't have to rely on the fertilizer company's marketing department for lawn advice.

How to Spread Fertilizer

You can broadcast granular fertilizer using a rolling fertilizer spreader, a hand-held spreader, or by hand (wear a glove). I will be completely honest with you. Spreading fertilizer is not an exact science. The calibrated settings on even the most expensive broadcast spreader are usually completely inaccurate. In addition, the majority of spreaders will clog, break, and jam.

I have had great success with a very simple and effective method. Begin by measuring your lawn and calculating the amount of fertilizer that you need to spread (see "How Much Fertilizer to Apply"). If you only need half of a 50-pound bag, remove it and set it aside. Next, shut off your fertilizer spreader and fill it. Begin moving and barely open the spreader only once

---

Here is an example using a 50-pound bag of 12-4-8 slow-release fertilizer:

1. Multiply the nitrogen percentage (12%) by the net weight of the bag (50 lbs.) to determine how many pounds of actual nitrogen are in the bag (6 lbs.).

2. Next, divide the actual nitrogen in the bag (6 lbs.) by the amount you want to apply per 1000 square feet (1.5 lbs.).

3. Multiply this number (4) by 1000 to determine how many square feet the bag will cover (4000).

4. If your lawn is only 3000 square feet, you will need to apply 75% of the 50-pound bag. Two cups of granular fertilizer weigh approximately 1 pound, so remove 25 cups.

you are up to speed. Try to spread as little fertilizer as possible while still broadcasting an even pattern. Continue covering the entire lawn at the same speed. If you must slow to turn around, turn off the spreader or you will drop too much fertilizer in a single location and burn your grass. Work across the entire lawn until you return to your starting point and turn off the fertilizer spreader. Now, see how much of the needed fertilizer is left. If 50% remains, repeat the entire process and you will be finished. If 25% remains, repeat the entire process but move twice as fast. Remember, it is impossible to be exact. Your foremost goal should be to spread the designated amount of fertilizer evenly over the entire lawn; avoid heavy doses in some areas and light doses in others.

When to Fertilize

When it comes to fertilizing, timing is everything. The following schedule will help you maintain a consistent level of nutrients in the soil without causing excessive growth.

• **Mid-Spring:** Saint Augustine begins to green when soil temperatures reach a consistent 60–65°. Depending on the particular year, this is usually in mid-March to early April. Do not fertilize when your grass first begins to turn green. Wait until the danger of frost has passed and your lawn is at least 50% green. This is usually in April around the time when the Dogwoods are in full bloom. Use a complete lawn fertilizer that contains a slow-release form of nitrogen. Apply at the rate of 1.5 pounds of actual nitrogen per 1000 square feet. This application will last about 2–3 months.

> ***Don't fertilize too early!*** It is hard to be patient. The minute the Saint Augustine begins to green I have an overwhelming desire to fertilize. I guess I feel that a green lawn will speed spring to my yard. Two things happen, though, if you fertilize early. First, you stimulate leaf growth at a time when the Saint Augustine roots should be growing foremost. Second, early leaf growth is particularly vulnerable to a late-season frost. Be patient!

• **Mid-Summer:** Fertilize again in mid-summer, approximately 3 months after your spring application. This is usually in late June/early July. I like to fertilize

the weekend before 4th of July so I can impress my father-in-law at the family barbeque. Use a complete lawn fertilizer that contains a slow-release form of nitrogen. If your lawn is healthy and a good color, apply at the rate of 1 pound of actual nitrogen per 1000 square feet. This will prevent excessive growth and insect problems.

• **Early Fall:** Fertilize your Saint Augustine lawn again in early September. You can use the same complete fertilizer you have been using, or switch to a fertilizer with little or no phosphorus, but a higher rate of potassium. This might be something like 12-4-14 or 12-0-12. Either way, make sure the fertilizer contains a slow-release form of nitrogen. Apply at the rate of 1.5 pounds of actual nitrogen per 1000 square feet.

> ***Winterizing Lawns:*** You will probably be bombarded with commercials in the fall encouraging you to "winterize" your lawn with a ***late Fall*** application of special fertilizer. Research has shown benefits and detriments to these applications. In my opinion, the benefits are so short-lived that they do not justify the costs. Growing up in a family of horticulturists, one of the first phrases I remember hearing was "sounds like he's trying to sell some fertilizer." I think this could be one of those times.

• **Winter:** Do not fertilize Saint Augustine lawns in the winter. You might encourage succulent top growth during a winter warm spell that will be damaged in the next cold snap. More likely, the fertilizer will not be absorbed by plant roots and will leach from the soil into nearby streams and lakes.

SOIL pH, LIME, AND IRON DEFICIENCIES

It is easy to focus entirely on the top growth of a lawn and forget that the soil affects its color, growth rate, and overall health. One particular soil measurement, soil pH, can be important in growing a Saint Augustine lawn. Soil pH is measured on a scale of 0–14 with 7 being neutral. A soil pH below 7 is considered acidic while a soil pH above 7 is considered basic (alkaline). Saint Augustine lawns grow best with a soil pH between 6.5 and 7. We can manipulate soil pH by applying lime to raise the pH and elemental sulfur to lower the pH. Many soils in the South are acidic, and may need moderate amounts of lime to increase the pH to the optimal range for Saint Augustine. Be careful, though, because a soil pH above 7 can cause Saint Augustine to turn yellow (due to iron chlorosis).

The best way to determine the exact pH of your soil is to have the soil tested by your local Cooperative Extension Service. If your soil pH is below the preferred range for Saint Augustine, the soil test results will recommend the amount of lime needed to raise the pH to the acceptable range. If your soil pH is above the preferred range for Saint Augustine, the soil test results will recommend the amount of elemental sulfur (usually sold as aluminum sulfate) needed to lower the pH to the acceptable range. Most acidic soils will need 50 pounds of pelletized lime per 1000 square feet. Lime can take up to three months to affect the pH of your soil and can be applied at any time of the year. Since lime moves slowly in the soil, the best time to apply it is when planting or just after core aerating.

Dealing with Light Green/Yellow Grass

A Saint Augustine lawn might lose its dark green color despite timely applications of fertilizer. This may be caused by one of several reasons. First, it could be chinch bugs. Pound a coffee can in the yellow turf as described in the "Insects and Pests" section on page 62. If you do not find chinch bugs, the problem is probably chlorosis. Saint Augustine Grass becomes chlorotic because of an iron deficiency in soils with high pH (7 and above). You can correct an iron deficiency in one of two ways. First, you can spray with iron for a short-term cure. Iron will help the Saint Augustine Grass to return to its natural green within a week or so. The

Saint Augustine lawns turn yellow in soils with a high pH.

darker color will last, however, for only about four weeks. Better yet, you can correct the iron deficiencies by lowering the soil pH with an elemental sulfur product. As you lower the pH, iron that is already in the soil will become available to the grass. The most common form of elemental sulfur is aluminum sulfate. It is usually available in 50-pound bags and should be applied at the rate recommended on the bag.

Occasionally, Saint Augustine lawns develop iron chlorosis because they are growing in compacted or soggy soil that is low in oxygen. You may see this problem in a low spot of the lawn near a surface drain. In these situations, grass roots have trouble absorbing iron from the soil. The best way to fix the problem is to correct your irrigation and add extra drainage if necessary. Compacted soils should be core aerated.

The same problem can occur in the spring if grass blades begin to emerge while soil temperatures are still cold. In these situations, the problem is short-lived and will correct itself within several weeks as the soil warms.

AERATING

Aerating is a method of increasing the flow of air, water, and nutrients into your lawn's root zone. In certain situations, aerating can have dramatic effects since Saint Augustine grass hates soil with poor drainage (low oxygen). Aerating each year will improve the quality and consistency of your lawn's growth. It can also be used to renovate areas like dry banks, poorly drained corners, and compacted dog paths.

A Saint Augustine lawn can be aerated any time during the growing season as long as it is not suffering from drought. Most of us, however, aerate once a year. The best time for a once-a-year aeration is in the late spring when your lawn is completely green and soil temperatures reach 80°. This is usually in May. I prefer not to aerate dormant Saint Augustine grass since it will disrupt my late winter pre-emergence weed control application and open the soil to weed seed infiltration. In addition, I avoid aerating during spring green-up since it will damage tender roots and stolons at a time when the grass is low on stored energy.

The only effective way to aerate a lawn is to use a core aerator. Core aerators are powered by an engine and remove cores of soil from the top layer of soil. Since most people do not own a core aerator, they rent one or have a lawn service aerate for them. Core aerators work best on moist soil so you will need to irrigate several days before you plan to aerate. A core aerator will bounce along the surface of dry soil. Make one or two passes across the entire lawn so that there is a hole every 4–6 inches. Afterwards, there will be cores of soil deposited all over the lawn. If the cores bother you, you can rake the lawn and most will break and drop below the level of the grass where they are not as visible. Otherwise, they will naturally disintegrate in a couple of weeks with the help of a few passing rainstorms. I prefer not to collect and remove the cores since they eventually return to the soil surface where they help thatch to decompose. Finally, irrigate the aerated lawn deeply to moisten exposed roots and rhizomes.

You will often see "spike aerators" of various sorts for sale. Some roll behind a riding lawn mower, others are attached to fertilizer spreaders, and manual types are like a pitch fork that you are supposed to press into the soil with your foot. There are even special spike-clad shoes that claim to aerate while you wander around the lawn. When a spike is forced into the soil, it creates an opening but compacts the surrounding areas. Even worse, you would need to take at least 10,000 steps with spike-clad shoes to even come close to core aerating. In my opinion, all of these products are useless and should be avoided.

DETHATCHING

Saint Augustine lawns often develop thatch. Thatch is a collection of dead plant parts like stems and grass clippings that accumulate on the soil surface below the grass stolons. Thatch becomes a problem when it is more than .5 inches thick. In these situations, grass roots grow into the thatch layer where they are more susceptible to drought. In addition, a thick layer of thatch is the perfect hideaway for insects like chinch bugs.

The best way to control thatch on a Saint Augustine lawn is to prevent it. Begin the year by mowing your Saint Augustine lawn to about 2 inches in the early spring before it turns green (see "Mowing"). If possible, rake your lawn at the same time with a metal-tined leaf rake. This can be very difficult since the grass is often woven into a tight web. It is easier, though, in areas that are thinning and you might be able to dredge up a significant about of thatch from the soil surface. Collect and remove as much of the debris as possible.

You can also prevent thatch problems by core aerating in early summer, mowing consistently at the right height, and avoiding excessive applications of fertilizer. If your lawn is growing rapidly and you are mowing more than once a week, it will also help to bag your grass clippings.

I prefer not to mechanically dethatch a Saint Augustine lawn unless I have discovered a major, sustained thatch problem (.5 inches thick or more) and want to renovate the lawn. Even then I will do my best with a core aerator and raking before I rent a vertical mower, or "dethatcher," from the local tool rental store. Vertical mowing is tricky and should be performed with extreme care. Do not cut too deeply or make more than one pass over the entire lawn. In addition, never vertical mow during periods of drought. After vertical mowing, rake and remove all thatch from the soil surface.

You may have heard about people burning a lawn during the winter to remove thatch and dead top-growth. Saint Augustine Grass has large, succulent stolons that are not completely dormant during the winter. Fire will injure them and kill large areas of your lawn. It is also extremely dangerous.

TOPDRESSING

Topdressing is a process by which a thin layer of soil or sand is distributed across the grass surface using a special topdressing machine. You may have heard the term because it is a common practice on golf courses. Golf course superintendents topdress golf greens to form a smoother putting surface. The idea is that grass roots and stolons grow into the topdressed soil and the grass shifts in response to the new, flatter soil surface.

Despite what many people may tell you, topdressing is not the answer to thinning turf or poor drainage. In fact, topdressing may compound these problems. For the typical homeowner, topdressing should be limited to filling gullies and holes that make mowing difficult. A single depression should be filled layer by layer over the entire growing season, never covering the surface with more than .25 inches of soil or sand at a time. Greater amounts will smother the grass and cause more harm than good.

There are only a few circumstances when you might consider topdressing your entire Saint Augustine lawn—

An excessive thatch accumulation becomes a haven for insect pests.

for instance, if your sod was laid poorly and the entire lawn is bumpy. It may also be helpful to topdress a lawn with a heavy thatch accumulation, although I prefer to try core aerating first (see "Aerating"). In either case, you may want to hire a lawn care professional who has a topdressing machine and access to high-quality topdressing soil mixtures. Topdressing with the wrong grade of soil or sand can cause the soil to "layer," which obstructs drainage and causes growth problems.

BLOWING AND EDGING

Many people own their own blower these days. Blowers are wonderful tools that take a lot of the backache out of lawn work. A blower can be used to clean debris from driveways, walks, and porches. It is also an invaluable tool in October when falling leaves are getting the best of us. I also use a blower to disperse grass clippings if they accumulate in lines along the surface of my lawn.

There are three types of blowers: electric blowers, backpack blowers, and rolling street blowers. If you are going to be doing yard work for many years to come, I would definitely invest in a gas-powered blower. Electric blowers are inexpensive, but the inevitable tangled power cord is a complete hassle. Backpack blowers are great if you need a versatile machine that can reach various nooks and crannies. Rolling street blowers are the best for blowing leaves, but they are expensive and difficult to maneuver if your property has hills or steps.

Lawn maintenance companies regularly edge lawns and flower beds with a special machine that has a vertically rotating blades. You can accomplish the same effect by rotating your string trimmer and letting the string dig into the soil. Edging is largely a matter of aesthetics, although it does keep Saint Augustine from creeping out across your driveway. Remember this, though. Edging opens the soil surface and will disrupt the chemical barrier of your pre-emergence weed control. It is common to see weeds sprouting in early March in the edged groove between a lawn and a driveway. If needed, it is safer to edge during June, July, and August.

WEED CONTROL

The majority of weeds you find in your lawn blew from surrounding areas as seeds and sprouted the minute they found enough bare soil, moisture, and light to grow. This is true for both annual weeds and perennial weeds. Annual weeds sprout, grow, flower, seed, and die within one year. Perennial weeds sprout from a seed as well, but the weed plant continues to grow and spread for more than one season (even though the top may die back in the winter).

> ☞ **TIP:** Neighboring lawns, woods, and adjacent untended areas produce enormous numbers of weed seeds that blow into your lawn. If possible, mow or "weed-eat" them to prevent seed formation.

Weeds will invade a Saint Augustine lawn for one reason: your lawn is not growing well. In fact, two common reasons for weeds in a Saint Augustine lawn are drought and insect damage. It is not that drought and insect damage increase the number of weeds or weed seeds trying to creep into your turf. Instead, drought and insect damage cause Saint Augustine lawns to thin, thus offering weed seeds an open space to germinate and grow. Your trouble may be different. Soil compaction, cold damage, flooding, steep slopes (causing dry soil), lack of fertilizer, and irregular pH can cause Saint Augustine grass to thin. The underlying point is that a dense mat of Saint Augustine grass is the most effective way to stop weeds. Even then, you will probably need to rely on several other weed control methods to keep your lawn free of weeds.

Weeds like Pennywort quickly enter a thinning lawn.

Types of Weed Control

There are two ways to control weeds in a lawn: as the weed seeds germinate (pre-emergence weed control) and after the weeds have already sprouted and are growing (post-emergence weed control). When using weed control products, always make sure the product is approved for use on Saint Augustine and your specific type of Saint Augustine. Some herbicides will be approved for use on Bermuda Grass and Zoysia, but *not Saint Augustine*. Follow the labeled directions carefully. Do not apply more than the recommended rate; it will not give you better results and may injure your lawn.

Pre-emergence weed controls kill immature weeds immediately after they germinate and before they emerge from the soil surface. Since annual weeds like annual bluegrass, chickweed, and henbit die and return from seed each year, a pre-emergence weed control will eradicate them from your Saint Augustine over several seasons. At the same time, it will prevent annual and perennial weed seeds that blow into your lawn from neighboring areas from emerging. Most pre-emergence products are sold in a granular form (with or without fertilizer) that you spread using a fertilizer spreader. It is important to spread the chemical "wall to wall" at the recommended rate. Areas that are not covered by the chemical will not be protected. After spreading the product, irrigate your lawn with at least .5 inches of water to activate the chemical (unless otherwise stated on the bag). Once activated, pre-emergence weed controls create a chemical barrier in the upper inches of soil that will prevent weed seeds from germinating. Do not cultivate, aerate, or disturb the soil after treating your lawn or you will open the soil to weed seed infiltration. Pre-emergence weed controls are usually effective for 2–3 months, depending on the temperature and amount of rainfall.

> **Pre-Emergence Weed Control:** Usually sold as a dry, granular product in a 10–30 pound bag. May be labeled as "crabgrass control" although it will stop other weeds as well.
> **Post-Emergence Weed Control:** Usually sold as a liquid concentrate you spray from a pressurized sprayer or a hose-end sprayer. May be labeled as "broadleaf weed killer" or "grassy weed killer."

Post-emergence weed controls kill established weeds like nutsedge and pennywort that are already growing in your lawn. These products are referred to as "selective" since they are targeted at specific annual and perennial weeds listed on the label. Usually, controls will either treat grassy weeds like crabgrass (monocotyledons) or broadleaf weeds like chickweed (dicotyledons). Choose the weed control spray that best fits your needs. You may need to purchase a spray for each category of weeds. In most cases, post-emergence products are designed to disrupt one of the weed's critical metabolic processes and should be sprayed when the weed is young and actively growing. If the weed is dormant because of cold weather or drought (i.e., not using the metabolic process), it may not die. Spray on a still day when air temperatures are between 60–80° and the grass is dry. Avoid spraying during the 4–6 weeks in the spring when your Saint Augustine is turning green. Pre-emergence products are sometimes available in granular form and should be spread with a fertilizer spreader when the grass is wet. The dry particles need the moisture to adhere to weed leaves.

☛ **WARNING:** Weed controls can have dramatic and damaging effects on ornamental trees, shrubs, and plants growing in or near your lawn. This is true for pre-emergence and post-emergence weed controls. For instance, some post-emergence sprays are absorbed by tree roots and can cause the leaves to burn or defoliate. Read the product label carefully for directions and never spray underneath shallow-rooted trees and shrubs like Dogwoods and Boxwoods.

There are other post-emergence weed controls like Round-Up that are non-selective. The term "non-selective" means they will kill all vegetation including your Saint Augustine. The trick is that non-selective weed sprays are absorbed through plant leaves. During the winter months, you may be able to spray green weeds without affecting the dormant Saint Augustine grass. WATCH OUT! Saint Augustine lawns are never truly dormant in the winter and they will die if you spray them. This may be your only option, however, if you are having trouble eradicating a troublesome patch of weeds.

When to Apply Weed Control

When it comes to weed control, a few weeks may mean the difference between controlling 95% of the weeds in your lawn and controlling only 50% of the weeds. This is especially true with pre-emergence weed controls since they have to be applied before weed seeds germinate or they are useless. Post-emergence weed control sprays and granules have to be applied when the weeds are young, tender, and actively growing. I have found that when it comes to weed control, it is always better to be a little early rather than a little late.

Under normal conditions, you can keep a Saint Augustine lawn relatively weed-free with two applications of granular pre-emergence weed control (late winter and early fall) and spot treatments of problem weeds with a post-emergence weed control spray in mid-winter and early summer. I have included two "optional" pre-emergence weed control applications for people trying to renovate a very weedy lawn and people that live near a major source of weeds like an old pasture.

• **Late Winter:** Apply a pre-emergence weed control when the soil temperature reaches a consistent 50°. This is usually in February/early March, when the Forsythia is in bloom. This application will control annual weeds and perennial weeds that germinate in the spring. Make sure the product is approved for use on Saint Augustine grass and apply at the rate recommended on the bag. Do not aerate for 3 months after you apply pre-emergence weed control, because it will affect the chemical barrier. Irrigate after applying unless otherwise stated on the bag. Do not use a pre-emergence weed control that contains fertilizer. If you fertilize now, you might stimulate your lawn to break dormancy during a warm spell, only to be damaged by freezing temperatures.

• **Late Spring and Summer:** Apply pre-emergence weed control without fertilizer around June 1 to control annual and perennial weeds that continue to germinate into the summer (optional application). If your lawn is mostly weed-free on June 1, and weeds do not usually blow in from surrounding areas, you can skip this application. Use a product approved for use on Saint Augustine lawns and apply it at the rate recommended on the bag. Remember not to aerate for 3 months after you apply pre-emergence weed control because it will affect the chemical barrier. Irrigate after applying unless otherwise stated on the bag.

Once your Saint Augustine grass is completely green and soil temperatures reach 75–80° (usually in May), begin treating weed outbreaks with a **post-emergence weed control** spray approved for use on Saint Augustine lawns. Do not spray weed control during March and April when your grass is turning green because it can harm your lawn. Most sprays should be used when the air temperature is 60–80° (check the product label) and weeds are young and tender. If you wait another month or two, weeds will be older, tougher, and require repeated applications to kill them.

If your lawn is still overrun with weeds in mid-summer, consider using a combination fertilizer/post-emergence weed control (granular form) when you fertilize around July 1. Follow the labeled instructions and make sure your lawn is wet when you broadcast the product.

• **Early Fall:** Wait until soil temperatures drop to 70° to apply pre-emergence weed control (without fertilizer) to your Saint Augustine lawn. This is usually October 15 in the lower South and late September in the middle South. If you think you will forget, you can apply pre-emergence weed control when you fertilize in early September but you will be sacrificing some effectiveness. This application will control weeds like annual bluegrass and henbit that germinate in the fall and winter.

Either way, make sure the pre-emergence product is approved for use on Saint Augustine grass and apply at the rate recommended on the bag. Irrigate after applying unless otherwise stated on the bag. This application will last 2–3 months.

• **Winter:** Apply a **pre-emergence weed control** without fertilizer 2–3 months after your fall application (optional application). This is usually in late November/early December. If your lawn is mostly weed-free, and weeds do not usually blow in from surrounding areas, you can skip this application. Use a product approved for use on Saint Augustine and apply at the rate recommended on the bag. Remember not to aerate for 3 months after you apply pre-emergence weed control because it may affect the chemical barrier. Irrigate after applying unless otherwise stated on the bag.

During the winter, treat winter weed outbreaks as soon as you see them (young weeds will die quickly) with a **post-emergence weed control** spray approved for use on Saint Augustine lawns. This is usually in January and February. Most of your problems this time of year will be from annual weeds like annual bluegrass and henbit. Spray on a warm afternoon (air tempera-ture is at least 60°) when the weeds are young and actively growing. It may take two applications to kill them. You can also spray tough perennial weeds during the winter with a non-selective weed control like Round-Up. Spray only the leaves of the weeds and expect some Saint Augustine grass in the vicinity to die.

INSECTS AND PESTS

Saint Augustine lawns are the perfect home for a variety of insects like crickets, beetles, grasshoppers, millipedes, and worms. Some feed on grass blades, some feed on grass roots, and some feed on each other. In most cases, Saint Augustine grass grows faster than the average insect can eat and we don't have to worry. There are, however, a few classes of insects that can increase in populations large enough to harm your lawn. If you do not treat them quickly, they have the potential to damage your lawn extensively. Be ready with soil insecticides and natural products like BT and Milky Spore. The best time for a once-a-year insect treatment is in late July or early August.

Insect damage is often defined as an irregularly shaped patch of discolored or brown grass in a lawn. If you take a drive around town, you will probably pass a thousand lawns that could fit that definition. The problem is this. Only about ten of those thousand lawns probably have an insect problem. Lawns are finicky and irregular patches of brown grass pop up because of different reasons. One of the most common is drought. You might think your lawn is evenly watered but even a slight rise or a different soil texture can alter the amount of water that penetrates the soil. When you think you have an insect problem, look for another cause first. Then, wait to see if the troubled lawn area expands. Only then should you worry about treating with a soil insecticide. Following is a list of insects that might cause problems in a Saint Augustine lawn. Don't panic! You may never see any of these bugs.

The most notorious insect problem to afflict Saint Augustine lawns is the chinch bug. These disgusting little creatures have numerous generations per year and can devastate a lawn. The first hatch is usually in the spring, at which time the young nymphs begin feeding in masses. They usually begin to damage a lawn, however, in July through September. Watch for dispersed patches of yellow turf in sunny areas of the lawn. These areas will eventually turn brown. There is a simple way to confirm their presence. Cut the top and bottom from a coffee can and pound it several inches into the off-color grass.

Check irregular patches of yellow or brown grass for chinch bugs.

Fill the inside of the can with several inches of water and maintain the water level for five minutes. The chinch bugs will float to the surface. Once you have confirmed their presence, treat the entire area with a soil insecticide approved for use on Saint Augustine grass. If you live in an area that has known chinch bug problems, and you are planning a new Saint Augustine lawn, you may want to consider a chinch bug "resistant" cultivar like Floratam or Floralawn Saint Augustine.

White grubs also cause problems on Saint Augustine lawns. White grubs are the larval, soil-inhabiting form of several different types of beetles. The most notorious beetle in the South is the Japanese Beetle, known for its voracious feeding on Crape Myrtle, grapes, ornamental cherry trees, and almost anything green. Japanese Beetles lay their eggs in lawns and grassy areas beginning in July. The eggs hatch as white grubs in late July and begin a two-month feeding frenzy on grass roots. As soil temperatures cool in October, the white grubs tunnel down 4–8 inches into the soil where they pass the winter. As the soil warms in the spring white grubs move to the surface, feed briefly in April/May, and then pupate. White grubs can be controlled with a granular soil insecticide applied in late July/early August according

to the labeled directions. Milky Spore is a natural product that contains spores of *Bacillus popilliae*, a disease that kills white grubs. Milky spore will not kill every last white grub, but spores will remain active in your lawn for many years.

There are several types of **larval worms** that feed on Saint Augustine leaf blades. They include cutworms and sod webworms. Unlike white grubs, larval worms can have several life cycles during a given growing season and are less predictable in their arrival. In addition, they are night-feeders and hide in tunnels beneath your lawn during the day. Insect damage appears as areas of brown or unevenly clipped grass. Sod webworms also leave a spidery web on grass blades that you notice early in the morning. Larval worms can be controlled with a soil insecticide approved for use on Saint Augustine grass. BT (*Bacillus thuringiensis*) is an effective natural product.

Armyworms feed in masses on Saint Augustine leaf blades throughout the day and night. They move quickly and can literally devour a lawn. Keep a lookout beginning in the late spring and through the growing season. Young larvae eat the edges of grass blades while the mature larvae eat the entire blade. Armyworms usually affect an entire subdivision/area at a time, so listen to your neighbors and state agencies for "army-worm alerts." The worst outbreaks of large populations usually occur from July to October. If they arrive in your lawn, apply a soil insecticide approved for use on Saint Augustine lawns. BT (*Bacillus thuringiensis*) is an effective natural product.

Mole crickets are a major concern in the lower South in sandy soils. These horrendous burrowing crickets tunnel through the soil at night, loosening the sandy soil and disrupting grass roots. Mole crickets are active throughout the growing season but are most common when night air temperatures remain above 60°. Damage usually appears as if someone cultivated areas of your lawn. Once you have located them, apply a soil insecticide labeled for control of mole crickets and approved for use on Saint Augustine lawns.

Fire ants are a complete pain in the neck. I have tried almost every chemical available, and a number of home remedies, and have only had average results. Every time I treat a mound it seems to pop up in another location. Sometimes the mounds seem to multiply. There are numerous entomologists working on the problem, so hopefully they will find a good cure soon.

If **moles** are tunneling through your lawn, they are probably after white grubs. Treat for white grubs in late July/early August and the moles will probably go away.

There is always another insect or pest that *might* plague your lawn. You might hear or read about ground pearls, billbugs, nematodes, mites, and a long list of other potential problems. In general, don't worry. Just keep an eye on things and treat problems when you find them. Your lawn is tougher than you think.

DISEASES AND VIRUSES

Under certain environmental conditions, Saint Augustine lawns are susceptible to a variety of fungal diseases including brownpatch, pythium blight, Helminthosporium, and gray leaf spot. These diseases are usually prevalent in the spring and fall when daytime air temperatures are 60–80°, nighttime air temperatures are around 60°, and there is plenty of moisture on the grass. During these critical times, irrigate during the daylight hours when moisture will evaporate quickly from the grass.

Since fungal diseases are very difficult to identify, it is important to keep a sharp watch for anything abnormal. In the early stages, a fungal disease like gray leaf

Saint Augustine lawns can be overseeded in the winter with Annual Ryegrass.

spot may appear as a discoloration on individual leaf blades. Most of us miss this stage, however, and we notice a disease as a brown or damaged patch of grass with smooth outlines. If you find a lawn area that fits this description, don't run out and spray the entire lawn with fungicide. Wait to see if the patch of damaged grass expands over the next day or two. It is quite possible that the fungal disease has already run its course. An "active" patch of diseased turf will grow and expand concentrically over a couple of days. Grass plants along the outline of the damaged patch will have the most telling signs: wilted plants, shriveled leaves, or discolored leaf blades. Once located, spray infected areas with a lawn fungicide approved for use on Saint Augustine grass.

If your lawn has a history of fungal problems, you may want to renovate the dead areas and then spray preventatively with a lawn fungicide the following year so that the disease does not recur. Follow the directions on the product label explicitly. You will probably need to spray several times over a 2–4 week period.

There is a virus known as Saint Augustine Decline (SAD) that causes yellowing of Saint Augustine leaf blades. There is no cure for SAD although good hygiene like bagging clippings and disinfecting mower blades are thought to prevent it from spreading. Luckily, Saint Augustine grass cultivars like Floratam, Floralawn, and Raleigh seem to be resistant to the disease.

In general, good maintenance practices like weekly mowing at the right height and limited fertilizer applications will go a long way toward preventing disease problems.

OVERSEEDING

Saint Augustine lawns can be overseeded with a cool-season grass in the fall to provide a green cover over the dormant lawn during the winter months. An overseeded Saint Augustine lawn will not be as thick and green as an overseeded Bermuda Grass lawn, but it is worth the try nonetheless. Here's how it works. The cool-season grass germinates in the fall and begins to grow as your Saint Augustine lawn enters dormancy. During the winter months, you continue to mow and maintain the cool-season grass as you would a normal lawn. As spring arrives, the Saint Augustine lawn will begin to green as normal. During this "spring transition," the cool-season grass and Saint Augustine lawn will both be green and will be competing with one another. As the heat of summer arrives, though, the cool-season grass will die and leave the Saint Augustine grass to prosper for the rest of the summer.

Saint Augustine grass can be overseeded with a variety of cool-season grasses. The key is to choose one that will not linger too long into summer, thus allowing your Saint Augustine lawn to recover fully. Annual Rye (a.k.a. Italian Rye) is a good, generic choice for the South. It cannot tolerate hot weather and will die quickly as heat approaches. Perennial Rye can also be used but it is more expensive and may linger into summer in shaded areas. Creeping Bentgrass is a good choice, but it is expensive and seldom available. Do not overseed Saint Augustine with Tall Fescue or Kentucky Bluegrass since they will last well into summer and compete with your Saint Augustine grass.

Steps in Overseeding

1. Do not apply pre-emergence weed control in the three months prior to overseeding.

2. Overseed Saint Augustine lawns when the soil temperature drops to 70°. This is usually around October 15 in the lower South and late September in the middle South.

3. Prepare the lawn before seeding by mowing your Saint Augustine to about 2 inches and raking the lawn vigorously with a metal-tined rake.

4. Sow 6–8 pounds of Annual Rye per 1000 square feet and apply a complete lawn fertilizer that contains a slow-release form of nitrogen, if you have not done so already. Apply at the rate of 1.5 pounds of actual nitrogen per 1000 square feet.

5. Keep the soil surface moist for 7–10 days to ensure even germination. After that, water weekly if there has been no significant rainfall.

6. Begin mowing as soon as the Annual Rye reaches 2.5 inches. This is a good time to install a new mower blade, or sharpen the old one. A dull blade will rip seedlings from the lawn.

7. Continue to mow throughout the winter at 2.5 inches, whenever the grass reaches 3.75 inches. Do not let the grass grow so tall that it flops over.

8. Fertilize lightly every 4–6 weeks throughout the winter whenever the Annual Rye is light green. Use a fertilizer like 10-10-10 that contains a soluble form of nitrogen, not a slow-release form of nitrogen. Slow-release forms of nitrogen are not effective during winter cold. Apply at the rate of .5 pounds of actual nitrogen per 1000 square feet. If using 10-10-10, this equals 5 pounds per 1000 square feet. Stop fertilizing in February, however, to slow its growth so it will not compete with your Saint Augustine grass during the spring green-up.

9. In March, mow your lawn to 2 inches as described in the "Mowing" section. This will stall the Annual Rye and give your Saint Augustine a chance to emerge. Continue to mow consistently at 2.5 inches during the spring transition until the Annual Rye begins to die in hot weather.

II. Renovating a Saint Augustine Grass Lawn

There is nothing worse than inviting the neighbors to a barbeque and realizing your lawn is a weedy mess. It wouldn't be a problem if you could be sure your gloating neighbor would not invite you for a tour of his immaculate turf. Luckily, a large percentage of "troubled" Saint Augustine lawns can be renovated without extreme effort. You might not have a prize-winning lawn in time for the barbeque, but it will certainly be ready for next season. The general rule is that if you can find one healthy clump of Saint Augustine grass in a given square foot of lawn, you can renovate. Otherwise, grab your wallet and head for the section entitled "Planting a New Saint Augustine Grass Lawn."

The first step in renovating a Saint Augustine lawn is to admit that there is a problem. There are two categories of problems that will ruin a Saint Augustine lawn: maintenance problems and fundamental problems. Unfortunately, the results of both often appear the same. For instance, a thinning lawn can be the result of drought, insects, or dense shade. Think about your lawn's history and work your way toward the logical cause.

CORRECTING MAINTENANCE PROBLEMS

As many a golfer has learned, your game will not improve miraculously by buying a new set of clubs. You have to address the underlying problem with your swing. Read through the maintenance section above and determine if you are skipping any critical steps. Are you fertilizing, mowing at the right height, mowing consis-

Saint Augustine runners will spread quickly if you correct underlying problems.

tently, aerating, irrigating, and applying pre-emergence weed control? Do you have an insect or disease problem? By addressing these problems, you can stimulate your grass to grow denser, fill voids, and darken in color. Below are two recipes for Saint Augustine lawn renovation. They cover approximately eight months of the year. Avoid renovation attempts in the two months when lawns are greening in the spring and the two months when lawns are going dormant in the fall.

CORRECTING FUNDAMENTAL PROBLEMS

There are times when even a perfect maintenance routine does not produce the perfect lawn. It is at these times that we are tempted to abandon lawn growing and settle for a nice collection of weeds. The first thing to remember is that Saint Augustine grass is not a miracle plant. It will not grow where all other plants have failed. In fact, in certain situations there may be hundreds of plants that will grow better in a particular area (see "ground cover" in the glossary). Remember this as you read the remedies below. The most efficient and inexpensive approach might be to reconfigure or abandon areas that are not suitable for a Saint Augustine lawn.

• **Shade.** While Saint Augustine grass tolerates moderate levels of shade, it will become thin and weak in dense shade. The only answer is remove a few tree branches or reduce the size of your lawn to avoid the shade. Raising the mowing height in the shaded areas may alleviate some of the problem but is often impractical. Also consider this. Areas of dense shade often have a high density of tree roots. Temporarily increase your irrigation in the shaded areas to see if the problem is actually drought.

• **Compacted soil.** Compacted soil is low in oxygen and will cause Saint Augustine grass to thin and die. This is especially true in clay-based soils. Consider aerating once or twice during the growing season when soil temperatures are 75–80°. Also, evaluate the cause of the compaction and correct continuing problems by creating walkways for people and pets.

• **Poor drainage.** Saint Augustine grass will thin and die in constantly wet, soggy soils. These are also some of most difficult and expensive problems to correct. Before you begin, determine the source of the water and where it is trying to flow. Occasionally, you can correct a poor drainage by diverting a water source

Recipe for Growing-Season Renovation *(May through August)*

1. Kill Weeds. Spray weedy areas with a post-emergence weed control as soon as possible. Young weeds die faster than mature weeds (see "Weed Control").

2. Rake. Rake the entire lawn vigorously with a metal-tined rake to remove thatch, leaves, dead weeds, grass clippings, rocks, etc. Consider renting a vertical mower if you have a thatch accumulation greater than .5 inches (see "Dethatching").

3. Mow. Check your mowing height. Mow frequently and consistently.

4. Irrigate. Water deeply once every week or so if there has been no rain. Don't drop the ball! Even short periods of drought can cause growth problems.

5. Fertilize/Lime. Fertilize immediately (if you have not done so) and again in late August/early September. Broadcast 50 pounds of lime per thousand square feet if your soil is acidic.

6. Aerate. Consider core-aerating to stimulate grass to grow and spread.

7. Do not topdress unless you are trying to smooth your lawn surface. It will not stimulate growth.

8. Control Future Weeds. Apply pre-emergence weed control ON TIME in the fall (see "Weed Control").

Recipe for Dormant-Season Renovation *(November through February)*

1. Kill Weeds. Spray weedy areas with a post-emergence weed control as soon as possible, on a warm day. Young weeds die faster than mature weeds (see "Weed Control"). Hand-pull problem weeds like bunches of fescue.

2. Control Future Weeds. Apply pre-emergence weed control ON TIME in late winter (see "Weed Control").

3. Rake. Rake your lawn vigorously in late February/early March and remove all the debris. The ideal is to have a good clean soil surface.

4. Wait until late April **to fertilize** and late May **to core aerate**.

(like a gutter outlet) or removing an obstruction (a clogged ditch). Other solutions include re-grading, French drains, and surface ditches. Once the soil dries, core-aerate to help renovate the root zone.

• **Improper pH.** In extremely acidic or basic soils, Saint Augustine will grow slowly, lose density, and be light green/yellow *despite* your best maintenance practices. Always consider your maintenance first, however, before you blame soil pH. If you suspect soil pH, take a soil sample to your local Cooperative Extension Service for testing. They will recommend the exact amount of lime or elemental sulfur to correct the problem.

III. Planting a New Saint Augustine Grass Lawn

Saint Augustine lawns are usually started from sod or plugs. Saint Augustine seeds are becoming available but are not yet a good option for the average homeowner. The most common method is to lay sod "wall to wall" so that you completely cover the entire new lawn area. This method is relatively quick and provides an instant lawn. Plugging is a variation of sodding in which you plant pieces of sod 1–2 feet apart. You save money because you are purchasing far less sod. The lawn will develop over 2–6 months as the Saint Augustine plugs spread to fill the gaps. During this time you will have to worry about weeds invading the bare intervals.

Whether you are sodding or plugging, the best time of year to begin is in the late spring once the danger of frost has passed and the sod is completely green. The optimal soil temperature for establishing a new Saint Augustine lawn is 75–80°, which usually occurs in May. You can continue to plant Saint Augustine lawns through the summer, as long as you water frequently while the roots are growing into the soil below. Try not to plant after mid-August because your lawn will not have enough warm weather to become established before winter weather.

A Sampling of Saint Augustine Grass Cultivars:

• **Floratam:** Coarse texture, vigorous, good resistance to SAD and chinch bugs.

• **Floralawn.** Coarse texture, vigorous, good resistance to SAD and chinch bugs.

• **Raleigh:** Medium texture, cold hardy, not resistant to chinch bugs.

• **Seville:** Semi-dwarf cultivar, some resistance to SAD and chinch bugs.

• **Palmetto:** A new cultivar with medium texture. Supposed to resist cold and drought.

☛ **TIP:** Soil-related problems cause all kinds of havoc with a lawn, and it is impossible to fix a soil problem once your lawn is established. Now is your only chance. Take the time to cultivate the soil deeply and amend it with humus before you plant.

STEPS IN PLANTING A SAINT AUGUSTINE GRASS LAWN

Planting a new lawn from sod or plugs is tough work and it is difficult to do a good job if you try to plant the entire lawn in one weekend. A good way to split the project into manageable parts is to cultivate one weekend and lay sod the next weekend. Even then, start as early in the morning as you can. Ninety-degree heat seems like 110° when you are bent over on your hands and knees laying sod.

STEP 1. Spray existing weeds. The first step in planting a new Saint Augustine lawn is to eliminate all weeds from the lawn area. Use a non-selective weed control like Round-Up. Plan ahead since you will need to wait 1–2 weeks after spraying before you sod or plug (check the product label for specifics).

STEP 2. Establish the grade. One of the best ways to guarantee a beautiful lawn is to establish the proper grade before you begin. This may be more than most of us can afford, but consider it nonetheless. A good slope has the potential to alleviate drought and poor drainage. It will also be easier to mow. In general, a 2–6% grade is optimal.

STEP 3. Cultivate the soil as deeply as possible. Whether you use sod or plugs, Saint Augustine grass roots will need to grow and become established in the existing soil. The deeper you can cultivate the soil, the more quickly your Saint Augustine lawn will become established and thrive. Remember to wait the allotted time after spraying a herbicide before cultivating. Begin by raking and removing debris like dead weeds, leaves, and rocks from the area. Next, cultivate the soil with a rear-tine rototiller. If you don't have a rototiller, consider renting one from a tool rental store. Rototill the entire area lengthwise, then again crosswise. Try to work at least 4–6 inches of soil into a nice pulverized soil mix. If you prefer not to rototill, cultivate as much of the area as you can with a hoe, garden rake, or shovel. Again, the deeper you work the soil, the better.

STEP 4. Amend the soil. Most of the soils you encounter will either be a sand-based soil or clay-based soil. Either way, amend the soil with humus before you plant. Humus is a general term for the organic material that naturally occurs in the top layer of soil. Unfortunately, most lawn areas are graded during home construction and the top layer of soil is buried or removed. Adding humus will renovate these soils by improving water retention in sandy soils and improving drainage in clay soils. Peat moss, composted bark products, and compost are all good choices. I usually add about two 3.8-cubic-foot bales of sphagnum peat moss per 1000 square feet. Work the peat moss into the top 4–6 inches of soil as you rototill.

STEP 5. Lime and fertilizer. A lawn is a big investment and it does not hurt to have the soil pH determined by your County Extension Service. Saint Augustine grass prefers a soil pH of 6.5–7. A soil test will recommend the specific amount of lime to add if the pH needs to be raised, and elemental sulfur to add if the pH needs to be lowered. Most Southern soils are acidic and will need approximately 50 pounds of lime per 1000 square feet. Whenever possible, purchase pelletized lime because it is easier to spread. Broadcast the pelletized lime with a fertilizer spreader, or by hand, and work it into the top layer of soil using a garden rake. At the same time, apply a complete lawn fertilizer that contains slow-release nitrogen. I prefer to start a Saint Augustine lawn with a 3-1-2 ratio fertilizer like 12-4-8. Apply at the rate of 1.5 pounds of actual nitrogen per 1000 square feet. Work the fertilizer into the top layer of cultivated soil using a garden rake.

Do not apply pre-emergence weed control when you sod or plug a new Saint Augustine lawn. Pre-emergence controls often stunt root growth and it will take longer for your Saint Augustine grass to become established. Wait until the late summer/early fall to begin using pre-emergence weed control products.

STEP 6. Sodding. Unless you are planting a small lawn, it is almost always cheaper and more efficient to order pallets of sod from your local nursery to be delivered to your house. Most people prefer to order enough sod to cover the entire lawn area "wall to wall." Plan on laying the sod soon after it arrives on pallets. Stacked sod should not sit for more than a day or two. It is usually a good idea to cultivate and amend the soil one weekend, and lime/fertilize and lay sod the next.

Begin by raking the entire cultivated area to prepare as smooth a surface as possible. Be careful because the sod will mimic the soil surface below, not compensate for it. It is best for the soil to be moist at the time you sod, but not wet. Start at the top of the lawn and lay the sod lengthwise, so that the long side of each piece of sod is running perpendicular to a hill or rise. As you place each piece of sod, work it tight against the surrounding pieces to prevent the edges from browning and ruts from forming. Sod is often cut on a slant so that the edges will overlap. Make sure the edges slant appropriately so that they interlock. Pound each block of sod with your palm to press it into the soil below and remove any air pockets. Stagger the second row of sod so that the perpendicular edges do not line up. The result should look like a brick wall, not a checkerboard. If you are placing sod along steep gradients, pin them in place with stakes or metal pins (available from sod distributors). Irrigate deeply once all the sod is placed.

STEP 7. Plugging. A plug is essentially a four-square-inch piece of sod. Plugs are sometimes available for purchase, but you may have to create your own by cutting sod into smaller pieces. The idea behind plugging is to plant each individual piece 1–2 feet apart and allow the grass to grow together over the coming months to form a solid grass surface. Unlike sodding, individual plugs must be planted in the ground so that the roots are surrounded by soil and the grass runners are flush with the soil surface. Once all the plugs are set, the lawn should be irrigated. Plugging is less expensive than sodding because you purchase less grass. It usually takes about the same time to plug as it does to lay sod.

STEP 8. Irrigation during establishment. Whether you begin with sod or plugs, nurse your lawn diligently over the coming 4–6 weeks. It may look like an established lawn but its root system is a fraction of what it should be. Begin by watering lightly and frequently. After a week or so, decrease the frequency of irrigation but increase the amount of water you apply. By six weeks, you should be applying an inch of water per week (in one application), if there has been no significant rainfall. If you are starting your lawn from plugs, follow these same guidelines but rely on your instinct. If the soil surface is eroding or remains excessively damp, skip a watering. If the soil surface near the plugs dries rapidly, irrigate more frequently.

STEP 9. Mowing during establishment. Begin mowing your new sod or plugs as soon as they reach the recommended height. Do not mow lower or higher: both have different negative effects.

STEP 10. Fertilizing during establishment. Fertilize six weeks after planting with a complete lawn fertilizer that contains a slow-release form of nitrogen. Apply at the rate of 1 pound of actual nitrogen per 1000 square feet. This application will last until you fertilize again in early fall (see "Fertilizer").

STEP 11. Weed control during establishment. Weeds are especially troublesome with a Saint Augustine lawn started with plugs. During the months it takes for the plugs to spread, weed seeds germinate and colonize each bare interval. Begin spraying weeds as soon as they appear with a post-emergence weed control approved for use on Saint Augustine. I would not risk spraying weedy areas between plugs with a non-selective herbicide like Round-Up. In all cases, begin applying pre-emergence weed control in early fall.

Rototill, amend the soil, and add fertilizer before you plant.

Saint Augustine plugs are often available in trays.

Individual plugs must be planted in the soil to cover the roots.

Plant Saint Augustine plugs 1–2 feet apart.

Continue planting in staggered rows.

Water thoroughly once all the plugs are planted.

Zoysia lawns are dense, fine-textured, and elegant.

CHAPTER FIVE

Zoysia
(Zoysia spp.)

ZOYSIA IS THE MOST ELEGANT, FINE-TEXTURED LAWN GRASS GROWN IN THE SOUTH. In many ways, it is the epitome of what we want and expect in a lawn. It is lush, dark green, and forms a dense cover. A well-grown Zoysia lawn is so thick that it physically prevents weeds from entering. It will thrive in the summer heat but it will not be bothered by freezing temperatures. It is also more resistant to insects and diseases than many other lawn grasses.

Zoysia lawns are not only elegant, they are a great lawn for a family. Once established, they are almost as durable as a Bermuda Grass lawn, but will also tolerate a moderate amount of shade. When you consider color, texture, durability, and elegance, a Zoysia lawn is certainly a step up from your neighbor's hybrid Bermuda Grass.

There is also a certain quality about Zoysia that makes you want to run your hands back and forth across its blades. It's almost like that urge to run your hands through your hair after leaving the barber. There are always detractors, though, who will claim that Zoysia is "wiry" and "prickly." This is only a problem with certain types of Zoysia if they are not mowed on time.

> **At a Glance:**
>
> - Fine textured, elegant grass
> - Dark green color
> - Will tolerate partial shade
> - Forms a dense stand, but spreads slowly
> - Should be sodded; plugging possible
> - Mowed at 1–2 inches when it reaches 1.5–3 inches
> - Needs approximately 1 inch of water per week during the growing season
> - Fertilized 2–3 times a year

I. Maintaining an Established Zoysia Lawn

Zoysia lawns are often characterized as high-maintenance lawns. I prefer not to think of them in this way. Instead, consider a Zoysia lawn as hit or miss. If you understand your maintenance program, and alter your "normal" techniques just a little, you will have a hit and grow an outstanding Zoysia lawn. If you think of Zoysia as any old lawn, there is a good chance you will miss entirely and lose your elegant lawn.

MOWING

It is hard to think of mowing as anything but the activity that can spoil a good Saturday afternoon. Let's face it, mowing seems mundane. There are a few finer points, however, that can drastically improve the appearance of your lawn. Even then, you'll have to mow every week. Sorry.

The mowing season actually begins while your Zoysia lawn is still dormant. Mow the entire lawn at about 1 inch to remove as much dead top growth as possible. Try to do this after the danger of hard freezes has passed, but before new grass blades emerge. This is usually in early to mid-March when the Bradford Pear trees are in full bloom. Bag or rake all of the dead top growth as you mow to prevent thatch accumulations and to start the year with a clean slate. Do not mow, however, below .5 inches because you may damage Zoysia rhizomes and stolons growing near the soil surface. In the middle and upper South, beware of mowing your dormant lawn too early. The dormant grass

Begin the growing season by mowing and removing dead top growth.

blades act as insulation and prevent hard freezes from affecting shallow roots and rhizomes.

> **Rhizomes:** a modified stem that grows horizontally on, or just below, the soil surface and sends up stems or leaves at the tip.
> **Stolon:** a shoot that grows horizontally near the soil surface, rooting at the nodes to form new plants.

Your lawn will begin to turn green several weeks later when the soil warms to 60–65°. This is usually in mid-March to mid-April, depending on the weather. Do not mow your lawn lower during spring green-up than you will mow during the rest of the growing season. Wait until it reaches the recommended height.

Zoysia lawns form a denser lawn cover than any other Southern lawn grass. In fact, they can be so dense that your lawn mower might have trouble cutting. There are two answers to this problem. If you are committed to Zoysia grass in the long term, and have a relatively small lawn, you may want to purchase a reel mower rather than a rotary mower. Reel mowers cut with a scissor action that is more suited to mowing dense grass at low heights. If you opt for one of the more versatile rotary mowers, choose one with plenty of horsepower and always mow with a sharp blade. Even then, experiment to see how low you can mow without having the rotary blade beat the grass in a circular pattern.

There are several types (species and cultivars) of Zoysia grass. The two most common are Emerald Zoysia and Meyer Zoysia. Both should be cut at 1–2 inches during the growing season. Emerald is slower growing and easier to maintain at lower heights. The two main criteria in determining your exact mowing height are your type of lawn mower (reel vs. rotary) and the frequency you are willing to mow. Reel mowers will be able to mow at one inch while some rotary lawn mowers will cause odd circular mowing patterns at that height. In addition, the lower you mow the more frequently you will have to mow. (For directions on how to accurately set your mower at the correct height, see **Rotary Mower** in the Glossary.)

Once you have set the mowing height for your Zoysia lawn, mow consistently! If you remove more than one-third of a grass blade at a time, you will shock the plant and stall its growth. During the ensuing recovery period, your lawn is more susceptible to stresses like heat, weed competition, and drought. The chart below will help you mow at the right height, at the right time.

> **The One-Third Rule:** Never reduce the height of your lawn by more than one-third when mowing.

There will be those times, like the family vacation, when your Zoysia lawn grows above the recommended height. When you return from your trip, mow the lawn twice over a two- or three-day period. Begin by temporarily raising the mowing height so that you do not remove more than one-third of the grass blade at a time. For instance, if the lawn has grown to 4.5 inches

Recommended Mowing Heights (in inches)

TYPE OF MOWER	MOW TO:	MOW WHEN GRASS IS:
Reel Mower	1	1.5
Reel Mower, Powerful Rotary Mowers	1.5	2.25
Reel or Rotary Mower	2	3

tall, mow at 3 inches. Two or three days later, mow the lawn again at the normal, recommended height.

As mentioned, Zoysia lawns have a tendency to accumulate thatch. Lawn clippings can contribute to this problem since they have difficulty falling through the dense turf to the soil surface where they naturally decompose. It is a good idea to bag your Zoysia lawn clippings or to rake your lawn after mowing. You might want to keep this fact in mind when buying a new mower so that you can purchase one with an easy and efficient bagging device.

Allow your Zoysia lawn to grow to 3 inches in the fall in preparation for cold weather. This extra height will act as winter insulation for roots, rhizomes, and stolons. Plan ahead because Zoysia grows slowly in the fall.

IRRIGATION

Zoysia lawns will need to be irrigated during the summer. While we do have significant rainfall (on average) during the summer months in the South, it is most often sporadic and undependable. A dry Zoysia lawn will lose its dark green color and eventually turn to straw. On the other hand, Zoysia lawns do not like poor drainage and overwatering can be just as detrimental as drought. Realize from the start that it will take a little finesse to water your lawn only when needed. In general, Zoysia lawns need 1 inch of water every week if there has been no significant rainfall. This amount will vary slightly depending on your type of soil. Sandy soils will need more water while clay soils will need less. Stop watering if water begins to run on the surface. Wait an hour and begin again.

Try to water deeply and infrequently. For example, apply 1 inch of water on a single day rather than .25 inches a day for four days. Zoysia grass has the ability to grow roots deep into the soil where there is more moisture, but it will not do so if you train it otherwise. Frequent, light irrigation encourages roots to stay near the soil surface where they are vulnerable to drought.

In a drought, dark green Zoysia grass (left) discolors (middle) and turns to straw (right).

If you have an automatic sprinkler system, take a moment to investigate your control box and settings. Place a rain gauge or straight-sided jar on the lawn and turn on the sprinklers. Monitor how much water is applied in a given period. Most systems will have several different types of sprinkler heads, so you might have to test each irrigation zone. I like to draw a rough diagram of the lawn and record the various sprinkler outputs for future reference. This helps me manipulate the irrigation system during the sporadic rain and drought periods of the coming season. Do not be shy about increasing the pre-set cycles during droughts or turning off the entire system after a heavy rainfall. While lack of water will affect your lawn's color and growth, excess water can kill a Zoysia lawn that does not drain well.

If you water your lawn with a manual sprinkler, place a rain gauge or straight-sided jar in the lawn to measure the amount of water applied. Try not to apply more, or less, than an inch at a time.

> **One Step Further:** A grass plant absorbs water from the soil to replace water that evaporates from its leaf blades. The perfect way to irrigate is to supply the soil with the exact same amount of water that evaporates. Search the Internet for a weather station in your area that records "pan evaporation rate" or "evapotranspiration." Water loss from Zoysia grass blades is roughly 75% of the pan evaporation rate.
> **Formula:** 75% x (Weekly Pan Evaporation Total) − Weekly Rainfall Total = Amount to irrigate that week

Zoysia lawns will occasionally need to be irrigated during the winter to prevent rhizomes, stolons, and roots near the soil surface from drying out. In general, you will need to apply only .25–.5 inches of water at a time. In addition, water dormant Zoysia lawns when temperatures are expected to drop below 20°. Wet soil will freeze and keep soil temperatures close to 32°, while dry soil allows damaging sub-20° air to penetrate the root zone.

FERTILIZER

Fertilizing is one of the most satisfying lawn activities. Within a matter of days, a fertilized lawn will turn dark green and look healthy. A Zoysia lawn will need a moderate amount of fertilizer during the growing season. The object is to supply enough nutrients for healthy growth and a rich green color, but not so much as to encourage excessively dense growth that is hard to mow and promotes thatch. If you apply more than the recommended amount, your lawn will not be any darker green, it will only grow faster and you will have to mow more often. The most efficient way to fertilize is to use the dry, granular fertilizers that are usually sold in 10–50 pound bags. Hose-end liquid fertilizers work, but they are difficult to use correctly and you will need to fertilize twice as often as with granular fertilizer.

> **Zoysia Fertilizer Facts:**
>
> • 3–4 pounds of actual nitrogen per 1000 square feet per year
>
> • Apply 1.5 pounds of actual nitrogen per 1000 square feet in mid-spring and early fall
>
> • Optional application of 1 pound of actual nitrogen per 1000 square feet in mid-summer depending on your lawn's color
>
> • Use slow-release fertilizers whenever possible
>
> • Water approximately 1 inch after fertilizing

What Kind of Fertilizer to Use

Fertilizer is described by the percentages of nitrogen (N), phosphorus (P), and potassium (K) contained in the bag. All fertilizer bags are clearly labeled with these three numbers, known as the N-P-K ratio. Whenever possible, I use a slow-release lawn fertilizer with a 3-1-2 ratio. An example would be a 12-4-8 fertilizer. A bag of 12-4-8 fertilizer contains 12% nitrogen, 4% phosphorus, and 8% potassium by weight. The remaining 76% is inert material that adds bulk to the mixture and makes it easier to spread.

It is important to use slow-release fertilizers whenever possible. Most major brands of lawn fertilizer will have a combination of soluble and slow-release forms of nitrogen (indicated on the label). Soluble nitrogen is available to the grass plant immediately while slow-release nitrogen becomes available over a period of two

Fertilize your Zoysia lawn in mid-spring after the danger of frost has passed.

to three months. In most situations it is best to have as much of the nitrogen in slow-release form as possible. Good brands of fertilizer will have 40–50% of the nitrogen in slow-release form. This is usually noted in a statement like "containing 6% nitrogen in slow-release form."

Be careful when using hose-end fertilizer sprayers or dry fertilizers in which all of the nitrogen is in a soluble, quick-release form. Soluble nitrogen will cause a major flush of growth for a week or two and will completely dissipate in 4–6 weeks. For most of us, it is almost impossible to fertilize with quick-release fertilizers without causing wild, fluctuating growth spurts. If you decide to use quick-release fertilizer, never apply more than 1 pound of actual nitrogen per 1000 square feet per application. You will need to fertilizer every 4–6 weeks during the growing season for a total of 3 or 4 applications. Stay on schedule throughout the season so that nitrogen levels will remain fairly constant in the soil.

Up to this point, I have only mentioned three major nutrients: nitrogen, phosphorus, and potassium. These three nutrients are used by grass plants in relatively large quantities and are known as macronutrients. Grass plants use other nutrients in relatively small quantities. Those nutrients are known as micronutrients or "minor elements." Most major brands of fertilizer contain the needed minor elements and you do not need to worry about them.

Common Forms of Nitrogen (indicated on the label)
Soluble: *Available immediately, lasts 4–6 weeks*
Ammonium nitrate, potassium nitrate, ammonium sulfate
Slow-Release: *Available slowly in small amounts, generally lasts 2–3 months*
Urea-Formaldehyde (UF), Isobutylidene diurea (IBDU), Sulfur Coated Urea (SCU), Polymer Coated Urea products (like "Polyon")

How Much Fertilizer to Apply

Most bags of fertilizer are covered from top to bottom with completely useless information that is written by the fertilizer company's marketing department. I continue to be amazed by the fact that the closest thing to directions is usually a vague phrase like "fertilizes up to 10,000 square feet." Luckily, there is a universal way to know how much fertilizer to apply, regardless of the brand or the specific N-P-K ratio. All you have to do is figure out how much "actual nitrogen" is contained in the bag. Zoysia lawns generally need 3–4 pounds of actual nitrogen per 1000 square feet each year, regardless of the brand of fertilizer you purchase. If you use a fertilizer that contains a slow-release form of nitrogen, you can apply the needed nitrogen in two applications of 1.5 pounds of actual nitrogen per 1000 square feet in mid-spring and early fall. Apply an additional 1 pound of actual nitrogen per 1000 square feet in mid-summer if your lawn is not dark green.

Unfortunately, the average bag of fertilizer does not tell you how much actual nitrogen it contains. It is easy to calculate, though, using two simple pieces of information: the N-P-K ratio and the weight of the bag. Multiply the percentage of nitrogen (the first number in the N-P-K ratio) by the weight of the bag and you will know the amount of actual nitrogen it contains. For instance, a 50-pound bag of 12-4-8 fertilizer has 6 pounds of actual nitrogen (12% of 50).

Determine the amount of coverage by dividing the amount of actual nitrogen in the bag by the amount of nitrogen you want to apply in a single application. With Zoysia, you want to apply 1.5 pounds of actual nitrogen per 1000 square feet. Therefore, a bag that contains 6 pounds of actual nitrogen will cover 4000 square feet (6 divided by 1.5 pounds per 1000 square feet). If your lawn is less than 4000 square feet, remove the amount you do not need. Two cups of granular fertilizer weigh about 1 pound.

All of this calculating may seem like a hassle, but it really is the best way to apply the correct amount of fertilizer to your lawn. It is also a great way to compare the cost of different fertilizers so that you get a good deal. The best part is that you won't have to rely on the fertilizer company's marketing department for lawn advice.

How to Spread Fertilizer

You can broadcast granular fertilizer using a rolling fertilizer spreader, a hand-held spreader, or by hand (wear a glove). I will be completely honest with you. Spreading fertilizer is not an exact science. The calibrated settings on even the most expensive broadcast spreader are usually completely inaccurate. In addition, the majority of spreaders will clog, break, and jam.

I have had great success with a very simple and effective method. Begin by measuring your lawn and calculating the amount of fertilizer that you need to spread (see "How Much Fertilizer to Apply"). If you only need 40 pounds of a 50-pound bag, remove 20 cups and set it aside. Next, turn off your fertilizer spreader and fill it. Begin moving and barely open the spreader only once you are up to speed. Try to spread as little fertilizer as possible while still broadcasting an even pattern. Continue covering the entire lawn at the same speed. If you must slow to turn around, shut off the spreader or you will drop too much in a single location and burn your grass. Work across the entire lawn

---

Here is an example using a 50-pound bag of 12-4-8 slow-release fertilizer:

1. Multiply the nitrogen percentage (12%) by the net weight of the bag (50 lbs.) to determine how many pounds of actual nitrogen are in the bag (6 lbs.).

2. Next, divide the actual nitrogen in the bag (6 lbs.) by the amount you want to apply per 1000 square feet (1.5 lbs.).

3. Multiply this number (4) by 1000 to determine how many square feet the bag will cover (4000).

4. If your lawn is only 3000 square feet, you will need to apply 75% of the 50-pound bag. Two cups of granular fertilizer weigh approximately 1 pound, so remove 25 cups.

until you return to your starting point and turn off the fertilizer spreader. Now, see how much of the needed fertilizer is left. If 50% remains, repeat the entire process and you will be finished. If 25% remains, repeat the entire process but move twice as fast. Remember, it is impossible to be exact. Your foremost goal should be to spread the designated amount of fertilizer evenly over the entire lawn; avoid heavy doses in some areas and light doses in others.

When to Fertilize

When it comes to fertilizer, timing is everything. This is especially important with Zoysia since you want your lawn to be healthy but not to grow excessively. The guidelines below will help you fertilize the right amount at the right time.

• **Mid-Spring:** Zoysia lawns begin to green when soil temperatures reach a consistent 60–65°. The best time to apply fertilizer is after the danger of frost has passed and when your Zoysia lawn is at least 50% green. Depending on the particular year, this is usually in mid-March to mid-April when the Dogwoods are in full bloom. Use a complete lawn fertilizer that contains a slow-release form of nitrogen. Apply at the rate of 1.5 pounds of actual nitrogen per 1000 square feet. Water approximately one inch after fertilizing.

Don't fertilize too early! It is hard to be patient in the spring. After mowing and removing the dead top growth, we are raring for action. At the first sign of new green growth, most of us want to drop everything and run out to buy fertilizer. Hold off! Two things will happen if you fertilize early. First, you will stimulate leaf growth at a time when Zoysia roots should be growing foremost. Second, early leaf growth is particularly vulnerable to late-season freeze damage.

• **Mid-Summer (Optional):** Fertilize again in mid-summer if your Zoysia lawn is not a healthy dark green. A good time to assess its condition is around the 4th of July. Use a complete lawn fertilizer that contains a slow-release form of nitrogen. Apply at the rate of 1 pound of actual nitrogen per 1000 square feet. Water approximately one inch after fertilizing.

• **Early Fall:** Fertilize your Zoysia lawn again in late

August/early September. You can use the same complete fertilizer you have been using, or switch to a fertilizer with little or no phosphorus, but a higher rate of potassium. This might be something like 12-4-14 or 12-0-12. Either way, make sure the fertilizer contains a slow-release form of nitrogen. Apply at the rate of 1.5 pounds of actual nitrogen per 1000 square feet. Water approximately one inch after fertilizing.

Winterizing Lawns: There is a lot of discussion these days about "winterizing" warm-season grass lawns like Zoysia with a *late fall* application of fertilizer. Studies have shown benefits and detriments to these applications. In my opinion, the benefits are so short-lived that they do not justify the costs. Growing up in a family of horticulturists, one of the first phrases I remember hearing was "sounds like he's trying to sell some fertilizer." I think this could be one of those times.

• **Winter:** Do not fertilize Zoysia lawns in the winter. You may stimulate your lawn to break dormancy during a winter warm spell only to be damaged in the next wave of freezing temperatures.

SOIL pH AND LIME

Liming a lawn is a way to raise the pH of the soil. Soil pH is measured on a scale of 0–14 with 7 being neutral. A soil pH below 7 is considered acidic while a soil pH above 7 is considered basic (alkaline). Zoysia grass prefers a soil pH of 6–7. The pH of a soil is important because it affects the availability of different nutrients. Nitrogen in the soil is more available at a pH of 6 than a pH of 5. Liming the lawn would actually increase the nitrogen available to grass roots. In addition, a soil pH below 5 or above 7.5 can decrease the effectiveness of slow-release fertilizers.

The best way to determine your lawn's pH is to have the soil tested by your local Cooperative Extension Service. The soil test result will recommend the amount of lime needed to raise the pH to the optimal level.

Many Southern soils are acidic and will need approximately 50 pounds of lime per 1000 square feet. Whenever possible, purchase pelletized lime since it is much easier to distribute. Broadcast pelletized lime with a fertilizer spreader, or by hand. Lime can take up to three months to affect the pH of your soil and can be applied at any time of the year. Since lime moves slowly in the soil, the best time to apply it is when planting or just after core aerating.

Occasionally, you may encounter an alkaline Southern soil with a pH above 7.5. In such a case, you can lower the soil pH to the 6–7 range with an elemental sulfur product. The most common form of elemental sulfur is aluminum sulfate. It is often available in 50-pound bags and should be applied at the rate recommended on the bag.

AERATING

Aerating increases the flow of air, water, and nutrients into the Zoysia root zone. Since Zoysia lawns form a dense, impenetrable grass cover, aerating can have marked effects on the quality and consistency of your lawn's growth. It can also be used to renovate areas like dry banks since it will increase water penetration.

A Zoysia lawn can be aerated any time during the growing season, as long as it is not suffering from drought. I prefer not to aerate a dormant Zoysia lawn, since it will disrupt my pre-emergence weed control and open the soil to weed seed infiltration. In addition, I avoid aerating during spring green-up since it will damage tender roots and shoots at a time when the grass is low on stored energy. The best time for a once-a-year aeration is in the late spring when your lawn is completely green and soil temperatures reach 75–80°. Zoysia grass roots grow best at that temperature and will capitalize on the additional air, water, and nutrients. This is usually in late May.

The only effective way to aerate a lawn is to use a core aerator. Core aerators are powered by an engine and remove cores of soil from the top layer of soil. Since most people do not own a core aerator, they rent one or have a lawn service aerate for them. Core aerators work best on moist soil so you will need to irrigate several days before you plan to aerate. Make one or two passes across the lawn so that there is a hole every 4–6 inches. Afterwards, there will be cores of soil deposited all over

Core aeration increases the flow of air and water into the soil by removing plugs of earth.

the lawn surface. If the cores bother you, you can rake the lawn and most will break and drop below the level of the grass where they are not as visible. Otherwise, they will naturally disintegrate in a couple of weeks with the help of a few passing rainstorms. I prefer not to collect and remove the cores since they eventually return to the soil surface where they help thatch to decompose. Finally, irrigate the aerated lawn deeply to moisten exposed roots and rhizomes.

"Spike aerators" are sometimes offered as an alternative to core aerators. Some spike aerators roll behind a riding lawn mower, others are attached to fertilizer spreaders, and manual types are a modified pitchfork that you poke into the soil. There are even special spike-clad shoes that claim to aerate while you wander around the lawn. When a spike is forced into the soil, it creates an opening but compacts the surrounding soil. Even worse, you would need to take at least 10,000 steps across the average lawn with spike-clad shoes to come close to core aerating. All of these products are useless and should be avoided.

DETHATCHING

Thatch is the worst potential problem associated with a Zoysia lawn and can be especially bothersome on the faster growing cultivars like 'Meyer.' Thatch is a collection of dead plant parts like stems and grass clippings that collect on the soil surface. Thatch is generally a problem when it becomes thicker than .5 inches and grass roots begin to grow into it as if it was soil. Thatch dries very quickly in hot summer conditions, and grass roots growing in it are much more susceptible to drought. In addition, thatch often encourages insect and disease problems.

The best way to control thatch on a Zoysia lawn is to prevent it. There are three ways to do this. First, begin each year with a clean slate by mowing your dormant lawn and raking/removing as much of the dead top growth as possible (see "Mowing"). Second, bag your lawn clippings during the growing season. Third, use slow-release fertilizers and fertilize moderately.

If your Zoysia lawn accumulates a thatch layer greater than .5 inches of thatch during the growing season, you may need to mechanically dethatch. Even then, I usually see if I can do any good with a metal-tined leaf rake before renting a vertical mower, or "dethatcher," from the local tool rental store. Vertical

mowing is tricky and should be performed with extreme care. Do not cut too deeply or make more than one pass over the entire lawn. In addition, never use a vertical mower during periods of drought. After vertical mowing, rake and remove all thatch from the lawn surface.

Methods to Prevent Thatch

1. Mow and remove dead top growth before spring green-up.

2. Remove lawn clippings during the mowing season.

3. Fertilize moderately on the correct schedule.

You may be tempted to burn your Zoysia lawn during the winter to remove thatch and dead top-growth. I do not recommend it. Fire can damage Zoysia rhizomes and stolons and kill areas of your lawn. Zoysia is very slow to re-grow, so these dead patches can ruin an otherwise beautiful Zoysia lawn. Besides, grass fires move quickly and are extremely dangerous.

TOPDRESSING

The term "topdressing" is fairly common these days because of the popularity of golf. It is a common practice for golf course superintendents to topdress a golf green with a thin layer of soil mix using a special topdressing machine. The purpose of topdressing is to create a smooth playing surface for putting. Grass roots grow into the topdressed soil and the grass shifts in response to the new, flatter soil surface.

In most cases, topdressing is a specialized activity that should only be used on golf courses. Despite what many people think, topdressing does not stimulate thinning grass to grow or improve poor drainage. In fact, topdressing may compound these problems.

For the typical homeowner, topdressing should be limited to filling gullies and holes that make mowing difficult. A single depression should be filled layer by layer over the entire growing season, never covering the surface with more than .25 inches of soil or sand at a time. Greater amounts will smother the grass and cause more harm than good.

There are a few situations when you might consider topdressing your entire lawn. For instance, if your sod was laid poorly and the entire lawn is bumpy, you may want to hire a lawn care professional who has a top-dressing machine and access to high-quality topdressing soil mixtures. Topdressing with the wrong grade of soil or sand can cause the soil to "layer," which obstructs drainage and causes growth problems.

BLOWING AND EDGING

Many people own their own blower these days. Blowers are wonderful tools that take a lot of the backache out of lawn work. A blower can be used to clean debris from driveways, walks, and porches. It is also an invaluable tool in the fall when leaves are getting the best of us. I also use a blower to disperse grass clippings if they accumulate in lines along the surface of my lawn.

There are three types of blowers: electric blowers, backpack blowers, and rolling street blowers. If you are going to be doing yard work for many years to come, I would definitely invest in a gas-powered blower. Electric blowers are inexpensive, but the inevitable tangled power cord is a complete hassle. Backpack blowers are great if you need a versatile machine that can reach various nooks and crannies. Rolling street blowers are the best for blowing leaves, but they are expensive and difficult to maneuver if your property has hills or steps.

Lawn maintenance companies regularly edge lawns and flower beds with a special machine that has a vertically rotating blade. Most homeowners can accomplish the same effect by rotating their string trimmer and letting the string dig into the soil. Edging is largely a matter of aesthetics, although it does keep Zoysia from hanging over your driveway. Remember this, though. Edging opens the soil surface and will disrupt the chemical barrier of your pre-emergence weed control. It is common to see weed sprouting in early March in the edged groove between a lawn and a driveway. If needed, it is safer to edge during June, July, and August.

WEED CONTROL

A good thick Zoysia lawn is a natural defense against weeds. This does not mean, however, that weed seeds do not regularly blow onto your lawn. They do. They are merely waiting for enough bare soil, moisture, and light to sprout and grow. This is true for both annual weeds and perennial weeds. Annual weeds sprout, grow, flower, seed, and die within one year. Perennial weeds sprout from a seed as well, but the weed plant continues to grow and spread for more than one season (even though the top may die back in the winter).

Weeds enter a lawn for one reason: your lawn is not growing well. With a Zoysia lawn, weeds usually enter voids like dead spots, damaged turf, or large areas that have died due to drought (i.e., near tree roots). Zoysia is very slow to spread, and weeds have plenty of time to drift onto exposed soil and germinate. Your trouble may be different. A Zoysia lawn will thin because of soil compaction, cold damage, insect/disease damage, flooding, steep slopes (causing dry soil), lack of fertilizer, or irregular pH. The best defense against weeds is to concentrate primarily on maintaining a thick, well-grown stand of Zoysia and secondarily on weed control.

> ☛ **TIP:** Neighboring lawns, woods, and adjacent untended areas produce enormous numbers of weed seeds that blow into your lawn. If possible, mow or cut these areas before they produce seeds.

Types of Weed Control

There are two ways to control weeds in a lawn: as the weed seeds germinate (pre-emergence weed control) and after the weeds have already sprouted and are growing (post-emergence weed control). When using weed control products, always make sure the product is approved for use on Zoysia and follow the labeled directions. Do not apply more than the recommended rate; it will not give you better results and may injure your lawn.

> **Pre-Emergence Weed Control:** Usually sold as a dry, granular product in a 10–30 pound bag. May be labeled as "crabgrass control" although it will stop other weeds as well.
>
> **Post-Emergence Weed Control:** Usually sold as a liquid concentrate you spray from a pressurized sprayer or a hose-end sprayer. May be labeled as "broadleaf weed killer" or "grassy weed killer."

In dense shade, a Zoysia lawn will thin and become weedy.

Pre-emergence weed controls kill immature weeds immediately after they germinate and before they emerge from the soil surface. Since annual weeds like annual bluegrass and henbit die and return from seed each year, a pre-emergence weed control will remove them from your Zoysia lawn over several seasons. At the same time, it will prevent annual and perennial weed seeds that blow into your lawn from emerging. Most pre-emergence products are sold in a granular form (with or without fertilizer) that you spread using a fertilizer spreader. It is important to spread the chemical "wall to wall" at the recommended rate. Areas that are not covered by the chemical will not be protected. After spreading the product, irrigate your lawn with at least .5 inches of water to activate the chemical (unless otherwise stated on the bag). Once activated, pre-emergence weed controls create a chemical barrier in the upper inches of your lawn that will kill weeds as they germinate. Do not cultivate, aerate, or disturb the soil after treating your lawn or you will disrupt the chemical barrier and open the soil to weed seed infil-

tration. Pre-emergence weed controls are usually effective for 2–3 months, depending on the temperature and amount of rainfall.

Post-emergence weed controls kill weeds that are already growing in your lawn. These products are referred to as "selective" since they are targeted at specific annual and perennial weeds listed on the label. Usually, a product will either treat grassy weeds like crabgrass (monocotyledons) or broadleaf weeds like chickweed (dicotyledons). Choose the weed control spray that best fits your needs. You may need to purchase one spray for grassy weeds and one spray for broadleaf weeds. In most cases, post-emergence products are designed to disrupt one of the weed's critical metabolic processes and should be sprayed when the weed is young and actively growing. If the weed is dormant because of cold weather or drought (i.e., not using the metabolic process), it may not die. Spray on a still day when air temperatures are between 60–80° and the grass is dry. Avoid spraying during the 4–6 weeks in the spring when your Zoysia is turning green. Post-emergence weed controls are sometimes available in a granular form that you apply with a fertilizer spreader when the grass is wet. The dry particles need moisture to adhere to weed leaves. Again, avoid using these products in the spring when your Zoysia lawn is turning green.

> ☛ **WARNING:** Weed controls can have dramatic and damaging effects on ornamental trees, shrubs, and plants growing in or near your lawn. This is true for pre-emergence and post-emergence weed controls. For instance, some post-emergence sprays are absorbed by tree roots and can cause the leaves to burn or defoliate. Read the product label carefully for directions and never spray underneath shallow-rooted trees and shrubs like Dogwoods and Boxwoods.

There are other post-emergence weed controls like Round-Up that are non-selective. The term non-selective means they will kill all vegetation including Zoysia grass. The trick is that non-selective weed sprays are absorbed through plant leaves. During the winter months when your Zoysia is brown, you can carefully spray green weeds without affecting the dormant Zoysa. WATCH OUT! Be very cautious and make sure Zoysia leaves and stolons have not emerged during a winter warm spell. Even then, spray only the weed and expect some Zoysia in the vicinity to be killed as well.

When to Apply Weed Controls

Zoysia lawns are usually so thick and dense that they will remain weed-free with two applications of granular pre-emergence weed control applied in late winter and early fall. Supplement this program by spot-treating problem weeds with a post-emergence weed control spray (approved for use on Zoysia) in early spring and summer. I have included two "optional" pre-emergence weed control applications for people trying to renovate a very weedy lawn and people that live near a major source of weeds like an old pasture.

• **Late Winter:** Apply a granular **pre-emergence weed control** when the soil temperature reaches a consistent 50°. This is usually late February/early March,

when the Forsythia is in bloom. Make sure the product is approved for use on Zoysia and apply at the rate recommended on the bag. Do not aerate or mechanically dethatch for 3 months after you apply pre-emergence weed control as it may affect the chemical barrier of the control. Irrigate after applying unless otherwise stated on the bag. Do not use a pre-emergence weed control that contains fertilizer. If you fertilize now, you might stimulate your Zoysia to break dormancy, only to be damaged in the next hard freeze.

• **Late Spring and Summer:** Apply granular **pre-emergence weed control** without fertilizer around June 1 to control annual and perennial weeds that continue to germinate during the summer (optional application). Most Zoysia lawns will be thick, healthy, and weed-free, and they will not need this application. Use a product approved for use on Zoysia and apply at the rate recommended on the bag. Remember not to aerate for 3 months after you apply pre-emergence weed control because it may affect the chemical barrier of the control. Irrigate after applying unless otherwise stated on the bag.

Begin treating weed outbreaks with a **post-emergence weed control** spray approved for use on Zoysia as soon as your lawn is completely green and soil temperatures reach 75–80°. This is usually in mid to late May. Do not spray weed control during March/April when your Zoysia is turning green because it may harm your lawn. Most sprays should be used when the air temperature is 60–80° (check the product label) and weeds are actively growing.

If your lawn is overrun with weeds in mid-summer, consider using a combination fertilizer/post-emergence weed control when you fertilize around July 1. Follow the labeled instructions. Most products should be applied when your lawn is wet.

• **Early Fall:** Wait until soil temperatures drop to 70° to apply granular pre-emergence weed control (without fertilizer) to your Zoysia lawn. This is usually September 15 in the upper South and October 15 in the lower South. If you think you will forget, you can apply pre-emergence weed control when you fertilize in early September but you will be sacrificing some effectiveness. This application will control weeds like annual bluegrass and henbit that germinate in the fall and winter.

Either way, make sure the pre-emergence product is approved for use on Zoysia and apply at the rate recommended on the bag. Irrigate after applying unless otherwise stated on the bag. This application will last 2–3 months.

• **Winter:** Apply a **pre-emergence weed control** without fertilizer 2–3 months after your fall application (optional application). This is usually in late November/early December. Most dormant Zoysia lawns will be thick and weed-free, and they will not need this application. Use a product approved for use on Zoysia and apply at the rate recommended on the bag. Remember not to aerate for 3 months after you apply pre-emergence weed control because it may affect the chemical barrier. Irrigate after applying unless otherwise stated on the bag.

During the winter, treat winter weed outbreaks as soon as you see them with a **post-emergence weed control** spray approved for use on Zoysia. This is usually in January and February. Most of your problems this time of year will be from annual weeds like annual bluegrass and henbit. Spray on a warm afternoon when the air temperature is at least 60°. It may take two applications to kill weeds during the winter. You can also spray during the winter with a non-selective weed control like Round-Up. Make sure your Zoysia is completely brown and spray only the leaves of the weeds. Be very careful because Zoysia stolons and rhizomes are often green during mild winter weather. Even then, expect some of the Zoysia around the weed to die.

INSECTS AND PESTS

A thick Zoysia lawn is the perfect home for a variety of crickets, beetles, grasshoppers, worms, and other insects. Some feed on grass blades, some feed on grass roots, and some happily feed on each other. In most cases, Zoysia grows faster than the average insect population can eat and we don't have to worry. In fact, a certain level of insect feeding (herbivory) can actually stimulate grass growth. Problems arise, however, when insect pests increase in populations large enough to damage our lawn. Luckily, lawn insects can be treated fairly easily with a soil insecticide or with natural products like BT and Milky Spore. The best time for a once-a-year insect treatment is in late July or early August.

Insect damage is often defined as an irregularly shaped patch of discolored or brown grass in a lawn. If you take a drive around town, you will pass a thousand lawns that could fit that definition. The problem is

this. Only about ten of those thousand lawns probably have an insect problem. Lawns are finicky and irregular patches of brown grass pop up for different reasons. One of the most common is drought. You might think your lawn is evenly watered but even a slight rise or a different soil texture can alter the amount of water that penetrates the soil. When you think you have an insect problem, look for another cause first. Then, wait to see if the troubled lawn area expands. Only then should you worry about treating with a soil insecticide. Following is a list of insects that might cause problems in a Zoysia lawn. Don't panic! You may never see any of these bugs.

The most common and problematic insects on Zoysia lawns in the South are **white grubs**. White grubs are the larval, soil-inhabiting form of several different types of beetles. The most notorious beetle in the South is the Japanese Beetle, known for its voracious feeding on Crape Myrtle, grapes, ornamental cherry trees, and almost anything green. Japanese Beetles lay their eggs in lawns and grassy areas beginning in July. The eggs hatch as white grubs in late July and begin a two-month feeding frenzy on grass roots. As soil temperatures cool in October, the white grubs tunnel down 4–8 inches into the soil where they pass the winter. As the soil warms in the spring white grubs move to the surface, feed briefly in April/May, and then pupate. White grubs can be controlled with a granular soil insecticide applied in early August according to the labeled directions. Milky Spore is a natural product that contains spores of *Bacillus popilliae*, a disease that kills white grubs. Milky spore will not kill every white grub, but spores will remain active in your lawn for many years.

Billbugs are black, hard-shelled beetles with a curved snout like a short elephant trunk. You may see them moving around in the spring as they prepare to lay their eggs. The eggs hatch into legless white grubs that feed on Zoysia roots during the late spring and summer. Damage usually appears as circular areas of brown or yellowing grass. Billbugs can be controlled with a soil insecticide approved for use on Zoysia.

There are several types of **larval worms** that may arrive to feed on Zoysia leaf blades. They include cutworms and sod webworms. Unlike white grubs, larval worms can have several life cycles during a given growing season and are less predictable in their arrival. In addition, they are night-feeders and hide in tunnels

Billbugs are the adult form of a legless grub that feeds on Zoysia roots.

beneath your lawn during the day. Sod webworms leave a spidery web on grass blades that you notice early in the morning. Cutworms leave patches of cut grass. Larval worms can be controlled with a soil insecticide approved for use on Zoysia. BT (*Bacillus thuringiensis*) is an effective natural product.

Armyworms feed in masses throughout the day and night. They move quickly and can literally devour a lawn. Keep a lookout beginning in the late spring and through the growing season. Young larvae eat the edges of grass blades while the mature larvae eat the entire blade. Armyworms usually affect an entire subdivision/area at a time, so listen to your neighbors and state agencies for "armyworm alerts." The worst outbreaks of large populations usually occur from July through October. If they arrive on your lawn, immediately apply a soil insecticide approved for use on Zoysia. BT (*Bacillus thuringiensis*) is an effective natural product.

Mole crickets are a major concern in the lower South in sandy soils. They occasionally damage Zoysia lawns, although they are most destructive to Bermuda Grass and Saint Augustine grass lawns. These horrendous burrowing crickets tunnel through the soil at night, loosening the sandy soil and disrupting grass roots. Mole crickets are active throughout the growing season but are most common when night air temperatures remain above 60°. They can be controlled with a soil insecticide labeled for control of mole crickets and approved for use on Zoysia.

Chinch bugs occasionally attack Zoysia lawns although they are most destructive to Saint Augustine and Centipede grass lawns. Damage usually appears as irregular patches of yellowing or wilted grass and is most common in July through September. To confirm their presence, cut the top and bottom from a coffee can and pound it several inches into the yellow grass. Fill the inside of the can with several inches of water and maintain the water level for five minutes. The chinch bugs will float to the surface. If you find any, apply a soil insecticide labeled for control of chinch bugs and approved for use on Zoysia.

Fire ants are disheartening. I have tried almost every chemical available, and a number of home remedies, and have had only average results. Every time I treat a mound it seems to pop up in another location. Sometimes the mounds seem to multiply. There are numerous entomologists working on the problem, so hopefully they will find a good cure soon.

If **moles** are tunneling through your lawn, they are probably after white grubs. Treat for white grubs in late July/early August and the moles will probably go away.

There is always another insect or pest that *might* plague your lawn. You might hear or read about ground pearls, nematodes, mites, viruses, and a long list of other potential problems. In general, don't worry. Just keep an eye on things and treat problems when you find them. Your lawn is tougher than you think.

DISEASES

Zoysia lawns are usually free of disease. Occasionally a fungal disease appears under the right environmental conditions, but they will often fade away as the weather changes. Nonetheless, always be prepared to act if brownpatch, dollar spot, leaf spot, pythium, or rust arrives on your lawn. These diseases are often prevalent in the spring and fall when daytime air temperatures are 60–80°, nighttime air temperatures are around 60°, and there is plenty of moisture on the grass. During these critical times, it is usually best to switch to a daytime or early morning (according to local regulations) irrigation schedule so that moisture will evaporate quickly from grass leaves.

Fungal diseases are difficult to identify and are often attributed to other problems. In fact, many spring disease outbreaks are ignored until the diseased area grows into a sizeable problem. The best advice is to take a good look at your lawn every couple of days and to be aware of any-

thing abnormal. In general, fungal diseases appear as brown or damaged patches of grass with clearly defined outlines. If you find a lawn area that fits this description, don't run out and spray the entire lawn with fungicide. Wait to see if the patch of damaged grass expands over the next day or two. It is quite possible that the fungal disease has already run its course. An "active" patch of diseased turf will grow and expand concentrically over a couple of days. Grass plants along the outline of the damaged patch will have the most telling signs: wilted plants, shriveled leaves, or discolored leaf blades. Rust is a common problem on Zoysia in the fall and appears as reddish brown spots on the leaf blades. Once you have identified a disease outbreak, spray the affected area with a lawn fungicide approved for use on Zoysia.

If your lawn has a history of fungal problems, you may want to renovate the dead areas and then spray preventatively with a lawn fungicide the following year so that the disease does not recur. Follow the directions on the product label explicitly. You will probably need to spray several times over a 2–4 week period.

OVERSEEDING

The primary reason we grow Zoysia is because it is an incredibly thick grass. Unfortunately, this makes it very hard, if not impossible, to overseed Zoysia lawns for a winter cover. If you were wondering, overseeding is a method by which you sow a cool-season grass like Annual Ryegrass into your dormant warm-season grass. The Annual Ryegrass sprouts and provides a green cover above your dormant warm-season lawn over the winter months. The problem with Zoysia is that it is so thick that it is nearly impossible for the Annual Rye seed to reach the soil surface and germinate. It is best to forget about overseeding and enjoy your Zoysia lawn for all of its wonderful attributes.

II. Renovating a Zoysia Lawn

A weed-infested Zoysia lawn is nothing short of heartbreaking.

If a beautiful, healthy Zoysia lawn is elegant, then a weak, struggling Zoysia lawn is nothing short of heartbreaking. This is especially true if you began with a healthy lawn and have watched it suffer and fade from glory. The good news is that many Zoysia lawns can be rehabilitated with a modest amount of effort. The bad news is that Zoysia lawns are slow to spread and it will probably take a good growing season for a troubled lawn to recover. The general rule is that an average square foot of lawn must have 60–70% Zoysia coverage to renovate. The grass may be thin and weak, but it has to be there. Otherwise, you are better off reading the section entitled "Planting a New Zoysia Lawn."

There is always a reason that a Zoysia lawn is struggling. Problems usually stem from one of two areas: maintenance problems and fundamental problems. Unfortunately, the results of both often appear the same. For instance, a thinning lawn can be the result of improper mowing or dense shade. Evaluate your particular situation and try to come up with the most logical culprit.

CORRECTING MAINTENANCE PROBLEMS

There is always room to improve your game. Before you rush out and order three pallets of new sod, read through the maintenance section above and determine if you are skipping any critical steps. Are you fertilizing, mowing at the right height, mowing consistently, acrating, irrigating, and applying pre-emergence weed control? Do you have an insect or disease problem? If

you address these problems accurately, you can stimulate your lawn to thicken, fill voids, and darken in color. Below are two "recipes" for Zoysia lawn renovation. They cover approximately 8 months of the year. Avoid renovation attempts in the two months when lawns are greening in the spring and the two months when lawns are going dormant in the fall.

CORRECTING FUNDAMENTAL PROBLEMS

There are times when growing a lawn that you are beaten before you start. These are the most frustrating of times and are especially painful if you have spent considerable sums of money on installation and maintenance. The first thing to remember is that Zoysia will not grow on every piece of ground. In fact, there may be situations where other plants like groundcovers or vines are more suitable (see "Ground Cover" in the glossary). Remember this as you read the remedies below. The most efficient and inexpensive approach might be to reconfigure or abandon areas that are not suitable for a Zoysia lawn.

• **Shade.** Zoysia is tolerant of light to moderate amounts of shade. In heavy shade, however, even a Zoysia lawn will become thin and weak. The only answer is to remove branches/trees, or reduce the size of your lawn to avoid the shade. Raising the mowing height to 2.5 inches in the shaded areas may alleviate some of the problem but is often impractical.

• **Compacted soil.** Compacted soil is low in oxygen and will cause Zoysia to thin and die. Consider aerat-

Proper maintenance is the first step in renovating a Zoysia lawn to its former glory.

Recipe for Growing-Season Renovation *(May through August)*

1. Rake. Rake the entire lawn vigorously with a metal-tined rake to remove thatch, leaves, dead weeds, grass clippings, rocks, etc.

2. Kill Weeds. Spray weedy areas with a post-emergence weed control as soon as possible. Young weeds die faster than mature weeds (see "Weed Control").

3. Mow. Check your mowing height, mow frequently.

4. Bag. Bag and remove the grass clippings.

5. Irrigate. Water deeply once every week or so if there has been no rain. Don't drop the ball! Even short periods of drought can cause discoloration.

6. Fertilize. Fertilize immediately (if you have not done so already) and again in late August/early September. DO NOT fertilize excessively.

7. Aerate. Consider core aerating to stimulate grass to grow and spread.

8. Do not topdress unless you are trying to smooth your lawn surface. It will not stimulate growth.

9. Control Future Weeds. Apply pre-emergence weed control ON TIME in the fall (see "Weed Control").

Recipe for Dormant-Season Renovation *(November through February)*

1. Kill Weeds. Spray weedy areas with a post-emergence weed control as soon as possible, on a warm day. Young weeds die faster than mature weeds (see "Weed Control"). Pull problem weeds like bunches of fescue by hand.

2. Control Future Weeds. Apply pre-emergence weed control ON TIME in late winter (see "Weed Control").

3. Scalp and rake. Be ready to scalp your lawn and rake it vigorously in late February/early March (see "Mowing").

4. Wait until late April **to fertilize** and late May **to core aerate**.

ing once or twice during the growing season when soil temperatures reach 75–80°. Also, evaluate the cause of the compaction and correct continuing problems by creating walkways for people and pets.

• **Poor drainage.** Zoysia lawns will thin and die in wet, soggy soils. These are also some of most difficult and expensive problems to correct. Before you begin, determine the source of the water and where it is trying to flow. Occasionally, you can correct poor drainage by diverting a water source (like a gutter outlet) or removing an obstruction (a clogged ditch). Other solutions include re-grading, French drains, and surface drains. Once the soil dries, core aerate to help renovate the root zone.

• **Improper pH.** Zoysia prefers a soil pH of 6–7. If pH levels stray from this range, your lawn will grow slowly, lose density, and be light green/yellow *despite* your best maintenance practices. Always consider maintenance problems first, however, before you blame soil pH. If you suspect soil pH, take a soil sample to your local Cooperative Extension Service for testing. They will recommend the needed lime or elemental sulfur to correct the problem.

III. Planting a New Zoysia Lawn

These days, Zoysia lawns are planted predominantly from sod or plugs. Seeds of *Zoysia japonica* and sprigs of various Zoysia grasses are occasionally available, but these methods tend to be filled with problems and homeowners should avoid them. The most common method is to lay sod "wall to wall" so that you completely cover the entire lawn area. This is the most satisfying method since Zoysia is slow to establish. Plugging is a variation of sodding in which you plant pieces of sod about one foot apart. The idea is that the lawn will develop over the growing season as the plugs grow to fill the gaps. Unfortunately, Zoysia is slow to spread and weeds will monopolize the bare ground. Some of the worst curses I have ever heard from a refined gardener came when she encountered a weed problem among her Zoysia plugs.

The two most common and available forms of Zoysia are Emerald and Meyer. Emerald has a fine texture and is slower growing. Meyer has a medium texture and grows faster. Both are good choices.

The best time of year to begin sodding or plugging is in the late spring once the danger of frost has passed and the sod is green. The optimal soil temperature for establishing a new Zoysia lawn is 75–80°. This usually occurs in May. With consistent watering, Zoysia lawns can be planted throughout June and July. Try not to plant after August 1 because your new lawn will not have enough warm weather to become established.

A Sampling of Zoysia Grass Cultivars:

• **Meyer** or Z-52 (Zoysia japonica): Dark green, medium texture

• **Emerald** (Zoysia japonica x Zoysia tenuifolia): Dark green, fine texture

• **El Toro** (Zoysia japonica): Dark green, medium texture, faster growth

• **Diamond** (Zoysia matrella): Dark green, fine texture, very dense, does not tolerate cold

---

☛ **TIP:** Zoysia sod is usually more expensive than other grasses so you do not want to plant twice. Do not ignore the soil when you plant. Cultivate the soil deeply and amend with humus before you plant. It will be too late to fix soil problems once your expensive sod is laid and is struggling.

STEPS IN PLANTING A NEW ZOYSIA LAWN

Planting a new Zoysia lawn is not a one-weekend project. Laying a sod lawn by yourself on single weekend is likely to kill you. This is especially true since temperatures will probably be in the 90s when you are working. Try to spread the various steps over two weekends. For instance, I would strongly suggest cultivating one weekend and planting the next.

STEP 1. Spray existing weeds. The first step in planting a new Zoysia lawn is to eliminate all weeds from the lawn area. Use a non-selective weed control like Round-Up. Plan ahead since you will need to wait approximately 1–2 weeks (check the product label) after spraying before you sod or plug.

STEP 2. Establish the grade. One of the best ways to guarantee a beautiful lawn is to establish the proper grade before you begin. This is probably more than most of us can afford, but consider it nonetheless. The proper slope has the potential to alleviate drought and poor drainage. It will also be easier to mow. In general, a 2–6% grade is optimal.

STEP 3. Cultivate the soil as deeply as possible. Whether you use sod or plugs, Zoysia grass roots will need to grow and become established in the existing soil. The deeper you can cultivate the soil, the more quickly your Zoysia lawn will become established and thrive. Remember to wait the allotted time after spraying a herbicide before cultivating. Begin by raking and removing debris like dead weeds, leaves, and rocks from the area. Next, cultivate the soil with a rear-tine rototiller. If you don't have a rototiller, consider renting one from a tool rental store. I prefer a "rear-tine rototiller" since they do not bounce as much and they cultivate deeply. Rototill the entire area lengthwise, then again crosswise. Try to work at least 4–6 inches of soil into a nice pulverized soil mix. If you prefer not to rototill, cultivate as much of the area as possible with a hoe, garden rake, or shovel. Again, the deeper you work the soil, the better.

STEP 4. Amend the soil. During home construction, most of the natural humus in the top layer of soil is often scraped away or buried. The remaining soil will be low in organic matter and will be greatly improved if you add humus. Adding humus will improve drainage in clay soils and improve water retention in sandy soils. Peat moss, composted bark products, and compost are all good choices. Be careful, however, if you use a soil amendment that contains a gel-like substance to retain water. These products can cause strange drainage problems. I prefer adding two 3.8-cubic-foot bales of sphagnum peat moss per 1000 square feet. Work the peat moss into the top 4–6 inches of soil as you rototill.

STEP 5. Lime and fertilizer. A lawn is a big investment and it does not hurt to have the soil pH determined by your County Extension Service. Zoysia grass prefers a soil pH 6–7 and your soil test results will recommend the specific amount of lime to add if the pH needs to be raised. Most Southern soils are acidic and will need approximately 50 pounds of pelletized limestone per thousand square feet. Spread the limestone with a fertilizer spreader, or by hand, and work it into the top layer of soil using a garden rake. At the same time, apply a complete lawn fertilizer that contains slow-release nitrogen. I prefer to start lawns with a 3-1-2 ratio fertilizer like 12-4-8. Fertilizers labeled as "starter fertilizer" are helpful, but not critical. Apply at the rate of 1.5 pounds of actual nitrogen per 1000 square. Work the fertilizer into the top layer of cultivated soil using a garden rake.

Do not apply pre-emergence weed control when you sod a new Zoysia lawn. Pre-emergence controls often stunt root growth and will slow or prevent your Zoysia sod from becoming established. Wait until the late summer/early fall to begin using pre-emergence weed control products.

STEP 6. Sodding. Unless you are planting a small lawn, it is almost always cheaper and more efficient to order pallets of sod from your local nursery to be delivered to your house. Most people prefer to order enough sod to cover the entire lawn area "wall to wall." Plan on laying the sod soon after it arrives on pallets. Stacked sod should not sit for more than a day or two. It is usually a good idea to cultivate and amend the soil one weekend, and lime/fertilize and lay sod the next.

Begin by raking the entire cultivated area to prepare as smooth a surface as possible. Be careful because the sod will mimic the soil surface below, not compensate for it. It is best for the soil to be moist at the time you sod, but not wet. Start at the top of the lawn and lay the sod lengthwise, so that the long side of each piece of sod is running perpendicular to a hill or rise. As you place each piece of sod, work it tight against the surrounding pieces to prevent the edges from browning and ruts from forming. Sod is often cut on a slant so that the edges will overlap. Make sure the edges slant appropriately so that they interlock. Pound each block of sod with your palm to press it into the soil below and remove any air pockets. Stagger the second row of sod so that the perpendicular edges do not line up ("running bond" pattern). The result should look like a brick wall, not a checkerboard. If you are placing sod along steep banks, pin them in place with stakes or metal pins (available from sod distributors). Irrigate deeply when the entire lawn is placed.

STEP 7. Plugging. A plug is essentially a 4-square-inch piece of sod. Plugs are sometimes available for purchase, but more often you will have to create your own by cutting sod into smaller pieces. The idea behind plugging is to set each individual piece 6–12 inches apart and allow the grass to grow together over the coming months to form a solid grass surface. Unlike sodding, individual plug roots must be worked into the top layer of soil for support. Once all the plugs are set, the lawn should be irrigated. Plugging is less expensive than sodding because you purchase less grass. It usually takes about the same time to plug as it does to lay sod.

STEP 8. Irrigation during establishment. Whether you begin with sod or plugs, nurse your lawn diligently over the coming 4–6 weeks. It may look like an established lawn but its root system is a fraction of what it should be. Begin by watering lightly every day. After a week or so, decrease the frequency of irrigation but increase the amount of water you apply. By six weeks, you should be applying an inch of water per week (in one application), if there has been no significant rainfall. If you are starting your lawn from plugs, follow these same guidelines but rely on your instinct. If the soil surface is eroding or remains excessively damp, skip a watering. If the soil surface near the plugs dries rapidly, irrigate more frequently.

STEP 9. Mowing during establishment. Begin mowing your new sod or plugs as soon as they reach the recommended height. Do not mow lower or higher: both have different negative effects.

STEP 10. Fertilizing during establishment. Fertilize six weeks after planting with a complete lawn fertilizer that contains a slow-release form of nitrogen. Apply at the rate of 1 pound of actual nitrogen per 1000 square feet. This application will last until you fertilize again in early Fall (see "Fertilizer").

STEP 11. Weed control during establishment. Weeds are especially troublesome with a Zoysia lawn started with plugs. With sod and plugs, begin spraying weeds as soon as they appear with a post-emergence weed control approved for use on Zoysia. I would not risk spraying weedy areas between plugs with a nonselective herbicide like Round-Up. In all cases, do not use pre-emergence weed control products when you plant because they hamper and retard Zoysia root growth. Wait until the following fall to begin using pre-emergence weed controls.

Cultivate deeply with a rototiller and amend the soil with a humus like sphagnum peat moss.

Work fertilizer into the top layer of soil with a garden rake.

Broadcast pelletized lime if your soil is acidic.

Place sod so that the overhanging (right) and underhanging (left) edges interlock.

Place sod blocks tight together to prevent brown edges and ruts from forming.

Stagger the rows so that the perpendicular edges do not line up.

Tall Fescue is a beautiful evergreen lawn grass for the middle and upper South.

CHAPTER SIX

Fescue

(Festuca spp.)

THERE ARE PEOPLE WHO WILL TELL YOU THAT FESCUE IS NOT A TRUE SOUTHERN LAWN grass. They are right. Fescue prefers cooler temperatures and grows vigorously in the South only during spring and fall. I grew up wrestling with a Golden Retriever on a Kentucky-31 Tall Fescue lawn, though, and I can tell you that a fescue lawn is well worth the extra nurturing it requires during a Southern summer. If you live in the middle or upper South, I would definitely encourage you to try Tall Fescue. How can it not be worth it? Fescue is the only evergreen grass that will grow well in these areas, and you can heartily enjoy its green color while your neighbor stares at his boring brown lawn all winter. Perhaps I am biased, but a good fescue lawn is still the perfect place to lounge with a Golden Retriever.

Tall Fescue is an evergreen grass that was introduced to the South for use in pastures. Its roots grow deeper in the soil than some of the other evergreen grasses, making it more resistant to periods of drought. Southerners admired these qualities and we soon began using Tall Fescue as a lawn grass as well. Back then, the only real choice was Kentucky-31 Tall Fescue. This old favorite has proved its mettle over the years and is still widely used. Beginning in the 1970s, new cultivars of Tall Fescue like 'Rebel' and 'Olympic' were developed and released specifically for use in lawns. These named cultivars have a finer texture than Kentucky-31 and are known collectively as Turf-type Tall Fescue.

Chewing Fescue and Creeping Red Fescue are a completely different species from Tall Fescue. They should be used in only specific, and limited, situations in the South. In general, Chewing and Creeping Red Fescue cannot stand the scorching summer sun and do very poorly in our long, hot summers. They have a beautiful fine texture, though, and are an excellent grass for shaded areas. They should only be considered for open lawn areas in the mountains and western Piedmonts of the upper South. In the middle and upper South, they should only be grown in shaded areas. Do not grow them in the lower South.

At a Glance:

- Deep-rooted evergreen grass that grows in clumps
- Has a dark green color
- Tall Fescues can be used as general-purpose lawn grass in the middle and upper South
- Creeping Red and Chewing Fescue do not tolerate heat and should be used only in shaded areas
- Can be started from seed or sod
- Fertilized 3 times a year, irrigated once a week

I. Maintaining an Established Fescue Lawn

Tall Fescue is a "cool-season" grass that prefers the mild temperatures of spring and fall in the South. It accomplishes the majority of its growth when soil temperatures are between 55 and 75° and air temperatures are in the 60s and 70s. Summer is a different story. As soil temperatures reach 80° and air temperatures soar into the 90s, fescue suffers tremendously.

To add insult to injury, this is also about the time when fescue plants produce their seed and are naturally weakened. The key to understanding fescue is to encourage it with timely fertilizer applications during the spring and fall, and to nurse it with consistent mowing and irrigation during the summer. Even then, the ravages of drought, heat, and weeds will take their toll and you may have to reseed thinning areas every couple of years.

Creeping Red and Chewing Fescue are similar to Tall Fescue in that they grow in clumps rather than spreading to form a mat. Again, they should only be used as a general lawn grass in the extreme upper South. In the middle and upper South, they should only be considered for shaded areas. They should not be used in the lower South. Creeping Red and Chewing Fescue should be nurtured with even irrigation and consistent mowing. Remember, lawn areas in the shade are usually competing with tree roots and may need more water than you expect.

MOWING

We often forget that a lawn is actually hundreds of individual plants growing together in a confined space. In fact, mowing is really a special term for pruning grass plants. When you remove the tops of the plants, you are encouraging fescue clumps to spread laterally and produce a thicker lawn. At the same time, you are trimming uneven growth so that all the indi-

vidual plants appear to be growing in unison at the exact same rate.

> **One Step Further:** Plants grow by dividing special cells at specific "meristem" regions of the plant. With a tree or shrub, these meristems are at the outermost tips of branches and roots. Pruning removes them and stalls growth in favor of other regions. Grasses are different. The meristems of grass plants are at the bottom of the grass blades, not the top. Grass continues to grow consistently when you mow because you are never removing the meristematic cells.

When you head out into the yard for a little "grass plant pruning," remember that fescue is a very different kind of grass from the warm-season grasses like Bermuda Grass and Zoysia. It grows in a clump, does not spread by rhizomes and stolons, and has a somewhat delicate growing point called a "crown" at the base of the grass blades. Unlike the warm-season grass-

Mow frequently and consistently to encourage fescue to spread and form a thick turf.

Recommended Mowing Heights (in inches)		
TYPE OF FESCUE	MOW TO:	MOW WHEN GRASS IS:
Kentucky-31 Tall Fescue	3 – 4	4.5 – 6
Turf-type Tall Fescue (Rebel, Olympic)	2.5 – 3	3.75 – 4.5
Chewing Fescue, Creeping Red Fescue	2 - 2.5	3 - 3.75

es, it is disastrous if you scalp a fescue lawn at any time during the year. Scalping will disrupt the crown (remove the meristems) and cause the middle of the clump to die. The result is an ugly creation called a "stooled" fescue plant. If you keep your mowing heights above 2.5 inches at all times, however, you should be fine.

There are three general categories of fescue lawns grown in the South: Kentucky-31 Tall Fescue, Turf-type Tall Fescue (Olympic, Rebel), and Creeping Red and Chewing Fescue. Kentucky-31 Tall Fescue should be mowed at 3–4 inches. The Turf-type Tall Fescues were developed for lawn situations and can be mown lower, at 2.5–3 inches. Creeping Red and Chewing Fescue should only be grown in shaded sites and is mowed at 2–2.5 inches. (For easy instructions on how to set your mower blade at the correct height, see **Rotary Mower** in the Glossary.)

> **The One-Third Rule:** Never reduce the height of your lawn by more than one-third at any single mowing.

Once you have determined the correct mowing height for your type of fescue, mow consistently! If you remove more than one-third of a grass blade in a single mowing, you will shock the plant and stall its growth. During the ensuing recovery period, your fescue lawn will be weakened and more susceptible to stresses like heat, weed competition, and drought. The chart above will help you mow at the right height, at the right time.

If you mow at the right height and at the right time, your grass clippings will never be more than a couple of inches long. Clippings of this size will fall to the soil surface and decompose quickly without building a layer of thatch. As they decompose, they will return nitrogen to the soil.

There will be those times, like the family vacation, when your fescue lawn is sure to grow beyond the recommended height. If possible, mow immediately before leaving and soon after you return. With kids and coolers and hundred-pound suitcases, this is easier said than done. If your lawn does grow out of control (well past 6 inches), mow the lawn at the highest setting the mower will allow. Return a day or two later and mow again at the recommended height. You may want to bag or rake your grass clippings during this process.

IRRIGATION

While there is usually significant rainfall (on average) during the summer months, it is often sporadic and undependable. Fescue has a deep root system, but it will discolor, thin, and eventually die under drought conditions. In general, a fescue lawn will need about an inch of water every 7–10 days, whether from rain or irrigation. Try to water deeply and infrequently. For example, apply an inch of water on a single day rather than .25 inches a day for four days. Deep and infrequent watering will help the roots to grow deep into the soil where it is cooler and there is more moisture. Stop watering, however, if water begins to pool or run

Fescue beyond the reach of a sprinkler often loses color and thins.

on the surface. Wait an hour or so until all the water is absorbed and begin again.

If you have an automatic sprinkler system, take a moment to investigate your control box and settings. Place a rain gauge or straight-sided jar on the lawn and turn on the sprinklers. Monitor how much water is applied in a given period. Most systems will have several different types of sprinkler heads, so you might have to test each irrigation zone. I like to draw a rough diagram of the lawn and record the various sprinkler outputs for future reference. This helps me manipulate the irrigation system during the sporadic rain and drought periods of the coming season. Do not be shy about increasing the pre-set cycles during drought or turning off the entire system after a heavy rainfall. While lack of water will affect your lawn's color and growth, excess water can kill a poorly drained fescue lawn.

One Step Further: A grass plant absorbs water from the soil to replace water that evaporates from its leaf blades. The perfect way to irrigate is to supply the soil with the exact same amount of water that is lost. Search the Internet for a weather station in your area that records "pan evaporation rate" or evapotranspiration. Water loss from fescue is approximately 80% of the pan evaporation rate. **Formula:** (80% x Weekly Pan Evaporation Total) − Weekly Rainfall Total = Amount to irrigate that week

If you water your lawn with a manual sprinkler, place a rain gauge or straight-sided jar in the lawn to measure the amount of water applied. Try not to apply more, or less, than an inch at a time.

FERTILIZER

There are few chores as satisfying as fertilizing a fescue lawn. This is especially true in the late winter when most of the landscape is still leafless and bare. Within a matter of days, the fescue is dark green and growing energetically. Fescue lawns thrive during these cooler periods and will respond immediately to a steady amount of fertilizer in the spring and fall. But remember: if you apply more than the recommended amount, your lawn will not be any darker green, it will only grow faster and you will have to mow more often. The most efficient way to fertilize is to use the dry, granu-

lar fertilizers that are usually sold in 10–50 pound bags. Hose-end liquid fertilizers work, but they are difficult to use correctly and you will need to fertilize twice as often as with a granular fertilizer.

Fescue Fertilizer Facts:

• 3–5 pounds of actual nitrogen per 1000 square feet per year

• Three applications: late winter, mid-spring, early fall

• Use slow-release fertilizers in mid-spring and early fall.

• Water approximately one inch after fertilizing.

What Kind of Fertilizer to Use

Fertilizer is described by the percentages of nitrogen (N), phosphorus (P), and potassium (K) contained in the bag. All fertilizer bags are clearly labeled with these three numbers, known as the N-P-K ratio. In the spring and fall, I prefer to use a lawn fertilizer with a 3-1-2 ratio. An example would be a 12-4-8 fertilizer. In late winter, use a lawn fertilizer with a higher percentage of nitrogen (the first number). A bag of 12-4-8 fertilizer contains 12% nitrogen, 4% phosphorus, and 8% potassium by weight. The remaining 76% is inert material that adds bulk to the mixture and makes it easier to spread.

It is important to use slow-release fertilizers in the spring and fall. Avoid hose-end fertilizer sprayers or dry fertilizers in which all of the nitrogen is in a soluble, quick-release form. Most major brands of lawn fertilizer will have a combination of soluble and slow-release forms of nitrogen (indicated on the label). Soluble nitrogen is available to the grass plant immediately while slow-release nitrogen becomes available over a period of two to three months. In most situations it is best to have as much of the nitrogen in slow-release form as possible. Good brands of fertilizer will have 40–50% of the nitrogen in slow-release form. This is usually noted in a statement like "containing 6% nitrogen in slow-release form."

The late winter fertilizer application should contain a soluble, quick-release form of nitrogen. Slow-release fertilizers are not as effective when soil temperatures are cold. Be careful, however, when using fertilizers in

By February, a fescue lawn is light green and the soil is warm enough to fertilize.

which all of the nitrogen is in a soluble, quick-release form. Never apply more than 1 pound of actual nitrogen per 1000 square feet or the nitrogen will be so concentrated that it could burn your lawn.

Common Forms of Nitrogen *(indicated on the label)*
Soluble: *Available immediately, lasts 4–6 weeks*
Ammonium nitrate, potassium nitrate, ammonium sulfate
Slow-Release: *Available slowly in small amounts, generally lasts 2–3 months*
Urea-Formaldehyde (UF), Isobutylidene diurea (IBDU), Sulfur Coated Urea (SCU), Polymer Coated Urea products (like "Polyon")

Up to this point, I have only mentioned three major nutrients: nitrogen, phosphorus, and potassium. These three nutrients are used by grass plants in relatively large quantities and are known as macronutrients. Grass plants use other nutrients in relatively small quantities. Those nutrients are known as micronutrients or "minor elements." Most brands of fertilizer contain the needed minor nutrients and you will not have to worry about them.

How Much Fertilizer to Apply

Most bags of fertilizer are covered from top to bottom with completely useless information that is written by the fertilizer company's marketing department. I continue to be amazed by the fact that the closest thing to directions is usually a vague phrase like "fertilizes *up* to 10,000 square feet." Luckily, there is a universal way to know how much fertilizer to apply, regardless of the brand or the specific N-P-K ratio. All you have to do is figure out how much "actual nitrogen" is contained in the bag. Fescue lawns grow best with 3–5 pounds of actual nitrogen per 1000 square feet applied each year, regardless of the brand of fertilizer you purchase. Apply 1 pound of actual nitrogen per 1000 square feet in late winter. Then, switch to a

Here is an example using a 50-pound bag of 12-4-8 slow-release fertilizer:

1. Multiply the nitrogen percentage (12%) by the net weight of the bag (50 lbs.) to determine how many pounds of actual nitrogen are in the bag (6 lbs.).

2. Next, divide the actual nitrogen in the bag (6 lbs.) by the amount you want to apply per 1000 square feet (1.5 lbs.).

3. Multiply this number (4) by 1000 to determine how many square feet the bag will cover (4000).

4. If your lawn is only 3000 square feet, you will need to apply 75% of the 50-pound bag. Two cups of granular fertilizer weigh approximately 1 pound, so remove 25 cups.

fertilizer with a slow-release form of nitrogen and apply 1.5 pounds of actual nitrogen per 1000 square feet in mid-spring and early fall.

Unfortunately, the average bag of fertilizer does not tell you how much actual nitrogen it contains in the bag. It is easy to calculate, though, using two simple pieces of information: the N-P-K ratio and the weight of the bag. Multiply the percentage of nitrogen (the first number in the N-P-K ratio) by the weight of the bag and you will know the amount of actual nitrogen it contains. For instance, a 50-pound bag of 12-4-8 fertilizer has 6 pounds of actual nitrogen (12% of 50).

Determine the amount of coverage by dividing the amount of actual nitrogen in the bag by the amount of nitrogen you want to apply in a single application. In the spring and fall, fescue needs 1.5 pounds of actual nitrogen per 1000 square feet. Therefore, a bag that contains 6 pounds of actual nitrogen will cover 4000 square feet (6 divided by 1.5 pounds per 1000 square feet). If your lawn is less than 4000 square feet, remove the amount you do not need. Two cups of granular fertilizer weigh about 1 pound.

All of this calculating may seem like a hassle, but it really is the best way to apply the correct amount of fertilizer to your lawn. It is also a great way to compare the cost of different fertilizers so that you get a good deal. This best part is that you won't have to rely on the fertilizer company's marketing department for lawn advice.

How to Spread Fertilizer

You can broadcast granular fertilizer using a rolling fertilizer spreader, a hand-held spreader, or by hand (wear a glove). I will be completely honest with you. Spreading fertilizer is not an exact science. The calibrated settings on even the most expensive broadcast spreader are usually completely inaccurate. In addition, the majority of spreaders will clog, break, and jam.

I have had great success with a very simple and effective method. Begin by measuring your lawn and calculating the amount of fertilizer that you need to spread (see "How Much Fertilizer to Apply"). If you only need 40 pounds of a 50-pound bag, remove 20 cups and set it aside. Next, turn off your fertilizer spreader and fill it. Begin moving and barely open the spreader only once you are up to speed. Try to spread as little fertilizer as possible while still broadcasting an even pattern. Continue covering the entire lawn at the same speed. If you must slow to turn around, turn off the spreader or you will drop too much in a single location and burn your grass. Work across the entire lawn until you return to your starting point and turn off the fertilizer spreader. Now, see how much of the needed fertilizer is left. If 50% remains, repeat the entire process and you will be finished. If 25% remains, repeat the entire process but move twice as fast. Remember, it is impossible to be exact. Your foremost goal should be to spread the designate fertilizer evenly over the entire lawn; avoid heavy doses in some areas and light doses in others.

When to Fertilize

When it comes to fertilizer, timing is everything. The following schedule will help you maintain a consistent level of nutrients in the soil that will be available to your lawn throughout the growing season.

• **Late Winter:** Fertilize fescue lawns in late winter when soil temperatures rise to a consistent 50° in order to stimulate deep root growth. This is usually in late February/early March, when the Forsythia is in bloom. Use a high-nitrogen, low-phosphorus fertilizer like 18-

0-4 that includes a pre-emergence weed control (unless you plan on reseeding in the spring). It is best if the nitrogen is NOT in a slow-release form. Apply at the rate of 1 pound of actual nitrogen per 1000 square feet.

• **Mid-Spring:** Fertilize again 4–6 weeks later. This is usually around April 1. Use a complete lawn fertilizer like 12-4-8 that contains a slow-release form of nitrogen. Apply at the rate of 1.5 pounds of actual nitrogen per 1000 square feet.

• **Summer (Optional):** It is best not to fertilize fescue lawns during the summer months. If your fescue lawn is light green or yellow, however, apply a light dose of a complete lawn fertilizer that contains a slow-release form of nitrogen. Apply no more than .5 pounds of actual nitrogen per 1000 square feet.

• **Early Fall:** Fertilize your fescue lawn again in early September. You can use the same complete fertilizer you have been using, or switch to a fertilizer with little or no phosphorus, but a higher rate of potassium. This might be something like 12-4-14 or 12-0-12. Either way, make sure the fertilizer contains a slow-release form of nitrogen and apply at the rate of 1.5 pounds of actual nitrogen per 1000 square feet.

It is common these days to hear about "winterizing" lawns with a *late fall* application of special fertilizer. If you fertilize with a slow-release fertilizer in early September, there is no need to fertilize again in late fall. Save your time and energy.

• **Winter:** There is often the temptation to fertilize a fescue lawn during our mild Southern winters. It is important to remember, however, that grass roots do not absorb nutrients when soil temperatures are below approximately 45°. While a warm spell seems the perfect time to fertilize an off-color fescue lawn, soil temperatures will rarely reach the minimal level for root activity. Fertilizer applied during the winter is most likely to leach from the soil into nearby stream and rivers.

SOIL pH AND LIME

Liming a lawn is a way to raise the pH of the soil. Soil pH is measured on a scale of 0–14 with 7 being neutral. A soil pH below 7 is considered acidic while a soil pH above 7 is considered basic (alkaline). Fescue prefers a soil pH of 6–6.5. The pH of a soil is important because it affects the availability of different nutrients. Nitrogen, for instance, is more available at a soil pH of 6 than a soil pH of 5. Liming a soil with a pH

of 5 would actually increase the amount of nitrogen available to grass roots.

The best way to determine your lawn's pH is to have the soil tested by your local Cooperative Extension Service. The soil test result will recommend the amount of lime needed to raise the pH to the optimal level.

Many Southern soils are acidic and will need approximately 50 pounds of lime per 1000 square feet. Whenever possible, purchase lime in pelletized form since it is much easier to distribute. Broadcast the pelletized lime with a fertilizer spreader, or by hand (wear a glove). Lime may take up to three months to affect the pH of your soil and can be applied at any time of the year. Since lime moves slowly in the soil, the best time to apply it is when planting or immediately after core aerating.

Occasionally, you may encounter a Southern soil with a pH above 7.5. In such a case, you can lower the soil pH to the 6–6.5 range with an elemental sulfur product. The most common form of elemental sulfur is aluminum sulfate. It is often available in 50-pound bags and should be applied at the rate recommended on the bag.

AERATING

Aerating a fescue lawn has two immediate effects. First, it allows air to move into the soil where it provides the oxygen needed for optimal root growth. Second, it creates passageways for water and nutrients to enter the soil. The best time of year to aerate a fescue lawn is in early September before you fertilize. The second best time is in late February/early March, just

The best way to aerate a fescue lawn is to rent a core aerator in September.

before fertilizing and applying pre-emergence weed control. In both cases, aerating will move fertilizer into the soil, increase water penetration, and provide plenty of oxygen for root growth.

Remember not to aerate after you have applied pre-emergence weed control. It will disrupt the chemical barrier of the control and reduce its effectiveness. Also, do not aerate during the summer months when your lawn is suffering from heat and drought.

The only effective way to aerate a lawn is to use a core aerator. Core aerators are powered by an engine and remove cores of soil from the top layer of soil. Since most people do not own a core aerator, they rent one or have a lawn service aerate for them. Core aerators work best on moist soil so you will need to irrigate several days before you plan to aerate. A core aerator will bounce along the surface of dry soil. Make one or two passes across the entire lawn so that there is a hole every 4–6 inches. Afterwards, there will be cores of soil deposited all over the lawn surface. If the cores bother you, you can rake the lawn and most will break and drop below the level of the grass where they are not as visible. Otherwise, they will naturally disintegrate in a couple of weeks with the help of a few passing rainstorms. I prefer not to collect and remove the cores since they eventually return to the soil surface where they help thatch to decompose. Finally, irrigate the aerated lawn deeply to moisten exposed roots and rhizomes.

You will often see "spike aerators" of various sorts. Some roll behind a riding lawn mower, others are attached to fertilizer spreaders, and manual types look like a pitch fork that you are supposed to press into the soil with your foot. There are even special spike-clad shoes that claim to aerate while you wander around the lawn. When a spike is forced into the soil, it creates an opening but compacts the surrounding soil. Even worse, you will need to take at least 10,000 steps across the average lawn with spike-clad shoes to even come close to core aeration. In my opinion, all of these products are useless and should be avoided.

DETHATCHING

Thatch is a collection of dead plant parts like stems and grass clippings that accumulate on the soil surface. Thatch is only a problem if it becomes thicker than .5 inches and grass roots begin to grow into the thatch as if it was soil. Thatch dries very quickly in hot summer conditions and grass roots growing in it are much more susceptible to drought. Luckily, fescue lawns seldom accumulate thatch if mowed properly.

A good way to prevent potential thatch problems is to give your lawn a good old-fashioned raking at least once a year. I like to do this in the late winter, using a metal-tined leaf rake. Try to work the tines down to the soil surface. Finally, collect and remove all of the debris.

Occasionally, a fescue lawn will accumulate more than .5 inches of thatch during the growing season. This is usually as a result of improper mowing or excessive fertilizing. Lawns like this will be weak and thin by the end of the summer. One way to handle such a problem is to rent a vertical mower, or "dethatcher," from a tool rental store in early fall. Vertical mowing is a way to cultivate the top layer of soil and remove thatch. It should be used on a fescue lawn only if you plan to reseed immediately afterwards. Even then, be extremely careful. Vertical mowing is tricky and will damage the fescue plants that remain. Make only one pass across your lawn. Thoroughly rake and remove all the subsequent debris prior to reseeding.

Never attempt to remove thatch by burning your fescue lawn. Besides being extremely dangerous, fire will damage the tender crown of the fescue plant and ruin your lawn.

TOPDRESSING

With the rise in popularity of golf, we hear a lot these days about topdressing. Topdressing is a technique used by golf course superintendents to create a smooth playing surface on golf greens. A thin layer of soil or sand is distributed across the grass surface using a special topdressing machine. The grass responds by growing roots and rhizomes into the new, flatter soil surface.

Fescue lawns do not benefit from topdressing. They do not have rhizomes and cannot easily shift their growth if soil is added around the crown. Topdressing may cause your fescue lawn to weaken, thin, and die.

There are those times when a low spot or pothole makes mowing difficult. Instead of topdressing, remove the section of turf and fill below the roots. This may not be practical on areas larger than two or three square feet. Large areas may need to be filled, rototilled, and reseeded in the fall.

BLOWING AND EDGING

Many people own their own blower these days. Blowers are wonderful tools that take a lot of the backache out of lawn work. A blower can be used to clean debris from driveways, walks, and porches. It is also an invaluable tool in October when falling leaves are getting the best of us. I also use a blower to disperse grass clippings if they accumulate in lines along the surface of my lawn.

There are three types of blowers: electric blowers, backpack blowers, and rolling street blowers. If you are going to be doing yard work for many years to come, I would definitely invest in a gas-powered blower. Electric blowers are inexpensive, but the inevitable tangled power cord is a complete hassle. Backpack blowers are great if you need a versatile machine that can reach various nooks and crannies. Rolling street blowers are the best for blowing leaves, but they are expensive and difficult to maneuver if your property has hills or steps.

Lawn maintenance companies regularly edge lawns and flower beds with a special machine that has a vertically rotating blades. Most homeowners can accomplish the same effect by rotating their string trimmer and letting the string dig into the soil. With a fescue lawn, edging is largely a matter of aesthetics since the grass will not creep out across your driveway. Keep in mind that edging opens the soil surface and disrupts the chemical barrier of your pre-emergence weed control. It is common to see weeds sprouting in early March in the edged groove between a lawn and a driveway. If needed, it is safer to edge during June, July, and August.

WEED CONTROL

While it may be hard to believe, most weeds blow into your lawn as seeds and sprout the minute they find enough bare soil, moisture, and light to grow. This is true for both annual weeds and perennial weeds. Annual weeds sprout, grow, flower, seed, and die within one year. Perennial weeds sprout from a seed as well, but the weed

Weed seeds blow in and sprout quickly in a thinning fescue lawn.

plant continues to grow and spread for more than one season (even though the top may die back in the winter).

> ☛ **TIP:** Neighboring lawns, woods, and adjacent untended areas produce enormous numbers of weed seeds that blow into your lawn. If possible, mow or cut them before they produce seeds.

Unfortunately, all fescue lawns weaken during our hot Southern summers and a thinning lawn is the perfect place for a weed seed to germinate and grow. Consequently, your ultimate goal becomes to grow a thick, luscious lawn that will naturally prevent weed seeds from germinating. There are two ways to accomplish this. First, correct fundamental problems like shade, poor drainage, and soil compaction that make growing a thick fescue lawn difficult at best. Second, stay on top of your lawn maintenance. Fescue lawns need to be nurtured during the summer and a couple of weeks without water or mowing can be devastating. Even then, you will need to incorporate a weed control program into your yearly maintenance activities.

Types of Weed Control

There are two ways to control weeds in a lawn: as the weed seeds germinate (pre-emergence weed control) and after the weeds have already sprouted and are growing (post-emergence weed control). When using weed control products, always make sure the product is approved for use on fescue and follow the labeled directions. Do not apply more than the recommended rate; it will not give you better results and may injure your lawn.

> **Pre-Emergence Weed Control:** Usually sold as a dry, granular product in a 10–30 pound bag. May be labeled as "crabgrass control" although it will stop other weeds as well.
> **Post-Emergence Weed Control:** Usually sold as a liquid concentrate you spray from a pressurized sprayer or a hose-end sprayer. May be labeled as "broadleaf weed killer" or "grassy weed killer."

Pre-emergence weed controls kill immature weeds immediately after they germinate and before they emerge from the soil surface. Since annual weeds like annual bluegrass and crabgrass die and return from seed each year, a pre-emergence weed control will eradicate them from your fescue lawn over several seasons. At the same time, it will prevent annual and perennial weed seeds that blow into your lawn from neighboring areas from emerging. Most pre-emergence products are sold in a granular form (with or without fertilizer) that you spread using a fertilizer spreader. It is important to spread the chemical "wall to wall" at the recommended rate. Areas that are not covered by the chemical will not be protected. Do not spread the chemical beyond your lawn since some pre-emergence controls can harm ornamental plants (check the product label). After spreading the product, irrigate your lawn with at least .5 inches of water to activate the chemical, unless otherwise stated on the bag. Once activated, pre-emergence weed controls create a chemical barrier in the upper inches of your lawn that will kill weeds as they germinate. Do not cultivate, aerate, or disturb the soil after treating your lawn or you will disrupt the chemical barrier and open the soil to weed seed infiltration. Pre-emergence weed controls are usually effective for 2–3 months, depending on the temperature and amount of rainfall. Be careful and plan ahead because a pre-emergence weed control will prevent fescue seeds from germinating as well.

Post-emergence weed controls kill weeds that are already growing in your lawn. These products are referred to as "selective" since they are targeted at specific weeds listed on the label. Usually, controls will either treat grassy weeds like crabgrass (monocotyledons) or broadleaf weeds like chickweed (dicotyledons). Choose the weed control spray that best fits your needs. You may need to purchase a spray for each category of weeds. In most cases, post-emergence products are designed to disrupt one of the weed's critical metabolic processes and should be sprayed when the weed is young and actively growing. If the weed is dormant because of cold weather or drought (i.e., not using the metabolic process), it may not die. Spray on a still day when air temperatures are between 60 and 80° and the grass is dry. Post-emergence weed controls are sometimes available in granular form and should be spread with a fertilizer spreader when the grass is wet. The dry particles need moisture to adhere to weed leaves. In either case, avoid using post-emergence weed controls immediately after seeding or sodding fescue because it can retard growth or damage tender grass. It is usually safe to spray after you have mowed at least twice.

> ☞ **WARNING:** Weed controls can have dramatic and damaging effects on ornamental trees, shrubs, and plants growing in or near your lawn. This is true for pre-emergence and post-emergence weed controls. For instance, some post-emergence sprays are absorbed by tree roots and can cause the leaves to burn or defoliate. Read the product label carefully for directions and never spray underneath shallow-rooted trees and shrubs like Dogwoods and Boxwoods.

There are other post-emergence weed controls like Round-Up that are non-selective. The term non-selective means they will kill all vegetation including your fescue. The trick is that non-selective weed sprays are absorbed through plant leaves. Large patches of weeds can be carefully sprayed with Round-Up without affecting the entire lawn. WATCH OUT! Sprays can drift very easily on a windy day and kill plants in surrounding areas. Wait at least 7–10 days before seeding or sodding the area.

When to Apply Weed Controls

When it comes to weed control in a fescue lawn, timing is critical. Pre-emergence weed controls have to be applied before weed seeds germinate or they are useless. Post-emergence weed control sprays and granules have to be applied when the weeds are young, tender, and actively growing. I have found that when it comes to weed control, it is always better to be a little early rather than a little late.

Under normal conditions, a well-grown fescue lawn will remain weed-free with two applications of granular pre-emergence weed control (late winter and early fall) and spot treatments of problem weeds with a post-emergence weed control spray in mid-winter and early summer. I have included two "optional" pre-emergence weed control applications for people trying to renovate a very weedy lawn and people that live near a major source of weeds like an old pasture.

• **Late Winter:** Apply a **pre-emergence weed control**

when the soil temperature reaches a consistent 50°. This is usually in February/early March, when the Forsythia is in bloom. This application will control annual weeds and perennial weeds that germinate in the spring. Make sure the product is approved for use on fescue and apply at the rate recommended on the bag. Do not aerate for 3 months after you apply pre-emergence weed control because it will affect the chemical barrier. Irrigate after applying unless otherwise stated on the bag. For convenience, you can combine this application with your fertilizer application (see "Fertilizer" above).

Do not apply pre-emergence weed control if you are planning to seed, sod, or reseed a fescue lawn in the spring. It will prevent fescue seed from germinating and retard fescue sod roots from growing.

• **Spring and Summer:** Begin treating weed outbreaks as soon as you see them with a **post-emergence weed control** spray approved for use on fescue. Weeds will die quickly when they are young and actively growing. Spray on a calm day when the air temperature is 60–80°. Avoid spraying newly seeded or sodded fescue, however, until you have mowed at least twice (follow the labeled directions).

If your lawn is still overrun with weeds in mid-spring, consider using a combination fertilizer/post-emergence weed control (granular form) when you fertilize in early April. Follow the labeled instructions. Most products should be applied when the lawn is wet.

Apply **pre-emergence weed control** without fertilizer 2–3 months after your late winter application to control annual and perennial weeds that continue to germinate into the summer (optional application). This is usually around June 1. If your lawn is mostly weed-free, and weeds do not usually blow in from surrounding areas, you can skip this application. Use a product approved for use on fescue and apply at the rate recommended on the bag. Remember not to aerate for 3 months after you apply pre-emergence weed control because it may affect the chemical barrier. Irrigate after applying unless otherwise stated on the bag.

• **Early Fall:** Apply **pre-emergence weed control** (without fertilizer) to fescue lawns when soil temperatures drop to 70°. This is usually mid-September in the upper South and late September in the middle South. If you think you will forget, you can apply pre-emergence weed control when you fertilize in early September but you will be sacrificing some effectiveness. This application will control weeds like annual bluegrass and henbit that germinate in the fall and winter.

Either way, make sure the pre-emergence product is approved for use on fescue and apply at the rate recommended on the bag. Remember to aerate before you apply pre-emergence weed control so you do not affect the chemical barrier. Irrigate after applying unless otherwise stated on the bag. This application will last 2–3 months.

Do not apply pre-emergence weed control if you are planning to seed, sod, or reseed your fescue lawn in the fall. It will prevent fescue seed from germinating and retard fescue sod roots from growing.

• **Winter:** Apply a **pre-emergence weed control** without fertilizer 2–3 months after your fall application (optional application). This is usually in late November/early December. If your lawn is mostly weed-free, and weeds do not usually blow in from surrounding areas, you can skip this application. Use a product approved for use on fescue and apply at the rate recommended on the bag. Remember not to aerate for 3 months after you apply pre-emergence weed control because it may affect the chemical barrier. Irrigate after applying unless otherwise stated on the bag.

During the winter, treat weed outbreaks as soon as you see them with a **post-emergence weed control** spray approved for use on fescue. Most of your problems this time of year will be from annual weeds like chickweed and henbit. Spray on a warm afternoon (air temperature is at least 60°) when the weeds are young and actively growing. Even then, it may take two applications to kill them.

INSECTS

A lush fescue lawn is the perfect habitat for a variety of insects. In fact, you could probably drive yourself crazy trying to figure out whether a given worm, grasshopper, cricket, or beetle is a friend or foe. In general, a fescue lawn grows faster than the average insect can eat and does not suffer any ill effects from their patronage. There are, however, a few classes of insects that arrive and increase in populations large enough to harm your lawn. These can be treated fairly easily with a soil insecticide or with natural products like BT and Milky Spore. The best time for a once-a-year insect treatment is in late July or early August.

Insect damage is often defined as an irregularly shaped patch of discolored or brown grass in a lawn. If you take a drive around town, you will probably pass a thousand lawns that could fit that definition. The problem is this. Only about ten of those thousand lawns probably have an insect problem. Lawns are finicky and irregular patches of brown grass pop up because of different reasons. One of the most common is drought. You might think your lawn is evenly watered but even a slight rise or a different soil texture can alter the amount of water that penetrates the soil. When you think you have an insect problem, look for another cause first. Then, wait to see if the troubled lawn area expands. Only then should you worry about treating with a soil insecticide. Following is a list of insects that might cause problems in a fescue lawn. Don't panic! You may never see any of these bugs.

White grubs are the most common and problematic insects on fescue lawns in the South. White grubs are the larval, soil-inhabiting form of several different types of beetles including Japanese Beetles, June Beetles, and Billbugs. The most notorious beetle in the South is the Japanese Beetle, known for its voracious feeding on Crape Myrtle trees, ornamental cherry trees, grapes, and almost anything green. Japanese Beetles lay their eggs in lawns and grassy areas beginning in July. The eggs hatch as white grubs in late July and begin a two-month feeding frenzy on grass roots. As soil temperatures begin to cool in late September, the white grubs tunnel 4–8 inches into the soil where they pass the winter. As the soil warms in the spring white grubs move to the surface, feed briefly in April/May, and then pupate. White grub damage looks very similar to drought damage and is most apparent in July and August. White grubs can be controlled with a granular soil insecticide applied in late July/early August according to the labeled directions. This is the best time to treat since the grubs are tender and easily killed. You can also treat with milky spore, a natural product that contains spores of *Bacillus popilliae*, a bacteria that kills white grubs. Milky spore will not kill every white grub, but spores will remain active in your lawn for many years.

Larval worms are another type of insect pest that feed on fescue leaf blades. They include cutworms and sod webworms. Unlike white grubs, larval worms can have several life cycles during a given growing season and are less predictable in their arrival. In addition, they are night-feeders and hide in tunnels beneath your lawn during the day. Sod webworms leave behind a spidery web that you notice on grass blades early in the morning. Insect damage appears as areas of brown or unevenly clipped grass. Larval worms can be controlled with a soil insecticide approved for use on fescue. BT (*Bacillus thuringiensis*) is an effective natural control.

Armyworms feed in masses throughout the day and night. They move quickly and can literally devour a lawn. Keep a lookout beginning in the late spring and through the growing season. Young larvae eat the edges of grass blades while the mature larvae eat the entire blade. Armyworms usually affect an entire subdivision/area at a time, so listen to your neighbors and state agencies for "armyworm alerts." The worst outbreaks of large populations usually occur from July to October. If they arrive on your lawn, immediately apply a soil insecticide approved for use on fescue. BT (*Bacillus thuringiensis*) is an effective natural product.

Fire ants once took up residence in a mulch pile I was moving. I will never forget that day and I will never forgive those ants. I have tried almost every chemical available, and a number of home remedies, and have only had average results. Every time I treat a mound it seems to pop up in another location. Sometimes the mounds seem to multiply. There are numerous entomologists working on the problem, so hopefully they will find a good cure soon.

If **moles** are tunneling through your lawn, they are probably after white grubs. Treat for white grubs in late July/early August and the moles will probably go away.

There is always another insect or pest that *might* plague your lawn. You might hear or read about ground pearls, nematodes, mites, viruses, and a long list of other potential problems. In general, don't worry. Just keep an eye on things and treat problems when you find them. Your lawn is tougher than you think.

DISEASES

Fungal diseases do occasionally appear on a fescue lawn, but there is no reason to panic. Fescue is not particularly prone to disease and most people will grow their lawn for years and years without spraying a single fungicide. Most of the time, a disease like brownpatch, dollar spot, or pythium blight will pop up if the moisture, humidity, and temperature are just right. It is pos-

sible to categorize individual diseases as more likely to appear during a specific season, but more likely they will follow the vagaries of the weather. In many cases, a disease will come and go without your ever knowing it was there. Since fungal diseases are very difficult to identify, it is important to keep a sharp watch for anything abnormal.

In general, fungal diseases appear as brown or damaged patches of grass with clearly defined outlines. If you find a lawn area that fits this description, don't run out and spray the entire lawn with fungicide. Wait to see if the patch of damaged grass expands over the next day or two. It is quite possible that the fungal disease has already run its course. An "active" patch of diseased turf will grow and expand concentrically over a couple of days. Grass plants along the outline of the damaged patch may have discolored, wilted, or spotted leaves. Once identified, treat the infected area with a lawn fungicide approved for use on fescue.

Many fungal diseases are exacerbated by water. This is especially true with fungal diseases like leaf spot that are prevalent in the spring and fall when daytime air temperatures are 60–80° and nighttime air temperatures are around 60°. During these critical times, do not irrigate unless it is necessary. When needed, water on a sunny day when moisture will evaporate quickly from grass leaves. If there is a daytime watering ban in effect for your area, irrigate immediately before dawn.

If your lawn has a history of fungal problems, you may want to reseed the dead areas and then spray preventatively with a lawn fungicide the following year so that the disease does not recur. Follow the directions on the product label explicitly. You will probably need to spray several times over a 2–4 week period.

OVERSEEDING

During the winter, many people sow a temporary, winter grass like Annual Ryegrass over their dormant warm-season grass lawns. Since fescue remains green during the winter, there is no reason to overseed. Thinning fescue lawns should be reseeded with fescue, not overseeded with Annual Ryegrass. Overseeding with Annual Ryegrass is a horrible idea since the ryegrass will compete with your fescue for nutrients, water, soil, and sunlight. Once hot weather arrives, the ryegrass will die and leave your fescue lawn weaker and thinner than before.

If your lawn has thinned to one or two plants per square foot, start over.

RESEEDING

Fescue lawns suffer during the heat and drought of a long, hot Southern summer. By the end of August, it is inevitable that you will have lost a few grass plants here or there. Most of the time, lawns will rebound with fer- tilizer, water, and cooler temperatures in September. In a bad year, however, your entire lawn may have weak- ened and thinned dramatically. If so, consider reseeding in early September.

The decision to reseed is not as clear-cut as you might think. Reseeding is not just a matter of throwing a few handfuls of seed here and there. Reseeding involves fore- going a pre-emergence weed control application, cultivat- ing the top layer of soil, and fertilizing and watering dili- gently. When you combine all of these components, you are providing fescue seeds, and winter weed seeds, the per- fect opportunity to germinate. In general, a decent stand of fescue will benefit more from aerating, fertilizing, and applying pre-emergence weed control than from reseeding.

A fescue lawn should be reseeded when the average dis- tance between any two given grass clumps is more than about three or four inches. If your lawn has thinned to about one or two grass clumps per square foot, you might as well start over. A lawn that has degenerated to this point will benefit greatly from the rototilling and soil amending described in the "Planting a New Fescue Lawn" section.

Steps in Reseeding

1. Do not apply pre-emergence weed control any time during the 3 months before you plan to reseed.

2. Before reseeding, mow Kentucky-31 Tall Fescue to 2.5 inches, Turf-type Tall Fescue to 1.5 inches, and Creeping Red and Chewing Fescue to 1.5 inches.

3. Rake the soil surface vigorously with a metal-tined leaf rake to remove thatch and other debris. This will also loosen the soil surface.

4. If possible, aerate with a rented core aerator. Rake the lawn afterwards to pulverize as many of the removed cores of soil as you can.

5. Apply a complete lawn fertilizer than contains a slow-release form of nitrogen. I prefer to start lawns with a 3-1-2 ratio fertilizer like 12-4-8. Fertilizers labeled as "starter fertilizer" are helpful, but not critical. Apply at the rate of 1.5 pounds of actual nitrogen per 1000 square. Rake the lawn to help the fertilizer drop to the soil surface. Do not use fertilizer that contains a pre-emergence weed control.

6. Apply pelletized lime to acidic soils according to soil test recommendations. This is often 50 pounds per 1000 square feet. Rake the lawn to help the pelletized lime drop to the soil surface.

7. Broadcast seed at a rate of 4–5 pounds per 1000 square feet.

8. Irrigate to keep the soil surface moist for the first two weeks. Afterwards, reduce consistently until you are applying 1 inch of water every 7–10 days if there has been no significant rainfall.

9. Continue to mow your fescue at the recommended height (see "Mowing"). Use a new mower blade or sharpen your old one. Bag your clippings until grass plants have toughened.

10. Do not use post-emergence weed control sprays until you have mowed the lawn two or three times.

II. Renovating a Fescue Lawn

Fescue is unique among Southern lawn grasses because it can be grown from seed with relative ease for a relatively low cost. Consequently, if a fescue lawn begins to wane our first impulse is to rush out and buy a bag of seed. This might be the appropriate move (see "Reseeding" above). Then again, you may be better off spending your time and effort renovating your existing lawn.

When a fescue lawn begins to lose color, weaken, and thin, it is easy to blame the weather. The very fact that fescue is a "cool-season grass" forces us to brand heat as the likely culprit. This may be true. But then again, there might be a dozen beautiful fescue lawns in your neighborhood (hopefully not next door) that force you to look beyond the weather for your problem. While intense heat will surely weaken a fescue lawn, it is more often improper mowing, shade, weed competition, or drought that kills it.

There are two categories of problems that will ruin a fescue lawn: maintenance problems and fundamental problems. Unfortunately, the results of both often appear the same. For instance, a thinning lawn can be the result of improper mowing or shade. Think about your lawn's history and work your way toward the logical cause.

CORRECTING MAINTENANCE PROBLEMS

When your golf game is suffering, it is easy to blame your clubs. More often, however, you need to address the underlying problem with your swing. Before buying another 50-pound bag of seed, read through the maintenance section above and determine if you are skipping any critical steps. Are you fertilizing, mowing at the right height, mowing consistently, aerating, irrigating, and applying pre-emergence weed control? Do you have an insect or disease problem? Address these problems accurately to stimulate your fescue to grow denser, darken in color, and remain healthy. Below is a "recipe" for fescue lawn renovation. This is a great way to boost the performance of your fescue lawn once or twice a year.

CORRECTING FUNDAMENTAL PROBLEMS

There are times when even a perfect maintenance schedule cannot cure a fescue lawn's troubles. These are the most frustrating of times and really try our patience with lawn growing. The first thing to remember is that a lawn is not a cure-all. Fescue is not meant to grow

---

Recipe for Fescue Renovation *(early September or late February)*

THREE WEEKS AHEAD:

• **Kill Weeds.** Spray weeds three weeks ahead of time with a post-emergence weed control approved for use on fescue. This will be either early August or early February. Repeat the application a week later for better control.

ALL AT ONCE:

• **Rake.** Rake the entire lawn vigorously with a metal-tined leaf rake and remove leaves, dead weeds, grass clippings, rocks, etc.

• **Aerate:** Aerate the lawn with a rented core aerator. Rake the lawn after core aerating to pulverize the cores and return them to the soil surface.

• **Fertilize.** Fertilize immediately after aerating with 1 pound of actual nitrogen per 1000 square feet in a quick-release form (see "Fertilizer" above).

• **Lime.** Apply 50 pounds of pelletized lime per 1000 square feet immediately after aerating (see "Soil pH and Lime" above).

• **Control Future Weeds.** Apply pre-emergence weed control after aerating (see "Weed Control").

everywhere. In fact, in certain situations there may be hundreds of more suitable plants for a particular area. Remember this as you read the remedies below. The most efficient and inexpensive approach might be to reconfigure or abandon areas that are not suitable for a fescue lawn.

• **Shade.** Tall Fescue is tolerant of partial shade. Partial shade is hard to define but usually means 2–3 hours of direct sunlight a day or a thin tree canopy like tall pines. In full shade, a Tall Fescue lawn will become thin and weak. The only answer is to remove a few tree limbs, cut down a few trees, or reduce the size of your lawn to avoid the shade. Raising the mowing height in the shaded areas may alleviate some of the problem but is often impractical. In the middle and upper South, consider sowing Creeping Red or Chewing Fescue in the shaded areas.

• **Compacted soil.** Compacted soil is low in oxygen and will cause a fescue lawn to thin and die. Consider core aerating once or twice during the growing season in late February or early September. Also, evaluate the cause of the compaction and correct continuing problems by creating walkways for people and pets. Do not topdress fescue lawns in an attempt to modify the soil.

• **Poor drainage.** Fescue is tolerant of a certain amount of moisture, but will thin and die in soggy soils. These are also some of most difficult and expensive problems to correct. Before you begin, determine the source of the water and where it is trying to flow. Occasionally, you can correct a drainage problem by diverting a water source (like a gutter outlet) or removing an obstruction (like a clogged ditch). Other solutions include re-grading, subsurface drains, and surface drains. Once the soil dries, core aerate to help renovate the root zone.

• **Improper pH.** Fescue prefers a soil pH between 6 and 6.5. It is tolerant of soil pH outside this range but will grow slowly, thin, and turn yellow *despite* your best maintenance practices. Always consider your maintenance before you blame soil pH. If you suspect soil pH, take a soil sample to your local Cooperative Extension Service for testing. They will recommend the needed lime or elemental sulfur to correct the problem.

III. Planting a New Fescue Lawn

Traditionally, fescue lawns have been planted from seed. In fact, it was not until recently that fescue sod became a viable option for starting a new fescue lawn. The decision to seed or sod is based largely on cost and availability. Fescue sod is much more expensive than seed (per square foot) and must be laid "wall to wall" rather than plugged since fescue does not spread well.

> ☞ **TIP:** Soil-related problems are the number-one killer of new and established fescue lawns. This is your only chance to fix soil problems! Cultivate the soil deeply and amend with humus before you plant.

Whether you seed or sod, early fall is the ideal planting time. Begin planting when soil temperatures drop into the 70s. This is usually in September. If you are pressed, early spring is a fair second choice. Begin planting in the spring when soil temperatures reach a consistent 55° and the danger of hard freezes has passed. This is usually in March, when the Bradford Pear trees are in bloom.

> **A Sampling of Tall Fescue Cultivars:**
> • Kentucky-31, Alta
>
> **A Sampling of Turf-type Fescue Cultivars:**
> • Rebel, Rebel II, Olympic, Winchester

Fescue sod laid in the summer is susceptible to widespread drought damage.

SEED MIXTURES AND BLENDS

A fescue seed mixture is a collection of several different grass species sold together in a single bag. An example would be a single bag containing Tall Fescue, Kentucky Bluegrass, and Perennial Ryegrass. A fescue seed blend is a collection of several different cultivars of Tall Fescue sold together in a single bag. An example would be a combination of Turf-type Tall Fescue cultivars. Either way, seed companies are required to divulge the exact components of their mixtures and blends by listing the percentages of grasses and grass cultivars on a special seed label attached or printed on the bag.

I do not believe in using grass mixtures in the South. The whole idea behind a grass mixture is to sow a variety of different types of grasses so that you have a better chance of one particular type flourishing while the others weaken, or even die. It is a shotgun approach to selecting seed. If you sow a mixture with 50% Kentucky Bluegrass and 50% Kentucky-31 Tall Fescue in the middle South, then half of your lawn will look horrible during the heat and drought of summer. Worse yet, if the Kentucky Bluegrass dies, your lawn will be thinned dramatically. The point is this. We know which types of grass do well in the South. So why court failure when we can ensure success?

More often than not, I stay away from grass blends as well. All too often, I will find a grass blend that contains 50% of a really well-known, proven Tall Fescue cultivar and 50% of a Tall Fescue cultivar that has consistently ranked poorly in university-level testing. The problem is not as bad as with a grass mixture, but I still avoid planting 50% of my lawn with a Tall Fescue cultivar that is known to be a poor performer.

Some grass mixtures and blends have a special marketing angle. For instance, they may claim to be a mixture of the best grasses for a certain geographic area, the best grasses for a specific situation like shade, or the best grasses to fix a lawn problem like a bare spot. Be extremely wary of these products. Some seed companies are known to "hide" cheap, useless seed in these types of grass mixtures and blends. For instance, you will often find Annual Ryegrass hidden in a blend claiming to repair your lawn. The Annual Ryegrass will sprout and look wonderful for a couple of weeks but will die in the summer heat. You might be told that the Annual Ryegrass is a "nurse grass"

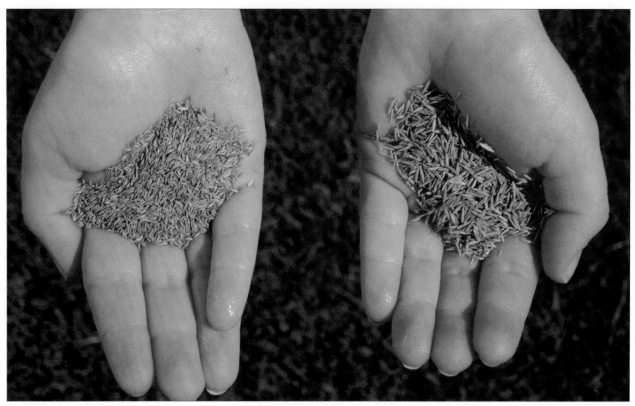

A 50/50 mix of Tall Fescue (right) and Kentucky Bluegrass (left) is actually 90% Kentucky Bluegrass because the seed weighs different amounts.

that will help your fescue along while it is germinating. This is wrong. It is the same as saying that annual bluegrass weeds help a fescue lawn to become established.

There is another reason that I avoid grass mixtures. The percentages listed on a grass seed mixture are most often percentages by weight. Unfortunately for us consumers, different grass species have different numbers of seeds per pound. Here's the problem. A 50-pound bag of a grass mixture with 50% Tall Fescue and 50% Kentucky Bluegrass by weight contains approximately 54 million Kentucky Bluegrass seeds and only about 6 million Tall Fescue seeds. If the germination is consistent, you will end up with a lawn that is 90% Kentucky Bluegrass and 10% Tall Fescue. If you live in areas of the middle South where Kentucky Bluegrass cannot grow, then 90% of your lawn will be dead by July 1.

Whenever possible I avoid grass mixtures and blends in favor of pure seed. I buy a single named cultivar like 'Rebel' Turf-type Tall Fescue or a single species of fescue like Creeping Red Fescue (for shade). This approach may cost a little more up front, but your lawn has a much greater chance of surviving, and flourishing, in the long run.

READING SEED LABELS

Seed companies are required to report several facts about the seed they are selling on a special label attached or printed on the bag. It is important to check this label because the information on the rest of the bag can be *very misleading*. First, make sure the bag contains only one type of seed (unless you want to buy a mixture). Second, make sure the germination test date is within the last year. Old seed will not germinate as well. Finally, make sure the bag does not contain seed for grasses like Perennial or Annual Ryegrass that will die during the summer heat of the South.

Kentucky-31 Tall Fescue	
Net. Wt. 50 lbs.	Origin: Oregon
98% Pure Seed	
1% inert matter	
1% weed seed	
Test Date: 2-1-20XX	
98% Kentucky-31 Tall Fescue	Germ: 85%

STEPS IN PLANTING A NEW LAWN

Starting a new lawn from scratch is not an overwhelming project. But then again, it is not for one weekend. Try to spread the various steps over two or three weekends. For instance, I would strongly suggest cultivating one weekend and planting the next. The best news is that fescue lawns are planted in cooler weather, so you can be thankful you are not laying Bermuda Grass sod on a 95° Saturday afternoon in July.

STEP 1. Spray existing weeds. The first step in planting a new fescue lawn is to remove as many weeds from the lawn area as possible. Use a non-selective herbicide like Round-Up. Plan ahead since you will need to wait 1–2 weeks after spraying before you seed or sod. Check the product label for specific directions.

STEP 2. Establish the grade. One of the best ways to guarantee a beautiful lawn is to establish a good grade before you begin. This may be more than most of us can afford, but consider it nonetheless. The proper grade can prevent both drought and poor drainage and will be a great benefit in the long run. In general, a 2% to 6% grade is the optimal.

STEP 3. Cultivate the soil as deeply as possible. Whether you seed or sod, fescue roots will need to grow into the existing soil surface. Fescue prefers cooler temperatures, so it is especially important for fescue roots to be able to grow deep into the soil. The deeper you can cultivate the soil, the more quickly your lawn will establish and thrive. Remember to wait the allotted time after spraying your herbicide before cultivating. Begin by raking and removing debris like dead weeds, leaves, and rocks from the area. Next, cultivate the soil with a rear-tine rototiller. If you do not own a rototiller, you might consider renting one from your local tool rental store. Rototill the entire area lengthwise, then again crosswise. Try to work the top 4–6 inches of soil into a nice pulverized soil mix. If you are planting a small lawn and do not have a rototiller, cultivate the entire area with a hoe, garden rake, or shovel. Again, the deeper you work the soil, the better.

STEP 4. Amend the soil. In most cases, the natural humus in the top layer of soil is scraped away or buried when a home is constructed. The remaining soil will probably be low in organic matter and will be greatly improved if you add humus. Adding humus will improve drainage in clay soils and improve water retention in sandy soils. Peat moss, composted bark products, and compost are all good choices. Be careful, however, if you use a soil amendment that contains a gel-like substance (indicated on the packaging) to retain water. These products can cause strange drainage problems. I prefer adding two 3.8-cubic-foot bales of sphagnum peat moss per 1000 square feet. Work the peat moss into the top 4–6 inches of soil as you rototill.

STEP 5. Lime and fertilizer. A lawn is a big investment and it does not hurt to have the soil pH determined by your County Extension Service. Fescue prefers a soil pH of 6–6.5 and your soil test results will recommend the specific amount of lime to add if the pH needs to be raised. Many Southern soils are acidic and will need approximately 50 pounds of lime per 1000 square feet. Whenever possible, purchase lime in a pelletized form because it is much easier to distribute. Spread the pelletized lime with a fertilizer spreader, or by hand, and work it into the top layer of cultivated soil using a garden rake. At the same time, apply a complete lawn fertilizer that contains slow-release nitrogen. I prefer to start lawns with a 3-1-2 ratio fertilizer like 12-4-8. Fertilizers labeled as "starter fertilizer" are helpful, but not critical. Apply at the rate of 1.5 pounds of actual nitrogen per 1000 square. Work the fertilizer into the top layer of cultivated soil using a garden rake.

STEP 6. Seeding. Plan on using approximately 6–8 pounds of Tall Fescue seed per 1000 square feet. You will need 4–5 pounds of Creeping Red or Chewing Fescue seed per 1000 square feet. Fescue seed usually takes 7–14 days to germinate. Begin by raking the area to provide as smooth a soil surface as possible. I like to use a plastic leaf rake because it creates tiny furrows and ridges on the soil surface that "capture" the seed. Measure the amount of seed needed for the lawn into a separate bucket or container (most of us approximate). Try not to use more seed than the recommended rate—an overpopulation of grass seedlings will weaken individual plants, cause strange growth problems, and make your lawn more susceptible to insects and diseases. Seed can be sown by hand or with a broadcast spreader. When using a spreader, sow one-half the seed lengthwise and one-half crosswise to avoid any skips. Once sown, lightly rake the entire lawn with a leaf rake to slightly cover the seed with no more than .25 inches of soil. The newly seeded lawn can be covered with a layer of wheat straw to prevent washing and erosion while the seed is germinating. You will need about one bale of wheat straw per 1000 square feet. Do not use hay since it is full of weed seeds.

STEP 7. Sodding. Before laying fescue sod, cultivate the soil as described in step 3. Do not skip this step! It is imperative that fescue sod roots grow deep into the soil before next summer.

Unless you are planting a small lawn, it is almost always cheaper and more efficient to order pallets of sod from your local nursery to be delivered to your house. Fescue is a clump-forming grass and will need to be sodded "wall-to-wall" since it is extremely slow to spread. Do not expect fescue sod to grow to fill empty areas of the lawn. Begin by measuring the entire new lawn area and ordering enough square footage of sod to completely cover every foot. Plan on laying the sod soon after it is delivered on pallets. If you won't be planting for a day or two, unstack the pallet and spread the blocks. Stacked fescue sod will turn yellow quicker than other grasses.

Begin by raking the entire cultivated area to prepare as smooth a surface as possible. It is best for the soil to be moist at the time of sodding, but not wet. Begin at the top of the lawn and lay the sod lengthwise, so that the long side of each piece of sod is running across, rather than down, a hill or rise. As you place each piece of sod, work it tight against the surrounding pieces to prevent the edges from browning and ruts from forming. Sod is often cut on a slant so that the edges will overlap. Make sure the edges slant appropriately so that they interlock. Pound each block of sod with your palm to press it into the soil below and remove any air pockets. Stagger the second row of sod so that the perpendicular edges do not line up. The result should look like a brick wall, not a checkerboard. If you are placing sod along steep gradients, pin them in place with stakes or metal pins (available from sod distributors). Irrigate deeply once all the sod is placed.

STEP 8. Irrigation during establishment. Whether you have seeded or sodded, it is essential to irrigate in the coming weeks. A newly seeded lawn should remain moist for about two weeks. Water lightly and frequently. Rely on your instinct. If the soil surface is eroding or becomes "soupy," skip a watering. If the soil surface dries rapidly, irrigate more frequently. After two weeks, decrease the frequency but increase the amount of water you are applying. By 4–6 weeks, your lawn will need about an inch of water per week, whether by irrigation or rainfall. If you have sodded your new fescue lawn, follow these same guidelines. Sodded lawns will require more water in the early stages than seeded lawns.

STEP 9. Initial mowing. Mow your newly seeded or sodded fescue lawn as soon as it reaches the recommended mowing height (see "Mowing"). This is a hard pill to swallow. A newly seeded lawn looks so delicate that most people wait and mow when the grass blades are 6 inches tall and flopped over. Do not hesitate! Use a mower with a sharp blade (this is a good time to buy a new blade) and cut frequently. Mowing will encourage the grass blades to toughen and spread. Bag your grass clippings since young growth is succulent and will mat easily.

STEP 10. Fertilizing during establishment. A fall-seeded fescue lawn may benefit from a light mid-winter application of soluble fertilizer. Use a 3-1-2 ratio fertilizer like 12-4-8 that does NOT contain nitrogen in a slow-release form. Apply at the rate of .5 pounds of actual nitrogen per 1000 square feet. If your new lawn is dark green and growing well, wait until late winter to begin the normal fescue fertilizer schedule.

STEP 11. Weed control during establishment. Weeds can be a problem in a newly seeded fescue lawn since weed seeds germinate under the same conditions that fescue seed germinates. Controlling weeds in a newly seeded lawn is a delicate maneuver. Even herbicides labeled for use on fescue have the potential of harming young, tender fescue seedlings. A general recommendation is to wait until you have mowed two or three times before using post-emergence weed control sprays approved for use on fescue. In most cases, you can begin using pre-emergence weed controls by the following February. Either way, check the product label for specific instructions.

Amend the soil with a humus like sphagnum peat moss before you plant.

Cultivate and pulverize the soil before sowing to ensure even germination.

Work fertilizer into the top layer of soil with a garden rake.

Plan on using 6–8 pounds of Tall Fescue and 4–5 pounds of Creeping Red Fescue per 1000 square feet.

Sow the seed evenly over the designated area.

Lightly rake the entire lawn with a leaf rake to slightly cover the seed with soil.

Kentucky Bluegrass is a beautiful lawn grass but is best-suited for cooler climates.

CHAPTER SEVEN

Kentucky Bluegrass
(Poa pratensis)

KENTUCKY BLUEGRASS IS ONE OF THE MOST POPULAR AND OFTEN-GROWN EVERGREEN grasses in the cooler climates of the United States. It forms a beautiful, fine-textured lawn with a handsome dark green color. Even better, it spreads by runners and forms a denser turf than the other evergreen grasses like Tall Fescue that grow in clumps.

Now that I have sold you on the beauty of a Kentucky Bluegrass lawn, here is the bad news. Kentucky Bluegrass cannot be grown in most of the South. It does not tolerate hot weather, dies during drought, and will burn up in our intense summer heat. It should not be considered as an all-purpose lawn grass in areas where summer air temperatures regularly rise into the 90s. This includes most of Texas, Louisiana, Mississippi, Alabama, Georgia, Florida, and South Carolina. It can be considered for the upper Piedmont and mountain regions of Virginia, North Carolina, Tennessee, and Arkansas. Even then, consider your options carefully and remember that a Turf-type Tall Fescue is a very good alternative.

Kentucky Bluegrass can be grown as a "shade grass" in lawn areas with moderate shade in the middle and upper South. It will need plenty of water, though, to grow well in these areas. It might seem that shaded lawns need less water, but they are usually competing with tree roots for every last drop of moisture. This is important to know if you don't have an irrigation system and will have to drag a hose out once or twice a week. Again, consider your options and remember that Creeping Red and Chewing Fescue are very good alternatives for shaded areas.

> **At a Glance:**
>
> - Evergreen grass that grows into a beautiful, dense turf
> - Can be used as a lawn grass in the mountains and western Piedmont regions of the upper South
> - Can be used in moderately shaded areas in the middle and upper South
> - Started from seed or sod
> - Fertilized 3 times a year, irrigated once a week

I. Maintaining an Established Kentucky Bluegrass Lawn

Kentucky Bluegrass thrives in the cooler months during spring and fall in the South. It grows best when air temperatures are in the 60s and 70s. Summer is a different story. As temperatures soar into the 90s, a Kentucky Bluegrass lawn suffers tremendously. The key to growing a Kentucky Bluegrass lawn in shaded areas of the middle and upper South, and sunny areas in the extreme upper South, is to encourage it to grow as much as possible during the spring and fall, and to nurse it with consistent mowing and irrigation during the summer. Even then, evaluate your lawn each September to see if the ravages of drought, heat, and weeds are too much for it to bear. If they are, switch to Tall Fescue.

MOWING

Mowing is one of the most important lawn activities. We often forget, but mowing is unique to growing a lawn. There is no other plant that we consistently "prune" every week for such a long period. Mowing also has a hidden component that is easy to overlook. It is more important to mow frequently than to mow

Do not allow your lawn to grow too tall before mowing.

Kentucky Bluegrass lawns should be mowed at 2.5–3 inches. (For an easy way to set your mower blade at the correct height, see **Rotary Mower** in the Glossary.) Once you have set the height of your mower, mow consistently! The chart below will help you mow at the right height, at the right time.

If you mow at the right height and at the right time, your grass clippings will never be more than about an inch long. Clippings of this size will fall to the soil surface and decompose quickly without building a layer of thatch. As they decompose, they will return nitrogen to the soil.

There are always those times, like the family vacation, when your Kentucky Bluegrass lawn is sure to grow beyond the recommended height. If possible, mow immediately before leaving and soon after you return. When you're packing three kids for the beach, this is easier said than done. If your lawn does grow out of control (well past 5 inches), mow at the highest setting your mower will allow. Return a day or two later and mow again at the recommended height. You may want to bag or rake your grass clippings during this process.

IRRIGATION

There is usually significant rainfall (on average) during the summer months in the South, but it is often sporadic and undependable. A Kentucky Bluegrass lawn needs plenty of water to grow well. In drought it will discolor, thin, and eventually die. In general, a Kentucky Bluegrass lawn will need 1–1.5 inches of water every 7–10 days during the summer, whether from rain or irrigation. Try to water deeply and infrequently. For example, apply 1 inch of water on a single day rather than .25 inches a day for four days. Deep

at the right height. If you remove large portions of a leaf blade in a single mowing, you will shock the grass plants and stall their growth. During the ensuing recovery period, your lawn will be weakened and more susceptible to stresses like heat, weed competition, and drought. As a general rule, always mow frequently enough so that you do not reduce the height of your lawn by more than one-third in a single mowing.

Recommended Mowing Heights (in inches)		
EXPOSURE	MOWING TO:	MOW WHEN GRASS IS:
Sun	2.5	3.75
Shade	3	4.5

In the South, Kentucky Bluegrass is highly susceptible to drought damage.

and infrequent watering will help the roots to grow deep into the soil where it is cooler and there is more moisture. Always stop irrigating, however, if water begins to run on the surface. Wait about an hour and begin again.

If you have an automatic sprinkler system, take a moment to investigate your control box and settings. Place a rain gauge or straight-sided jar on the lawn and turn on the sprinklers. Monitor how much water is applied in a given period. Most systems will have several different types of sprinkler heads, so you might have to test each irrigation zone. I like to draw a rough diagram of the lawn and record the various sprinkler outputs for future reference. This helps me manipulate the irrigation system during the sporadic rain and drought periods of the coming season. Do not be shy about increasing the pre-set cycles during droughts or turning off the entire system after a heavy rainfall. Your lawn will lose some of its dark green color in a drought, but it might die if swamped in poorly drained soil.

One Step Further: A grass plant absorbs water from the soil to replace water that evaporates from its leaf blades. The perfect way to irrigate is to supply the soil with the exact same amount of water that is lost. Search the Internet for a weather station in your area that records "pan evaporation rate" or "evapotranspiration." Water loss from Kentucky Bluegrass is approximately 85% of the pan evaporation rate.
Formula: (85% x Weekly Pan Evaporation Total) – Weekly Rainfall Total = Amount to irrigate that week

If you water your lawn with a manual sprinkler, place a rain gauge or straight-sided jar in the lawn to measure the amount of water applied. Try not to apply more, or less, than an inch at a time.

FERTILIZER

Fertilizing a lawn is one of the most satisfying and instantly rewarding lawn activities. Kentucky Bluegrass responds well to fertilizer and will darken in color and look much healthier. Without fertilizer, your lawn will become light green, thin, and will be easily invaded by weeds. Don't get carried away, though, and apply more fertilizer than is recommended. An over-fertilized lawn will not be any darker green, it will only grow faster and you will have to mow more often. The most efficient way to fertilize is to use the dry, granular fertilizers that are usually sold in 10–50 pound bags. Hose-end liquid fertilizers work, but they are difficult to use correctly and you will need to fertilize twice as often as with granular fertilizer.

Kentucky Bluegrass Fertilizer Facts:

• 4 lbs. of actual nitrogen per 1000 square feet per year

• Apply 1.5 lbs. of actual nitrogen per 1000 square feet in mid-spring and early fall

• Apply 1 lb. of actual nitrogen per 1000 square feet in late winter

• Use slow-release fertilizers in mid-spring and early fall

• Water approximately 1 inch after fertilizing

What Kind of Fertilizer to Use

Fertilizer is described by the percentages of nitrogen (N), phosphorus (P), and potassium (K) contained in the bag. All fertilizer bags are clearly labeled with these three numbers, known as the N-P-K ratio. In the spring and fall, I prefer to use a lawn fertilizer with a 3-1-2 ratio. An example would be a 12-4-8 fertilizer. In late winter, use a lawn fertilizer with a higher percentage of nitrogen (the first number). A bag of 12-4-8 fertilizer contains 12% nitrogen, 4% phosphorus, and

Without fertilizer, Kentucky Bluegrass loses its dark green color.

a soluble, quick-release form of nitrogen. Slow-release fertilizers are not as effective when the soil is cold. Be careful, however, when using fertilizers in which all of the nitrogen is in a soluble, quick-release form. Never apply more than 1 pound of actual nitrogen per 1000 square feet or the nitrogen will be so concentrated that it could burn your lawn.

> **Common Forms of Nitrogen** *(indicated on the label)*
> **Soluble:** *Available immediately, lasts 4–6 weeks*
> Ammonium nitrate, potassium nitrate, ammonium sulfate
> **Slow-Release:** *Available slowly in small amounts, generally lasts 2–3 months*
> Urea-Formaldehyde (UF), Isobutylidene diurea (IBDU), Sulfur Coated Urea (SCU), Polymer Coated Urea products (like "Polyon")

Up to this point, I have only mentioned three major nutrients: nitrogen, phosphorus, and potassium. These three nutrients are used by grass plants in relatively large quantities and are known as macronutrients. Grass plants use other nutrients in relatively small quantities. Those nutrients are known as micronutrients or "minor elements." Most brands of fertilizer contain the needed minor nutrients and you will not have to worry about them.

How Much Fertilizer to Apply

Most bags of fertilizer are covered from top to bottom with completely useless information that is written by the fertilizer company's marketing department. I continue to be amazed by the fact that the closest thing to directions is usually a vague phrase like "fertilizes up to 10,000 square feet." Luckily, there is a universal way to know how much fertilizer to apply, regardless of the brand or the specific N-P-K ratio. All you have to do is figure out how much "actual nitrogen" is contained in the bag. Kentucky Bluegrass lawns grow best with 4 pounds of actual nitrogen per 1000 square feet applied each year, regardless of the brand of fertilizer you purchase. Apply 1 pound of actual nitrogen per 1000 square feet in late winter. Then, switch to a fertilizer with a slow-release form of nitrogen and apply 1.5 pounds of actual nitrogen per 1000 square feet in mid-spring and early fall.

8% potassium by weight. The remaining 76% is inert material that adds bulk to the mixture and makes it easier to spread.

It is important to use slow-release fertilizers in the spring and fall. Avoid hose-end fertilizer sprayers or dry fertilizers in which all of the nitrogen is in a soluble, quick-release form. Most major brands of lawn fertilizer will have a combination of soluble and slow-release forms of nitrogen (indicated on the label). Soluble nitrogen is available to the grass plant immediately while slow-release nitrogen becomes available over a period of two to three months. In most situations it is best to have as much of the nitrogen in slow-release form as possible. Good brands of fertilizer will have 40–50% of the nitrogen in slow-release form. This is usually noted in a statement like "containing 6% nitrogen in slow-release form."

The late winter fertilizer application should contain

Here is an example using a 50-pound bag of 12-4-8 slow-release fertilizer:

1. Multiply the nitrogen percentage (12%) by the net weight of the bag (50 lbs.) to determine how many pounds of actual nitrogen are in the bag (6 lbs.).

2. Next, divide the actual nitrogen in the bag (6 lbs.) by the amount you want to apply per 1000 square feet (1.5 lbs.).

3. Multiply this number (4) by 1000 to determine how many square feet the bag will cover (4000).

4. If your lawn is only 3000 square feet, you will need to apply only 75% of the 50-pound bag. Two cups of granular fertilizer weigh approximately 1 pound, so remove 25 cups.

Unfortunately, the average bag of fertilizer does not tell you how much actual nitrogen it contains in the bag. It is easy to calculate, though, using two simple pieces of information: the N-P-K ratio and the weight of the bag. Multiply the percentage of nitrogen (the first number in the N-P-K ratio) by the weight of the bag and you will know the amount of actual nitrogen it contains. For instance, a 50-pound bag of 12-4-8 fertilizer has 6 pounds of actual nitrogen (12% of 50).

Determine the amount of coverage by dividing the amount of actual nitrogen in the bag by the amount of nitrogen you want to apply in a single application. In the spring and fall, Kentucky Bluegrass needs 1.5 pounds of actual nitrogen per 1000 square feet. Therefore, a bag that contains 6 pounds of actual nitrogen will cover 4000 square feet (6 divided by 1.5 pounds per 1000 square feet). If your lawn is less than 4000 square feet, remove the amount you do not need. Two cups of granular fertilizer weigh about 1 pound.

All of this calculating may seem like a hassle, but it really is the best way to apply the correct amount of fertilizer to your lawn. It is also a great way to compare the cost of different fertilizers so that you get a good deal. This best part is that you won't have to rely on the fertilizer company's marketing department for lawn advice.

How to Spread Fertilizer

You can broadcast granular fertilizer using a rolling fertilizer spreader, a hand-held spreader, or by hand (wear a glove). I will be completely honest with you. Spreading fertilizer is not an exact science. The calibrated settings on even the most expensive broadcast spreader are usually inaccurate. In addition, the majority of spreaders will clog, break, and jam.

I have had great success with a very simple and effective method. Begin by measuring your lawn and calculating the amount of fertilizer that you need to spread (see "How Much Fertilizer to Apply"). If you only need 40 pounds of a 50-pound bag, remove 20% and set it aside. Next, turn off your fertilizer spreader and fill it. Begin moving and barely open the spreader only once you are up to speed. Try to spread as little fertilizer as possible while still broadcasting an even pattern. Continue covering the entire lawn at the same speed. If you must slow to turn around, turn off the spreader or you will drop too much in a single location and burn your grass. Work across the entire lawn until you return to your starting point and shut off the fertilizer spreader. Now, see how much of the needed fertilizer is left. If 50% remains, repeat the entire process and you will be finished. If 25% remains, repeat the entire process but move twice as fast. Remember, it is impossible to be exact. Your foremost goal should be to spread the designated amount of fertilizer evenly over the entire lawn; avoid heavy doses in some areas and light doses in others.

When to Fertilize

When it comes to fertilizer, timing is everything. The following schedule will help you maintain a consistent level of nutrients that will be available to your lawn throughout the growing season.

• **Late Winter:** Fertilize Kentucky Bluegrass lawns in late winter when soil temperatures rise to a consistent 50° in order to stimulate deep root growth. This is usually late February/early March, when the Forsythia is in bloom. Use a high nitrogen, low phosphorus fertilizer like 18-0-4 that includes a pre-emergence weed control (unless you plan on reseeding in the spring). It is best if the nitrogen is NOT in a slow-release form.

Apply at the rate of 1 pound of actual nitrogen per 1000 square feet. Irrigate after fertilizing to wash fertilizer from leaf blades and move it to the soil surface.

• **Mid-Spring:** Fertilize again 4–6 weeks later. This is usually around April 1. Use a complete lawn fertilizer like 12-4-8 that contains a slow-release form of nitrogen. Apply at the rate of 1.5 pounds of actual nitrogen per 1000 square feet. Irrigate after fertilizing to wash fertilizer from leaf blades and move it to the soil surface.

• **Summer (Optional):** It is best not to fertilize Kentucky Bluegrass lawns during the summer months. If your Kentucky Bluegrass lawn is light green or yellow, however, apply a light dose of a complete lawn fertilizer that contains a slow-release form of nitrogen. This should be no more than .5 pounds of actual nitrogen per 1000 square feet. Irrigate immediately after fertilizing to prevent burning.

• **Early Fall:** Fertilize your Kentucky Bluegrass lawn again in early September. You can use the same complete fertilizer you have been using, or switch to a fertilizer with little or no phosphorus, but a higher rate of potassium. This might be something like 12-4-14 or 12-0-12. Either way, make sure the fertilizer contains a slow-release form of nitrogen and apply at the rate of 1.5 pounds of actual nitrogen per 1000 square feet. Irrigate after fertilizing to wash fertilizer from leaf blades and move it to the soil surface.

It is common these days to hear about "winterizing" lawns with a *late fall* application of special fertilizer. If you fertilize with a slow-release fertilizer in early September, there is no need to fertilize again in late fall. Save your time and energy.

• **Winter:** You may be tempted to fertilize your Kentucky Bluegrass lawn during our mild Southern winters. It is important to remember, however, that grass roots do not absorb nutrients when soil temperatures are below approximately 45°. While a warm spell seems like the perfect time to fertilize an off-color Kentucky Bluegrass lawn, soil temperatures will rarely reach the minimal level for root activity. Fertilizer applied during the winter will most likely leach from the soil into nearby streams and waterways.

SOIL pH AND LIME

Liming a lawn is a way to raise the pH of the soil. Soil pH is measured on a scale of 0–14 with 7 being neutral. A soil pH below 7 is considered acidic while a soil pH above 7 is considered basic (alkaline). Kentucky Bluegrass prefers soil pH of 6–7. The pH of a soil is important because it affects the availability of different nutrients. Nitrogen, for instance, is more available at a soil pH of 6 than a soil pH of 5. Liming a soil with a pH of 5 would actually increase the amount of nitrogen available to grass roots.

The best way to determine your lawn's pH is to have the soil tested by your local Cooperative Extension Service. The soil test result will recommend the amount of lime needed to raise the pH to the optimal level.

Many Southern soils are acidic and will need approximately 50 pounds of lime per 1000 square feet. Whenever possible purchase lime in pelletized form since it is much easier to distribute. Broadcast the pelletized lime with a fertilizer spreader, or by hand (wear a glove). Lime may take up to three months to affect the pH of your soil and can be applied at any time of the year. Since lime moves slowly in the soil, the best time to apply it is when planting or immediately after core aerating.

Occasionally, you may encounter a Southern soil with a pH above 7.5. In these cases, Kentucky Bluegrass may develop iron chlorosis. This appears as a yellowing between the veins of a grass blade. In such a case, you can correct the problem by lowering the soil pH to the 6–7 range with an elemental sulfur product. The most common form of elemental sulfur is aluminum sulfate. It is often available in 50-pound bags and should be applied at the rate recommended on the bag. A temporary cure of iron chlorosis is to spray with iron at the rate recommended on the bottle.

AERATING

Aerating a Kentucky Bluegrass lawn is a good way to encourage a healthy root system. In turn, your lawn will look better and withstand the heat of summer better. Aerating has two immediate effects. First, it allows air to move into the soil where it provides the oxygen needed for optimal root growth. Second, it creates passageways for water and nutrients to enter the soil. The best to time of year to aerate a Kentucky Bluegrass lawn is in early September before you fertilize. The second best time is in late February/early March, just before fertilizing and applying pre-emergence weed control. In both cases, aerating will move fertilizer into the soil, increase water penetration, and provide plenty of oxygen for root growth.

Remember not to aerate after you have applied pre-emergence weed control. It will disrupt the chemical barrier of the weed control and reduce its effectiveness. Also, do not aerate during the summer months when your lawn is suffering from heat and drought.

The only effective way to aerate a lawn is to use a core aerator. Core aerators are powered by an engine and remove cores of soil from the top layer soil. Since most people do not own a core aerator, they rent one or have a lawn service aerate for them. Core aerators work best on moist soil so you will need to irrigate several days before you plan to aerate. Make one or two passes across the lawn so that there is a hole every 4–6 inches. Afterwards, there will be cores of soil deposited all over the lawn surface. If they bother you, you can rake the lawn and most will break and drop below the level of the grass where they are not as visible. Otherwise, they will naturally disintegrate in a couple of weeks with the help of a few passing rainstorms. I prefer not to collect and remove the cores since they eventually return to the soil surface where they help thatch to decompose. Finally, irrigate the aerated lawn deeply to moisten exposed roots and rhizomes.

You will often see "spike aerators" of various sorts. Some roll behind a riding lawn mower, others are attached to fertilizer spreaders, and manual types look like a pitch fork that you are supposed to press into the soil with your foot. There are even special spike-clad shoes that claim to aerate while you wander around the lawn. When a spike is forced into the soil, it creates an opening but compacts the surrounding soil. Even worse, you will need to take at least 10,000 steps across the average lawn with spike-clad shoes to even come close to core aeration. In my opinion, all of these products are useless and should be avoided.

DETHATCHING

Thatch is a collection of dead plant parts like stems and grass clippings that accumulate on the soil surface. Thatch is not a problem unless it becomes thicker than .5 inches and grass roots begin to grow into it as if it was soil. Thatch dries very quickly in hot summer conditions and grass roots growing in it are much more susceptible to drought. If you mow and fertilize properly, your Kentucky Bluegrass lawns should not develop a thatch problem.

A good way to prevent any potential thatch prob-

lems is to give your lawn a good old-fashioned raking at least once a year. If your lawn is huge, don't bother. If your lawn is manageable, pick a nice day in late winter and use a metal-tined leaf rake. Try to work the tines down to the soil surface. Finally, collect and remove all of the debris.

Occasionally, a Kentucky Bluegrass lawn will accumulate greater than .5 inches of thatch during the growing season. This is usually as a result of improper mowing or excessive fertilizing. Lawns like this will be weak and thin by the end of the summer. One way to handle such a problem is to rent a vertical mower, or "dethatcher," from a tool rental store in early fall. Vertical mowing is a way to cultivate the top layer of soil and remove thatch. It should be used on a Kentucky Bluegrass lawn only if you plan to reseed immediately afterwards. Even then, be extremely careful. Vertical mowing is tricky and will damage the Kentucky Bluegrass plants that remain. Make only one pass across your lawn. Thoroughly rake and remove all the subsequent debris prior to reseeding.

Do not attempt to burn a Kentucky Bluegrass lawn during the winter to remove thatch. Unlike a warm-season grass lawn, Kentucky Bluegrass is alive and active throughout the year. Fire will damage the grass plants and ruin your lawn.

TOPDRESSING

With the rise in popularity of golf, we hear a lot these days about topdressing. Topdressing is a technique used by golf course superintendents to create a smooth playing surface on golf greens. A thin layer of soil or sand is distributed across the grass surface using a special topdressing machine. The grass responds by growing roots and rhizomes into the new, flatter soil surface.

Despite what many people think, topdressing is not a remedy for thinning turf or poor drainage. In fact, topdressing may compound these problems. For the typical homeowner, topdressing should be limited to filling gullies and holes that make mowing difficult. A single depression should be filled layer by layer over the entire growing season, never covering the surface with more than .25 inches of soil or sand at a time. Greater amounts will smother the grass and cause more harm than good.

There are a few situations when you might consider topdressing your entire lawn, for instance, if your sod was laid poorly and the entire lawn is bumpy. In that case, you may want to hire a lawn care professional who has a topdressing machine and access to high-quality topdressing soil mixtures.

BLOWING AND EDGING

Many people own their own blower these days. Blowers are wonderful tools that take a lot of the backache out of lawn work. A blower can be used to clean debris from driveways, walks, and porches. It is also an invaluable tool in the fall when leaves are getting the best of us. I also use a blower to disperse grass clippings if they accumulate in lines along the surface of my lawn.

There are three types of blowers: electric blowers, backpack blowers, and rolling street blowers. If you are going to be doing yard work for many years to come, I would definitely invest in a gas-powered blower. Electric blowers are inexpensive, but the inevitable tangled power cord is a complete hassle. Backpack blowers are great if you need a versatile machine that can reach various nooks and crannies. Rolling street blowers are the best for blowing leaves, but they are expensive and difficult to maneuver if your property has hills or steps.

Lawn maintenance companies regularly edge lawns and flower beds with a special machine that has a vertically rotating blade. You can accomplish the same effect by rotating your string trimmer and letting the string dig into the soil. Edging is largely a matter of aesthetics, although it does keep Kentucky Bluegrass from hanging out over your driveway. Remember this, though. Edging opens the soil surface and will disrupt the chemical barrier of your pre-emergence weed control. It is common to see weeds sprouting in March in the edged groove between a lawn and a driveway. If needed, it is safer to edge during June, July, and August.

WEED CONTROL

While it may be hard to believe, most weeds blow into your lawn as seeds and sprout the minute they find enough bare soil, moisture, and light to grow. This is true for both annual weeds and perennial weeds. Annual weeds sprout, grow, flower, seed, and die within one year. Perennial weeds sprout from a seed as well, but the weed plant continues to grow and spread for more than one season (even though the top may die back in the winter).

> ☛ **TIP:** Neighboring lawns, woods, and adjacent untended areas produce enormous numbers of weed seeds that blow into your lawn. If possible, mow or cut them before they produce seeds.

Unfortunately, all Kentucky Bluegrass lawns weaken during our hot Southern summers and a thinning lawn is the perfect place for a weed seed to germinate and grow. Consequently, your ultimate goal should be to grow a thick, luscious lawn that will naturally prevent weed seeds from germinating. There are two ways to accomplish this. First, correct fundamental problems like poor drainage and soil compaction that make growing a dense lawn difficult at best. Second, do not neglect your lawn maintenance. Kentucky Bluegrass lawns need to be nurtured during the summer and a couple of weeks without water or mowing can be devastating. The best defense against weeds is to concentrate primarily on maintaining a thick, well-grown stand of Kentucky Bluegrass and secondarily on weed control.

Types of Weed Control

There are two ways to control weeds in a lawn: as the weed seeds germinate (pre-emergence weed control) and after the weeds have already sprouted and are growing (post-emergence weed control). When using weed control products, always make sure the product is approved for use on Kentucky Bluegrass and follow the labeled directions. Do not apply more than the recommended rate; it will not give you better results and may injure your lawn.

> **Pre-Emergence Weed Control:** Usually sold as a dry, granular product in a 10–30 pound bag. May be labeled as "crabgrass control" although it will stop other weeds as well.
> **Post-Emergence Weed Control:** Usually sold as a liquid concentrate you spray from a pressurized sprayer or a hose-end sprayer. May be labeled as "broadleaf weed killer" or "grassy weed killer."

Pre-emergence weed controls kill immature weeds immediately after they germinate and before they

Weeds can ruin a beautiful Kentucky Bluegrass lawn.

emerge from the soil surface. Since annual weeds like crabgrass and annual bluegrass die and return from seed each year, a pre-emergence weed control will eradicate them from your lawn over several seasons. At the same time, it will prevent annual and perennial weed seeds that blow into your lawn from neighboring areas from emerging. Most pre-emergence products are sold in a granular form (with or without fertilizer) that you spread using a fertilizer spreader. Make sure the product is approved for use on Kentucky Bluegrass. It is important to spread the chemical "wall to wall" at the recommended rate. Areas that are not covered by the chemical will not be protected. Do not spread the chemical beyond your lawn since some pre-emergence controls can harm ornamental plants (check the product label). After spreading the product, irrigate your lawn with at least .5 inches of water to activate the chemical (unless otherwise stated on the bag). Once activated, pre-emergence weed controls create a chemical barrier in the upper inches of your lawn that will

kill weeds as they germinate. Do not cultivate, aerate, or disturb the soil after treating your lawn or you will disrupt the chemical barrier and open the soil to weed seed infiltration. Pre-emergence weed controls are usually effective for 2–3 months, depending on the temperature and amount of rainfall. Be careful and plan ahead, because a pre-emergence weed control will prevent Kentucky Bluegrass seeds from germinating as well.

Post-emergence weed controls kill weeds that are already growing in your lawn. These products are referred to as "selective" since they are targeted at specific annual and perennial weeds listed on the label. Usually, controls will either treat grassy weeds like crabgrass (monocotyledons) or broadleaf weeds like chickweed (dicotyledons). Choose the weed control spray that best fits your needs. You may need to purchase a spray for each category of weeds. In most cases, post-emergence products are designed to disrupt one of the weed's critical metabolic processes and should be sprayed when the weed is young and actively growing. If the weed is dormant because of cold weather or drought (i.e., not using the metabolic process), it may not die. Spray on a still day when air temperatures are between 60 and 80° and the grass is dry. Post-emergence weed controls are sometimes available in a granular form that should be spread with a fertilizer spreader when the grass is wet. The dry particles need the moisture to adhere to weed leaves. In either case, avoid using post-emergence weed controls immediately after seeding or sodding Kentucky Bluegrass because it can retard growth or damage tender grass. It is usually safe to spray after you have mowed at least twice.

> ☞ **WARNING:** Weed controls can have dramatic and damaging effects on ornamental trees, shrubs, and plants growing in or near your lawn. This is true for pre-emergence and post-emergence weed controls. For instance, some post-emergence sprays are absorbed by tree roots and can cause the leaves to burn or defoliate. Read the product label carefully for directions and never spray underneath shallow-rooted trees and shrubs like Dogwoods and Boxwoods.

There are other post-emergence weed controls like Round-Up that are non-selective. The term "non-selective" means they will kill all vegetation including your Kentucky Bluegrass. The trick is that non-selective weed sprays are absorbed through plant leaves. Large weed patches can be specifically sprayed with Round-Up without affecting the entire lawn. WATCH OUT! Sprays can drift very easily on a windy day. Wait at least 7–10 days before seeding or sodding the area (follow the directions on the label).

When to Apply Weed Controls

When it comes to weed control in a Kentucky Bluegrass lawn, timing is critical. Pre-emergence weed controls have to be applied before weed seeds germinate or they are useless. Post-emergence weed control sprays and granules have to be applied when the weeds are young, tender, and actively growing. I have found that when it comes to weed control, it is always better to be a little early rather than a little late.

Under normal conditions, a well-grown Kentucky Bluegrass lawn will remain weed-free with two applications of granular pre-emergence weed control (late winter and early fall) and spot treatments of problem weeds with a post-emergence weed control spray in mid-winter and early summer. I have included two "optional" pre-emergence weed control applications for people trying to renovate a very weedy lawn and people that live near a major source of weeds like an old pasture.

• **Late Winter:** Apply a **pre-emergence weed control** when the soil temperature reaches a consistent 50°. This is usually in February/early March, when the Forsythia is in bloom. This application will control annual weeds and perennial weeds that germinate in the spring. Make sure the product is approved for use on Kentucky Bluegrass and apply at the rate recommended on the bag. Do not aerate for 3 months after you apply pre-emergence weed control because it will affect the chemical barrier of the weed control. Irrigate after applying unless otherwise stated on the bag. For convenience, you can combine this application with fertilizer in late winter (see "Fertilizer" above).

Do not apply pre-emergence weed control if you are planning to seed, sod, or reseed a Kentucky Bluegrass lawn in the spring. It will prevent Kentucky Bluegrass seed from germinating and retard Kentucky Bluegrass sod roots from growing.

• **Spring and Summer:** Begin treating weed outbreaks as soon as you see them with a **post-emergence weed control** spray approved for use on Kentucky Bluegrass. Weeds will die quickly when they are young and actively growing. Spray on a calm day when the air temperature is 60–80°. Avoid spraying newly seeded or sodded Kentucky Bluegrass, however, until you have mowed at least twice (follow the labeled directions).

If your lawn is still overrun with weeds in mid-spring, consider using a combination fertilizer/post-emergence weed control (granular form) when you fertilize in April. Follow the labeled instructions. Most products should be applied when the lawn is wet.

Apply **pre-emergence weed control** without fertilizer 2–3 months after your late winter application to control annual and perennial weeds that continue to germinate into the summer (optional application). This is usually around June 1. If your lawn is mostly weed-free, and weeds do not usually blow in from surrounding areas, you can skip this application. Use a product approved for use on Kentucky Bluegrass and apply at the rate recommended on the bag. Remember not to aerate for 3 months after you apply pre-emergence weed control because it may affect the chemical barrier of the weed control. Irrigate after applying unless otherwise stated on the bag.

• **Early Fall:** Apply **pre-emergence weed control** (without fertilizer) to Kentucky Bluegrass lawns when soil temperatures drop to 70°. This is usually occurs in mid-September in the upper South. If you think you will forget, you can apply pre-emergence weed control when you fertilize in early September but you will be sacrificing some effectiveness. This application will control weeds like annual bluegrass and henbit that germinate in the fall and winter.

Either way, make sure the pre-emergence product is approved for use on Kentucky Bluegrass and apply at the rate recommended on the bag. Remember to aerate before you apply pre-emergence weed control so you do not affect the chemical barrier. Irrigate after applying unless otherwise stated on the bag. This application will last 2–3 months.

Do not apply pre-emergence weed control if you are planning to seed, sod, or reseed your Kentucky Bluegrass lawn in the fall. It will prevent Kentucky Bluegrass seed from germinating and retard Kentucky Bluegrass sod roots from growing.

• **Winter:** Apply a **pre-emergence weed control** without fertilizer 2–3 months after your fall application (optional application). This is usually in late November/early December. If your lawn is mostly weed-free, and weeds do not usually blow in from surrounding areas, you can skip this application. Use a product approved for use on Kentucky Bluegrass and apply at the rate recommended on the bag. Remember not to aerate for 3 months after you apply pre-emergence weed control because it may affect the chemical barrier. Irrigate after applying unless otherwise stated on the bag.

During the winter, treat weed outbreaks as soon as you see them with a **post-emergence weed control** spray approved for use on Kentucky Bluegrass. Most of your problems this time of year will be from annual weeds like chickweed and henbit. Spray on a warm afternoon (air temperature is at least 60°) when the weeds are young and actively growing. Even then, it may take two applications to kill them.

INSECTS

A lush, dense Kentucky Bluegrass lawn is the perfect habitat for a variety of insects. In fact, you could probably drive yourself crazy trying to figure out whether a given worm, grasshopper, cricket, or beetle is a friend or foe. In general, a Kentucky Bluegrass lawn grows faster than the average insect can eat and does not suffer any ill effects from their patronage. There are, however, a few classes of insects that arrive and increase in populations large enough to harm your lawn. They can be treated fairly easily with a soil insecticide or with natural products like BT and Milky Spore. The best time for a once-a-year insect treatment is in late July or early August.

Insect damage is often defined as an irregularly shaped patch of discolored or brown grass in a lawn. If you take a drive around town, you will probably pass a thousand lawns that could fit that definition. The problem is this. Only about ten of those thousand lawns probably have an insect problem. Lawns are finicky and irregular patches of brown grass pop up because of different reasons. One of the most common is drought. You might think your lawn is evenly watered but even a slight rise or a different soil texture can alter the amount of water that penetrates the soil. When you think you have an insect problem, look for another cause first. Then, wait to see if the troubled lawn area expands. Only then should you worry about treating with a soil insecticide. Following is a list of insects that might cause problems in a Kentucky Bluegrass lawn. Don't panic! You may never see any of these bugs.

White grubs are the most common and problematic insects on Kentucky Bluegrass lawns in the South. White grubs are the larval, soil-inhabiting form of several different types of beetles including Japanese Beetles and June Beetles. The most notorious beetle in the South is the Japanese Beetle, known for its voracious feeding on Crape Myrtle trees, ornamental cherry trees, grapes, and almost anything green. Japanese Beetles lay their eggs in lawns and grassy areas beginning in July. The eggs hatch as white grubs in late July and begin a two-month feeding frenzy on grass roots. As soil temperatures begin to cool in late September, the white grubs tunnel 4–8 inches into the soil where they pass the winter. As the soil warms in the spring white grubs move to the surface, feed briefly in

Green June Beetles are an adult form of root-eating white grubs.

April/May, and then pupate. White grubs can be controlled with a granular soil insecticide applied in late July/early August according to the labeled directions. This is the best time to treat since the grubs are tender and easily killed. You can also treat with milky spore, a natural product that contains spores of *Bacillus popilliae*, a disease that kills white grubs. Milky spore will not kill every white grub, but spores will remain active in your lawn for many years.

Larval worms are another type of insect pest that feed on Kentucky Bluegrass leaf blades. They include cutworms and sod webworms. Unlike white grubs, larval worms can have several life cycles during a given growing season and are less predictable in their arrival. In addition, they are night-feeders and hide in tunnels beneath your lawn during the day. Sod webworms leave behind a spidery web that is noticeable on grass blades early in the morning. Insect damage appears as areas of brown or unevenly clipped grass. Larval worms can be controlled with a soil insecticide approved for use on Kentucky Bluegrass. BT (*Bacillus thuringiensis*) is an effective natural product.

Fire ants once took up residence in a mulch pile I was moving. I will never forget that day and I will never forgive those ants. I have tried almost every chemical available, and a number of home remedies, and have only had average results. Every time I treat a mound it seems to pop up in another location. Sometimes the mounds seem to multiply. There are numerous entomologists working on the problem, so hopefully they will find a good cure soon.

If **moles** are tunneling through your lawn, they are probably after white grubs. Treat for white grubs in late July/early August and the moles will probably go away.

There is always another insect or pest that *might* plague your lawn. You might hear or read about ground pearls, nematodes, mites, viruses, and a long list of other potential problems. In general, don't worry. Just keep an eye on things and treat problems when you find them. Your lawn is tougher than you think.

DISEASES

Diseases can be a problem on Kentucky Bluegrass lawns in the South since most of them prefer the same temperature and moisture as your grass. Fungal diseases like leaf spot, powdery mildew, and rust can be prevalent under the right environmental conditions. While individual diseases appear at different times of the year (depending on the weather), it is almost impossible to predict when your lawn will be afflicted. In many cases, a disease will come and go without you ever knowing it. Since fungal diseases are very difficult to identify, it is important to keep a sharp watch for anything abnormal.

In general, fungal diseases appear as brown or damaged patches of grass with clearly defined outlines. If you find a lawn area that fits this description, don't run out and spray the entire lawn with fungicide. Wait to see if the patch of damaged grass expands over the next day or two. It is quite possible that the fungal disease has already run its course. An "active" patch of diseased turf will grow and expand concentrically over a couple of days. Grass plants along the outline of the damaged patch may have discolored, wilted, or spotted leaves. If you find one of these problems, treat the infected area with a lawn fungicide approved for use on Kentucky Bluegrass.

Many fungal diseases are exacerbated by water. This is especially true with fungal diseases like leaf spot that are prevalent in the spring and fall when daytime air temperatures are 60–80° and nighttime air temperatures are around 60°. During these critical times, do not irrigate unless it is necessary. When needed, water on a sunny day when moisture will evaporate quickly from grass leaves. If there is a daytime watering ban in effect for your area, irrigate immediately before dawn.

If your lawn has a history of fungal problems, you may want to reseed the dead areas and then spray preventatively with a lawn fungicide the following year so that the disease does not recur. Follow the directions on the product label explicitly. You will probably need to spray several times over a 2–4 week period.

OVERSEEDING

During the winter, many people sow a temporary, cool-season grass like Annual Ryegrass over their dormant warm-season grass lawns. Since Kentucky

Fungal diseases appear as brown patches of grass with clearly defined outlines.

Bluegrass remains green during the winter, there is no reason to overseed. Thinning Kentucky Bluegrass lawns should be reseeded with Kentucky Bluegrass, not overseeded with ryegrass. Overseeding with ryegrass is a horrible idea since the ryegrass will compete with your Kentucky Bluegrass for nutrients, water, soil, and sunlight. Once hot weather arrives, the ryegrass will die and leave your Kentucky Bluegrass lawn weaker and thinner than before.

RESEEDING

Kentucky Bluegrass lawns do not like hot weather. Most will suffer and thin during a long, hot Southern summer. By the end of August, it is inevitable that you will have lost a few grass plants here or there. Most of the time, lawns will rebound with fertilizer, water, and cooler temperatures in September. In a bad year, however, your entire lawn may have weakened and thinned dramatically. If so, consider reseeding in early September.

The decision to reseed is not as clear-cut as you might think. Reseeding is not just a matter of throwing a few handfuls of seed here and there. Reseeding involves foregoing a pre-emergence weed control application, cultivating the top layer of soil, and fertilizing and watering diligently. When you combine all of these components, you are providing not only Kentucky Bluegrass seeds, but winter weed seeds like annual bluegrass, the perfect opportunity to germinate. In general, a decent stand of Kentucky Bluegrass will benefit more from aerating, fertilizing, and applying pre-emergence weed control than from reseeding. Kentucky Bluegrass lawns should be reseeded when there is roughly 3–4 inches of bare ground between grass plants. If your lawn has thinned to about one or two grass clumps per square foot, you might as well start over. A lawn that has degenerated to this point will benefit greatly from the rototilling and soil amending described in the "Planting a New Kentucky Bluegrass Lawn" section.

Steps in Reseeding

1. Do not apply pre-emergence weed control any time during the 3 months before you plan to reseed.

2. Before reseeding, mow your Kentucky Bluegrass to 1.5 inches.

3. Rake the soil surface vigorously with a metal-tined leaf rake to remove thatch and other debris. This will also loosen the soil surface.

4. If possible, aerate with a rented core aerator. Rake the lawn afterwards to pulverize as many of the removed cores of soil as you can.

5. Apply a complete lawn fertilizer that contains a slow-release form of nitrogen. I prefer to start lawns with a 3-1-2 ratio fertilizer like 12-4-8. Fertilizers labeled as "starter fertilizer" are helpful, but not critical. Apply at the rate of 1.5 pounds of actual nitrogen per 1000 square feet. Rake the lawn to help the fertilizer drop to the soil surface. Do not use fertilizer that contains a pre-emergence weed control.

6. Apply pelletized lime to acidic soils according to soil test recommendations. This is often 50 pounds per 1000 square feet. Rake the lawn to help the pelletized lime drop to the soil surface.

7. Broadcast seed at a rate of 2–3 pounds per 1000 square feet.

8. Irrigate to keep the soil surface moist for the first two weeks. Afterwards, reduce consistently until you are applying 1 inch of water every 7–10 days if there has been no significant rainfall.

9. Mow your Kentucky Bluegrass at 2.5–3 inches over the winter and spring months. Use a new mower blade or have your old one sharpened. Bag your clippings until grass plants have toughened.

10. Do not use post-emergence weed control sprays until you have mowed the lawn two or three times.

II. Renovating a Kentucky Bluegrass Lawn

Kentucky Bluegrass is one of the few Southern lawn grasses that can be grown from seed with relative ease. If your Kentucky Bluegrass lawn thins, your first impulse might be to rush out and buy a bag of seed. This might be the appropriate move (see "Reseeding" above). Then again, you may be better off spending your time and effort renovating your existing lawn.

When a Kentucky Bluegrass lawn begins to lose color, weaken, and thin, it is easy to blame the weather. Kentucky Bluegrass is not really meant for the South, and heat should always be a likely suspect. Then again, your vainglorious neighbor might be growing a beautiful Kentucky Bluegrass lawn and offering to give you a few pointers.

There are two categories of problems that will ruin a Kentucky Bluegrass lawn: maintenance problems and fundamental problems. Unfortunately, the results of both often look the same. For instance, a thinning lawn can be the result of improper mowing or dense shade. Think about your lawn's history and work your way toward the logical cause.

CORRECTING MAINTENANCE PROBLEMS

When your golf game is suffering, it is easy to blame your clubs. More often, however, you need to address the underlying problem with your swing. Before buying another 50-pound bag of seed, read through the maintenance section above and determine if you are skipping any critical steps. Are you fertilizing, mowing at the right height, mowing consistently, aerating, irrigating, and applying pre-emergence weed control? Do you have an insect or disease problem? Address these problems accurately to stimulate your Kentucky Bluegrass to grow denser, darken in color, and remain healthy. Below is a "recipe" for Kentucky Bluegrass lawn renovation. This is a great way to boost the performance of your Kentucky Bluegrass lawn once or twice a year.

CORRECTING FUNDAMENTAL PROBLEMS

There are times when a lawn looks horrible even though you are maintaining it perfectly. These are the most frustrating of times and really try our patience

---

Recipe for Kentucky Bluegrass Renovation *(early September or late February)*

THREE WEEKS AHEAD:

• **Kill Weeds.** Spray weeds three weeks ahead of time with a post-emergence weed control approved for use on Kentucky Bluegrass. This will be either early August or early February. Repeat the application a week later for better control.

ALL AT ONCE:

• **Rake.** Rake the entire lawn vigorously with a metal-tined leaf rake and remove leaves, dead weeds, grass clippings, rocks, etc.

• **Aerate:** Aerate the lawn with a rented core aerator. Rake the lawn after core aerating to pulverize the cores and return them to the soil surface.

• **Fertilize.** Fertilize immediately after aerating in the fall with 1.5 pounds of actual nitrogen in slow-release form. Fertilize immediately after aerating in the spring with 1 pound of actual nitrogen per 1000 square feet in quick-release form.

• **Lime.** Apply 50 pounds of pelletized lime per 1000 square feet immediately after aerating (see "Soil pH and Lime" above).

• **Control Future Weeds.** Apply pre-emergence weed control after aerating (see "Weed Control").

Kentucky Bluegrass will thin and die in waterlogged soils, only to be replaced by weeds.

with lawn growing. Before going any farther, re-read the beginning of this chapter. Make sure you are living in one of the specific areas of the South where Kentucky Bluegrass will grow. There is no need to waste money on a lawn grass that is unsuitable for your area. Next, remember that a lawn is not a cure-all. In fact, there may be hundreds of plants besides a lawn grass that are more suitable for a particular area (see **ground cover** in the glossary). Remember this as you read the remedies below. The most efficient and inexpensive approach might be to reconfigure or abandon areas that are not suitable for a lawn.

• **Shade.** Kentucky Bluegrass will grow in partial shade. Partial shade is hard to define but usually means 2–3 hours of direct sunlight a day or a thin tree canopy like tall pines. In dense shade, a Kentucky Bluegrass lawn will become thin and weak. The only answer is to remove a few tree limbs, cut down a few trees, or reduce the size of your lawn to avoid the shade. Raising the mowing height in the shaded areas may alleviate some of the problem but is often impractical since the grass might flop over.

• **Compacted soil.** Compacted soil is low in oxygen and will cause a Kentucky Bluegrass lawn to thin and die. Consider core aerating once or twice during the growing season in late February or early September. Also, evaluate the cause of the compaction and correct continuing problems by creating walkways for people and pets. Do not topdress Kentucky Bluegrass lawns in an attempt to modify the soil. You will only cause the soil to "layer," which prevents good drainage.

• **Poor drainage.** Kentucky Bluegrass is tolerant of a certain amount of moisture, but will thin and die in soggy soils. These are also some of most difficult and expensive problems to correct. Before you begin, determine the source of the water and where it is trying to flow. Occasionally, you can correct a drainage problem by diverting a water source (like a gutter outlet) or removing an obstruction (a clogged ditch). Other solutions include re-grading, subsurface drains, and surface drains. Once the soil dries, core aerate to help renovate the root zone.

• **Improper pH.** Kentucky Bluegrass prefers a soil pH between 6 and 7. It is tolerant of soil pH outside this range but will grow slowly, lose density, and be light green/yellow *despite* your best maintenance practices. Always consider your maintenance before you blame soil pH. If you suspect soil pH, take a soil sample to your local Cooperative Extension Service for testing. They will recommend the needed lime or elemental sulfur to correct the problem.

III. Planting a New Kentucky Bluegrass Lawn

A new Kentucky Bluegrass lawn can be started from seed or sod. Your decision to seed or sod is based primarily on cost and availability. Kentucky Bluegrass sod is much more expensive than seed (per square foot) and should be laid "wall to wall" for best results. A final consideration might be rate of establishment. If you have dogs or kids, it might be hard to keep them off a germinating lawn long enough for the seedlings to become tough and established.

> ☛ **TIP:** Soil-related problems can devastate a new or established Kentucky Bluegrass lawn. This is your only chance to fix soil problems! Cultivate the soil deeply and amend with humus before you plant.

Whether you seed or sod, early fall is the ideal planting time. Begin planting when soil temperatures drop into the 70s. This is usually in September. If you miss this window of opportunity, early spring is an average second choice. Begin planting in the spring when soil temperatures reach a consistent 55° and the danger of hard freezes has passed. This is usually in March, when the Bradford Pear trees are in bloom.

> **A Sampling of Kentucky Bluegrass Cultivars:**
> • Adelphi, Baron, Glade, Vantage, Victa
> **A Sampling of Kentucky Bluegrass Cultivars Promoted as Shade Tolerant:**
> • Bristol, Glade, Nugget, Touchdown

SEED MIXTURES AND BLENDS

A Kentucky Bluegrass seed mixture is a collection of several different grass species sold together in a single bag. An example would be a single bag containing Kentucky Bluegrass, Perennial Ryegrass, and Creeping Red Fescue. A Kentucky Bluegrass seed blend is a collection of several different cultivars of Kentucky Bluegrass sold together in a single bag. An example would be a combination of "shade-tolerant" Kentucky Bluegrass cultivars. Either way, seed companies are required to divulge the exact components of their mixtures and blends by listing the percentages of grasses

and grass cultivars on a special seed label attached or printed on the bag.

I do not believe in using grass mixtures in the South. The whole idea behind a grass mixture is to sow a variety of different types of grasses so that you have a better chance of one particular type flourishing while the others weaken, or even die. It is a shotgun approach to selecting seed. If you sow a mixture with 50% Kentucky Bluegrass and 50% Perennial Ryegrass, then half of your lawn will look horrible during the heat and drought of summer. Worse yet, if the Perennial Ryegrass dies, your lawn will be thinned dramatically. The point is this. We know which types of grass do well in the South. So why not increase our odds of success?

More often than not, I stay away from grass blends as well. All too often, I will find a grass blend that contains 50% of a well-known, proven Kentucky Bluegrass cultivar and 50% of a Kentucky Bluegrass cultivar that has consistently ranked poorly in university-level testing. The problem is not as bad as with a grass mixture, but I still avoid planting 50% of my lawn with a Kentucky Bluegrass cultivar that is known to be a poor performer.

Some grass mixtures and blends have a special marketing angle. For instance, the seed bag may claim to be a mixture of the best grasses for a certain geographic area, the best grasses for a specific situation like shade, or the best grasses to fix a lawn problem like a bare spot. Be extremely wary of these products. Some seed companies are known to "hide" cheap, useless seed in these types of grass mixtures and blends. For instance, you will often find Annual Ryegrass hidden in a blend claiming to repair your lawn. The Annual Ryegrass will sprout and look wonderful for a couple of weeks but will die in the summer heat. You might be told that the Annual Ryegrass is a "nurse grass" that will help your Kentucky Bluegrass along while it is germinating. This is wrong. It is the same as saying that annual bluegrass weeds help your Kentucky Bluegrass lawn to become established.

Whenever possible I avoid grass mixtures and blends in favor of pure seed. For instance, I might buy a bag containing only 'Adelphi' Kentucky Bluegrass. You can often rely on the cost as an indicator of the quality. A bag containing a single, top-rated Kentucky Bluegrass cultivar will usually cost more than a blend, but it is usually well worth the extra money.

Creeping Red Fescue will form isolated and noticeable clumps in a mixed Kentucky Bluegrass lawn.

READING SEED LABELS

Seed companies are required to report several facts about the seed they are selling on a special label attached or printed on the bag. It is important to check this label because the information on the rest of the bag can be *very misleading*. First, make sure the bag contains only one type of seed (unless you want to buy a blend). Second, make sure the germination test date is within the last year. Old seed will not germinate as well. Finally, make sure the bag does not contain seed for grasses like Perennial or Annual Ryegrass that will die during the summer heat of the Sou

'Adelphi' Kentucky Bluegrass	Lot: XXX-1234-XXX
Net. Wt. 50 lbs.	Origin: Oregon

98% Pure Seed	
1% inert matter	
1% weed seed	
Test Date: 2-1-20XX	Germ: 85%

STEPS IN PLANTING A NEW LAWN

Starting a new Kentucky Bluegrass lawn from scratch is not an overwhelming project. But then again, it is not a one-weekend project. Try to spread the various steps over two or three weekends. For instance, I would strongly suggest cultivating one weekend and planting the next. This is especially true if you are cultivating areas under trees. The best news is that Kentucky Bluegrass lawns are planted in cooler weather, so you can be thankful you are not laying Bermuda Grass sod on a 95° Saturday afternoon in July.

STEP 1. Spray existing weeds. The first step in planting a new Kentucky Bluegrass lawn is to remove as many weeds from the lawn area as possible. Use a non-selective herbicide like Round-Up. Plan ahead since you will need to wait 1–2 weeks after spraying before you seed or sod. Check the product label for specific directions.

STEP 2. Establish the grade. One of the best ways to guarantee a beautiful lawn is to establish a good grade before you begin. This may be more than most of us can afford, but consider it nonetheless. The proper grade can prevent both drought and poor drainage and will be a godsend in the long run. In general, a 2% to 6% grade is the optimal.

STEP 3. Cultivate the soil as deeply as possible. Whether you seed or sod, Kentucky Bluegrass roots will need to grow into the existing soil surface. Kentucky Bluegrass prefers cooler temperatures, so it is especially important for roots to be able to grow deep into the soil. The deeper you can cultivate the soil, the more quickly your lawn will establish and thrive. Remember to wait the allotted time after spraying your herbicide before cultivating. Begin by raking and removing debris like dead weeds, leaves, and rocks from the area. Next, cultivate the soil with a rear-tine rototiller. If you do not own a rototiller, you might consider renting one from your local tool rental store. Rototill the entire area lengthwise, then again cross-wise. Try to work the top 4–6 inches of soil into a nice pulverized soil mix. If you are planting a small lawn and do not have a rototiller, cultivate the entire area with a hoe, garden rake, or shovel. Again, the deeper you work the soil, the better.

STEP 4. Amend the soil. During home construction, most of the natural humus in the top layer of soil is scraped away or buried. The remaining soil will probably be low in organic matter and will be greatly improved if you add humus. Adding humus will improve drainage in clay soils and improve water retention in sandy soils. Peat moss, composted bark products, and compost are all good choices. Be careful, however, if you use a soil amendment that contains a gel-like substance (indicated on the packaging) to retain water. These products can cause strange drainage problems. I prefer adding two 3.8-cubic-foot bales of sphagnum peat moss per 1000 square feet. Work the peat moss into the top 4–6 inches of soil as you rototill.

STEP 5. Lime and fertilizer. A lawn is a big investment and it does not hurt to have the soil pH determined by your County Extension Service. Kentucky Bluegrass prefers a soil pH of 6–7, and your soil test results will recommend the specific amount of lime to add if the pH needs to be raised. Many Southern soils are acidic and will need approximately 50 pounds of lime per thousand square feet. Whenever possible, purchase lime in a pelletized form because it is much easier to distribute. Spread the pelletized lime with a fertilizer spreader, or by hand, and work it into the top layer of cultivated soil using a garden rake. At the same time, apply a complete lawn fertilizer that contains a slow-release form of nitrogen. I prefer to start lawns with a 3-1-2 ratio fertilizer like 12-4-8. Fertilizers labeled as "starter fertilizer" are helpful, but not critical. Apply at the rate of 1.5 pounds of actual nitrogen per 1000 square feet. Work the fertilizer into the top layer of cultivated soil using a garden rake.

STEP 6. Seeding. Plan on using approximately 4–5 pounds of Kentucky Bluegrass seed per 1000 square feet. Seed may take 2–4 weeks to germinate, so be patient. Begin by raking the area to provide as smooth a soil surface as possible. I like to use a plastic leaf rake because it creates tiny furrows and ridges on the soil surface that "capture" the seed. Measure the amount of seed needed for the lawn into a separate bucket or container (most of us approximate). Try not to use more seed than the recommended rate—an overpopulation of grass seedlings will weaken individual plants, cause strange growth problems, and make your lawn more susceptible to insects and diseases. Seed can be sown by hand or with a broadcast spreader. When using a spreader, sow one-half the seed lengthwise and one-half crosswise to avoid any skips. Once sown, lightly rake the entire lawn with a leaf rake to slightly cover the seed with no more than .25 inches of soil. Cover the newly seeded lawn with a layer of wheat straw to prevent washing and erosion while the seed is germinating. You will need about one bale of wheat straw per 1000 square feet. Do not use hay since it is full of weed seeds.

STEP 7. Sodding. Before laying Kentucky Bluegrass sod, cultivate the soil as described in step 3. Do not skip this step! It is imperative that Kentucky Bluegrass sod roots grow deep into the soil before next summer.

Unless you are planting a small lawn, it is almost always cheaper and more efficient to order pallets of sod from your local nursery to be delivered to your house. Begin by measuring the entire new lawn area and ordering enough square footage of sod to completely cover every foot. Plan on laying the sod soon after it is delivered. Stacked sod should not sit for more than a day or two.

Begin at the top of the lawn and lay the sod lengthwise, so that the long side of each piece of sod is running across, rather than down, a hill or rise. As you place each piece of sod, work it tight against the surrounding pieces to prevent the edges from browning and ruts from forming. Sod is often cut on a slant so that the edges will overlap. Make sure the edges slant appropriately so that they interlock. Pound each block of sod with your palm to press it into the soil below and remove any air pockets. Stagger the second row of sod so that the perpendicular edges do not line up. The result should look like a brick wall, not a checkerboard. If you are placing sod along steep gradients, pin them in place with stakes or metal pins (available from sod distributors). Irrigate deeply once all the sod is placed.

STEP 8. Irrigation during establishment. Whether you have seeded or sodded, it is essential to irrigate in the coming weeks. A newly seeded lawn should remain moist for about two weeks. Water lightly and frequently. Rely on your instinct. If the soil surface is

eroding or becomes "soupy," skip a watering. If the soil surface dries rapidly, irrigate more frequently. After two weeks, decrease the frequency but increase the amount of water you are applying. By 4–6 weeks after germination, your lawn will need about an inch of water per week, whether by irrigation or rainfall. If you have sodded your new Kentucky Bluegrass lawn, follow these same guidelines. Sodded lawns will require more water in the early stages than seeded lawns.

STEP 9. Initial mowing. Mow your newly seeded Kentucky Bluegrass lawn as soon as it reaches 3.75 inches. This is a hard pill to swallow. A newly seeded lawn looks so delicate that most people wait and mow when the grass blades are 6 inches tall and flopped over. Do not hesitate! Use a mower with a sharp blade (this is a good time to buy a new blade) and cut frequently. Mowing will encourage the grass blades to toughen and spread. Bag your grass clippings since young growth is succulent and will mat easily. Lawns started from sod should be mowed at 2.5 inches as soon as they reach 3.75 inches.

STEP 10. Fertilizing during establishment. A fall-seeded Kentucky Bluegrass lawn may benefit from a light mid-winter application of soluble fertilizer. Use a 3-1-2 ratio fertilizer like 12-4-8 that does NOT contain nitrogen in a slow-release form. Apply at the rate of .5 pounds of actual nitrogen per 1000 square feet. If your new lawn is dark green and growing well, wait until late winter to begin the normal Kentucky Bluegrass fertilizer schedule.

STEP 11. Weed control during establishment. Weeds like annual bluegrass can be a problem in a newly seeded Kentucky Bluegrass lawn since weed seeds germinate under the same conditions that Kentucky Bluegrass seed germinates. Controlling weeds in a newly seeded lawn is a delicate maneuver. Even herbicides labeled for use on Kentucky Bluegrass have the potential of harming young, tender Kentucky Bluegrass seedlings. A general recommendation is to wait until you have mowed two or three times before using post-emergence weed control sprays approved for use on Kentucky Bluegrass. In most cases, you can begin using pre-emergence weed controls by the following February. Either way, check the product label for specific instructions.

Cultivate the soil deeply with a rototiller before planting.

Amend the soil with a humus like sphagnum peat moss prior to planting.

Work fertilizer into the top layer of soil with a garden rake.

Plan on using 4–5 pounds of Kentucky Bluegrass seed per 1000 square feet.

Sow the seed evenly over the designated area.

Lightly rake the entire lawn with a leaf rake to slightly cover the seed with soil.

CHAPTER EIGHT

Other Lawn Grasses

The preceding chapters have covered the best lawn grasses for the South. These grasses, and their named cultivars, are the result of a hundred years of research, breeding, and innovation. Every year it becomes a little bit easier to grow a gorgeous lawn in our hot climate.

There are other grasses out there. Some are relatively unknown and some are absolutely outstanding in other parts of the country. My philosophy is this. While you may want to grow an exotic plant to impress your friends and neighbors, there is no reason to grow an "exotic" lawn. When it comes to a lawn, a trusted, tried, and true Southern lawn grass should be your first and only choice.

Following is a list of other grasses you may hear about or find for sale.

WARM-SEASON GRASSES

Bahiagrass (*Paspalum notatum*): My father firmly believes that a Bahiagrass lawn is the ugliest lawn you will ever see. I will not disagree. I have been told that Bahiagrass is "absolutely wonderful" along the side of the highway and does well in soggy soil. Hopefully your lawn area is not soggy and you don't want it to look like the side of a highway.

Carpetgrass (*Axonopus affinis*): Carpetgrass will grow into a more appealing lawn than Bahiagrass, but it requires frequent mowing to remove hundreds and thousands of seed stalks. It is not very tolerant of cold and would have problems in the middle South. In the lower South, it grows well in soils that are too wet for Centipede and Bermuda Grass. Despite this, Centipede and Saint Augustine are better choices.

Native Grasses: There are several grasses indigenous to the United States that are occasionally offered or discussed as an alternative lawn grass for the South. These include Buffalograss (*Buchloe dactyloides*) and Blue Grama (*Bouteloua gracilis*), both of which are native to the American Midwest and West. Do not consider them for a lawn in the South. If you are looking for the perfect drought-resistant, low-maintenance, trouble-free native grass, why spend money? Rototill your lawn area and a grass native to the South is sure to blow in and sprout for free.

EVERGREEN GRASSES

Annual Ryegrass (*Lolium multiflorum*): Annual Ryegrass is also known as Italian Ryegrass. It is a true annual plant and will grow, produce seed, and die within one year. It germinates quickly, grows quickly, and produces a fast cover. It is a great grass with which to overseed Bermuda Grass, Centipede, and Saint Augustine lawns for a green winter cover. It should never be purchased, however, as a permanent lawn grass. In the old days in the South, Annual Ryegrass was known as "Real Estate Grass." Disreputable real estate agents would sow it over a lawn area to fool prospective buyers into thinking the house had a perfect lawn. The new owners would move in, and two weeks after "closing," the lawn would burn up in the summer heat. To overseed, sow 6–8 pounds of Annual Ryegrass per 1000 square feet when soil temperatures drop to 70°. This is usually around September 15 in the upper South and October 15 in the lower South.

Perennial Ryegrass (*Lolium perenne*): Perennial Ryegrass is the more refined cousin of Annual Ryegrass. It is a perennial plant and it does not complete its life cycle in one year. Consequently, it can be used as a permanent lawn grass in the cooler areas of the country. It does not like heat, grows poorly in drought, and seldom survives a true Southern summer. Perennial Ryegrass cultivars are sometimes used instead of Annual Ryegrass to overseed Bermuda Grass, Centipede, and Saint Augustine lawns for a green winter cover. Some of these named cultivars have a more consistent texture and are more durable than Annual Ryegrass. There is a problem, though. Perennial Ryegrass does not die as quickly as Annual Ryegrass and will often linger into summer in shaded areas. This might sound like a benefit but it is not. The Perennial Ryegrass will look like a weed in the shaded area, not a handsome turf. To overseed, sow 6–8 pounds of Perennial Ryegrass per 1000 square feet when soil temperatures drop to 70°. This is usually around September 15 in the upper South and October 15 in the lower South.

Creeping Bentgrass (*Agrostis palustris*): Creeping Bentgrass is an outstanding grass where it will grow, but it will not grow here. In the Northeast, Creeping Bentgrass is heralded and admired for its fine texture and dense growth. It forms a beautiful green carpet and is the top choice for golf greens. In fact, many Southern golf courses switched to Creeping Bentgrass

greens in hopes of enjoying these attributes. Most are switching back because of the extraordinary efforts they have to perform to keep it alive. Creeping Bentgrass can be used to overseed Bermuda Grass, Centipede, and Saint Augustine lawns for a green winter cover, but it is usually hard to find. To overseed, sow 1–2 pounds of Creeping Bentgrass seed per 1000 square feet around September 1 in the upper South and September 15 in the lower South. Creeping Bentgrass takes longer to germinate and establish than other overseeded grasses.

Rough Bluegrass (*Poa trivialis*): Rough Bluegrass is sometimes grown in the northern states as a permanent lawn grass or a lawn grass for shaded areas. It will grow in the South and can be used as a fine-textured grass for shaded areas in the middle and upper South. The problem is that Rough Bluegrass is seldom available and it is usually very expensive. If you find some and want to try it in the shade, sow 3–4 pounds of Rough Bluegrass per 1000 square feet.

*Southern lawns are occasionally
covered by snow.*

Month-by-Month
Southern Lawn Care

I. JANUARY ACTIVITIES

IF WE ARE GOING TO HAVE WINTER WEATHER IN THE SOUTH, IT IS LIKELY TO ARRIVE THIS month. A frigid cold front will sweep down across the Midwest and send temperatures into the teens. Then suddenly, the front will pass and temperatures may be back up into the sixties. That is the beauty of a Southern winter. There are those wonderful respites when we can wander the yard, pruning here and there, playing backyard football with the kids, and believing that spring has arrived unusually early this year.

Plants take advantage of these warm spells, too. The January Jasmine bursts into bloom with a little warm weather alongside Winter Honeysuckle and an assortment of Camellia. I always keep an eye on the Flowering Quince because a few buds always swell and bloom early. January is a good time to cut a branch and "force" the blooms inside. It isn't hard. Just cut the branch about two feet long and place it in a vase.

Warm-season lawns are pleasantly dormant this month and their boring tan color is a little bit more palatable when you consider the alternative—mowing. Even a healthy fescue lawn needs only the occasional cut. It is so nice to be free from mowing for a while. By January I haven't quite rid myself of that draining feeling you get when you know you have to mow once again. It seems hard to believe, but in a couple of months, the dread will be gone and I'll be raring to crank up my mower and head out into the warm spring sunshine.

WARM-SEASON LAWN ACTIVITIES FOR JANUARY:

(Bermuda Grass, Centipede, Saint Augustine, Zoysia)

☛ **Planting:** Wait until late spring when soil temperatures reach 75–80° to begin planting warm-season lawns from seed or plugs, or to sod a new warm-season lawn. This is usually in May.

☛ **Mowing:** Warm-season grass lawns are dormant this month and will not need to be mowed. It is a good idea to leave grass at about 3 inches over the winter months to provide insulation for tender roots, rhizomes, and stolons growing near the soil surface. Uneven or weedy lawns can be mowed when dormant, however, to provide a more kempt appearance. You will only need to remove about .25 inch.

Centipede, Bermuda Grass, and Saint Augustine lawns overseeded with a temporary cool-season grass like Annual Ryegrass should be mowed at 2–2.5 inches whenever the grass reaches 3 inches. Do not allow the overseeded grass to grow over 3 inches at any time. It will begin to clump and become ugly.

☛ **Irrigation:** Dormant warm-season lawns seldom need to be watered in January. Occasionally, we will have a warm, dry spell that may cause shallow roots, rhizomes, and stolons to desiccate. Apply about .5 inches of water if the top .25 inches of soil is dry to the touch.

If possible, water dormant lawns when temperatures are expected to drop below 20°. Wet soil will freeze and keep soil temperatures close to 32°, while dry soil allows damaging sub-20° air to penetrate the root zone.

☛ **Fertilizer:** Wait until mid-spring to begin fertilizing warm-season lawns. Dormant lawns will not absorb fertilizer and it may leach into nearby streams and rivers.

☛ **Aerating:** The best time to aerate warm-season lawns is in late spring/early summer when soil temperatures reach 80º. Aerating now will disrupt your pre-emergence weed control, open the soil to weed seed infiltration, and allow damaging cold temperatures to penetrate the root zone.

☛ **Dethatching:** Do not worry about thatch this month. Mechanical and manual dethatching will only expose stolons, roots, and rhizomes to colder temperatures. Wait until March to mow dead top growth and to rake and remove debris.

☛ **Topdressing:** Do not topdress warm-season lawns this month. Warm-season grass lawns are not growing actively and topdressing could smother your lawn.

☛ **Weed Control:** Weeds are easily recognized and located on a tan, dormant warm-season lawn. Spray newly emerging annual weeds (henbit, chickweed) and established perennial weeds (ground ivy, pennywort) with a post-emergence weed control approved for use on your specific type of grass. Spray on a warm afternoon when air temperatures are between 60 and 80° and follow the labeled directions. You may have to spray twice (over a week or so) to kill tough, mature weeds.

Remember that weed control products like Round-Up are non-selective and will kill your lawn grass as well. You can use Round-Up on dormant Bermuda Grass, but check to make sure its leaves and stolons have not emerged from dormancy in a winter warm spell. Even then, spray only the weed and stop spraying if it begins to drip from the leaves.

☛ **Insects and Diseases:** Problem insects and disease are not active this month.

☛ **Overseeding:** It is too late to effectively overseed Bermuda, Centipede, and Saint Augustine lawns with a temporary cool-season grass like Annual Ryegrass (a.k.a. Italian Ryegrass). Annual Ryegrass might germinate despite the cold, but it will look more like a weed than a beautiful green cover.

☛ **Other:** Rake any remaining leaves. Wet leaves can smother even a dormant lawn.

EVERGREEN LAWN ACTIVITIES FOR JANUARY:

(Tall Fescue, Creeping Red Fescue, Chewing Fescue, Kentucky Bluegrass)

☛ **Planting:** The best time of year to plant an evergreen lawn is in early September. The second best time is in the spring when soil temperatures are above 55° and the danger of hard freezes has passed. This is usu-

ally in mid-March when the Bradford Pear trees are in full-bloom.

If you are planning to seed an evergreen lawn this spring, remember not to apply pre-emergence weed control in February.

☛ **Mowing:** Mow lawns consistently at the recommended height. Do not to let your lawn grow beyond these heights, even in the winter. If you reduce the height of your lawn by more than one-third in a single mowing, you will shock the grass plants and stall their growth.

Recommended Mowing Heights (in inches)

	Height:	Mow When:
Kentucky 31 Fescue	3–4	4.5–6
Turf-type Fescue	2.5–3	3.75–4.5
Creeping Red and		
Chewing Fescue	2–2.5	3–3.75
Kentucky Bluegrass	2.5–3	3.75–4.5

Mow fall-seeded lawns with a sharp blade as soon as they reach the recommended mowing height. Do not allow them to grow beyond 4 inches. Mowing consistently will cause the grass plants to toughen and spread.

Continue to bag your grass clippings when mowing a fall-seeded lawn. Succulent young grass clippings mat easily on the lawn surface and can damage your new lawn.

☛ **Irrigation:** Evergreen lawns seldom need to be watered in January. During the occasional warm, dry spell you may need to apply .5 inches of water if the top .25 inches of soil is dry to the touch.

By this time, evergreen lawns seeded this past fall should not need more water than an established lawn. Remember that frequent, light irrigation encourages a shallow root system. Evergreen lawns need to develop a deep root system in advance of the coming summer season.

☛ **Fertilizer:** Wait until next month to begin fertilizing evergreen lawns and applying pre-emergence weed control. The best time to begin is when soil temperatures reach a consistent 50°. This is usually in late February/early March, when the Forsythia is in bloom.

Fall-seeded lawns should not need additional fertilizer this month.

☛ **Aerating:** Aerate evergreen lawns next month, immediately before applying pre-emergence weed control. Grass roots will be growing more vigorously at that time and aerating will be more effective.

☛ **Dethatching:** Evergreen lawns do not usually have thatch problems. If needed, however, lawns can be raked with a metal-tined leaf rake this month to remove thatch and other debris.

☛ **Weed Control:** Spray newly emerging annual weeds (henbit, chickweed) and established perennial weeds (ground ivy, pennywort) with a post-emergence weed control approved for use on your specific type of grass. Spray on a warm afternoon when air temperatures are between 60 and 80° and follow the directions on the label. You may have to spray twice (over a week or so) to kill tough, mature weeds.

Remember that weed control products like Round-Up are non-selective and will kill your lawn grass as well.

Wait until next month to begin fertilizing evergreen lawns and applying pre-emergence weed control. The best time to begin is when soil temperatures reach a consistent 50°. This is usually in February/early March, when the Forsythia is in bloom.

Brown (dead) patches in your lawn might be due to summer annual weeds that died in the first winter frost. Spraying these areas will not help. Instead, wait until mid-March to cultivate and reseed.

☛ **Insects and Diseases:** Insects and diseases are usually not active this month. Relax!

☛ **Reseeding:** January is not a good time to reseed an evergreen lawn. Wait until soil temperatures are above 55° and the danger of hard freezes has passed. This is usually in mid-March when the Bradford Pear trees are in full bloom. Remember not to apply pre-emergence weed control if you are planning to reseed.

☛ **Other:** Rake leaves. Heavy, wet leaves can kill areas of your lawn.

In the lower South, it is common to overseed warm-season grass lawns.

II. FEBRUARY ACTIVITIES

FEBRUARY IS FICKLE. IT CAN EITHER BE COLD AND SOMBER OR WARM AND SUNNY. IT MAY even be both. This kind of weather is tough on plants, especially the ones from other countries like Oriental Magnolias. They are often tricked by oscillating temperatures into blooming early. We can be sure of one thing, though. It will be cold again. In fact, it will probably be very cold.

Southern rose gardeners know about February. They always wait until the very end of the month, or even the beginning of next month, to prune. If they prune early in the month, it might prompt roses to sprout and grow in a February warm spell. A devilish wave of cold weather is sure to follow and will quickly kill the delicate new growth.

Just like rose pruning, there are some specific lawn activities that are unique to February. As the soil slowly begins to warm, evergreen lawns like fescue are beginning to grow new roots. February is a great time to zap fescue with fertilizer to encourage a deep root system before summer arrives. Evergreen lawns will also need pre-emergence weed control when the Forsythia is in bloom (soil temperatures reach 50°). Do not fertilize warm-season lawns but do give them pre-emergence weed control. Be careful because the pre-emergence weed control is often sold in combination with fertilizer. Don't buy it! Look for a product that is only weed control.

WARM-SEASON LAWN ACTIVITIES FOR FEBRUARY:

(Bermuda Grass, Centipede, Saint Augustine, Zoysia)

☛ **Planting:** February is not a good time to start a new warm-season grass lawn. Wait until late spring when soil temperatures reach 75–80° to begin planting warm-season lawns from seed, plugs, or sod. This is usually in May.

☛ **Mowing:** Leave your warm-season grass lawn at about 3 inches over the winter months to provide insulation for tender roots, rhizomes, and stolons growing near the soil surface. Temperatures will surely drop below freezing once more before spring truly arrives. Uneven or weedy lawns can be mowed when dormant, however, to provide a more kempt appearance. Only remove about .25 inches at a time.

Centipede, Bermuda Grass, and Saint Augustine lawns overseeded with a temporary cool-season grass like Annual Ryegrass should be mowed at 2–2.5 inches whenever the grass reaches 3 inches. Do not allow the overseeded grass to grow over 3 inches at any time. It will begin to clump and become ugly.

☛ **Irrigation:** Dormant lawns will occasionally need to be watered during a winter warm spell (if it hasn't rained for a while). This will prevent roots/rhizomes near the soil surface from drying out. Apply about .5 inches of water if the top .25 inches of soil is dry to the touch.

If possible, water dormant lawns when temperatures are expected to drop below 20°. Wet soil will freeze and keep soil temperatures close to 32°, while dry soil allows damaging sub-20° air to penetrate the root zone.

☛ **Fertilizer:** Do not fertilize warm-season grasses this month. Fertilizing might encourage your lawn to emerge prematurely from dormancy, only to be damaged in the next hard freeze.

Make sure the pre-emergence weed control you broadcast at the end of the month does not include fertilizer.

☛ **Aerating:** The best time to aerate warm-season lawns is in late spring/early summer when soil temperatures reach 80º. Aerating now will open the soil to weed seed infiltration and allow damaging cold temperatures to penetrate the root zone.

☛ **Dethatching:** Wait until next month to mow, rake, and remove last year's dead top-growth. Removing dead top-growth is one of the best ways to prevent thatch accumulation.

☛ **Topdressing:** Do not topdress warm-season lawns this month. Warm-season grass lawns are not growing actively and topdressing could smother your lawn.

☛ **Weed Control:** Begin applying granular pre-emergence weed control to warm-season grass lawn when soil temperatures reach a consistent 50°. This is usually in late February/early March, when the Forsythia is in bloom. Use a pre-emergence weed control that does not contain fertilizer. Warm-season grasses do not need fertilizer until they become green and active later in the spring. This application will last 2–3 months.

Irrigate your lawn after applying pre-emergence weed control in order to activate the chemical (unless otherwise stated on the bag).

Winter weeds like wild onion and henbit love this time of year. Henbit is often in bloom, in fact, preparing a new batch of weed seeds to plague us next year. Spray annual weeds (henbit, chickweed) and established perennial weeds (ground ivy, pennywort) as soon as you see them with a post-emergence weed control approved for use on your specific type of grass. Spray on a warm afternoon when air temperatures are between 60 and 80° and follow the directions on the label. You may have to spray twice (over a week or so) to kill tough, mature weeds.

Remember that weed control products like Round-Up are non-selective and will kill your lawn grass as well. You can use Round-Up on dormant Bermuda Grass, but check to make sure leaves and stolons have not emerged from dormancy in a winter warm spell. Even then, spray only the weed and stop spraying if it begins to drip from the weed leaves.

☞ **Insects and Diseases:** Insects and diseases are not active this month.

☞ **Overseeding:** Do not try to overseed warm-season grasses this late in the winter.

EVERGREEN LAWN ACTIVITIES FOR FEBRUARY:

(Tall Fescue, Creeping Red Fescue, Chewing Fescue, Kentucky Bluegrass)

☞ **Planting:** Wait until next month to begin seeding or sodding a new evergreen lawn. Early spring is the second best time of the year to plant. Wait until soil temperatures rise above 55° and the danger of hard freezes has passed. This is usually in March when the Bradford Pear trees are in full bloom.

Remember not to apply pre-emergence weed control this month if you are planning to seed an evergreen lawn during the spring.

☞ **Mowing:** Continue to mow consistently at the recommended height.

Mow fall-seeded lawns frequently with a sharp blade to encourage the grass plants to expand and form a dense stand.

☞ **Irrigation:** There is usually plenty of rain in February. If we have a warm, dry spell, check the soil

Recommended Mowing Heights (in inches)		
	Height:	Mow When:
Kentucky 31 Fescue	3–4	4.5–6
Turf-type Fescue	2.5–3	3.75–4.5
Creeping Red and Chewing Fescue	2–2.5	3–3.75
Kentucky Bluegrass	2.5–3	3.75–4.5

and apply approximately .5 inches of water if the top .25 inches of soil is dry to the touch.

Lawns that were seeded in the fall should not need more water than established lawns. Remember that light, frequent irrigation encourages a shallow root system. Evergreen lawns need to develop a deep root system in advance of the coming summer season.

☞ **Fertilizer:** Begin fertilizing evergreen lawns once the soil temperature reaches a consistent 50°. This is usually in February/early March, when the Forsythia is in bloom. Use a high nitrogen, low phosphorus fertilizer like 18-0-4 that includes a pre-emergence weed control approved for use on your specific type of grass. It is best if the nitrogen is NOT in a slow-release form. It should be in a soluble form like ammonium nitrate, ammonium sulfate, urea, or potassium nitrate. Apply at the rate of 1 pound of actual nitrogen per 1000 square feet. This application will last 4–6 weeks.

Do not apply pre-emergence weed control if you plan to seed an evergreen lawn next month.

☞ **Aerating:** February is the second best time of the year to aerate evergreen lawns. Use a core aerator, available at most tool rental stores. Aerate before you fertilize so that fertilizer, water, and oxygen can move easily into the root zone. Do not aerate after applying pre-emergence weed control because you will disrupt the chemical barrier.

☞ **Dethatching:** Evergreen lawns do not usually have thatch problems. If needed, however, lawns can be raked with a metal-tined leaf rake this month to remove thatch and other debris.

☞ **Weed Control:** Apply a granular pre-emergence weed control, along with fertilizer, when soil temperatures reach a consistent 50°. This is usually in February/early March, when the Forsythia blooms. Make sure the product is approved for use on your specific type of evergreen grass and apply at the rate recommended on the bag.

Irrigate your lawn after broadcasting granular pre-emergence weed control in order to activate the chemical (unless otherwise stated on the bag).

Winter annual weeds like chickweed, henbit, and wild onion are usually growing quickly this month. They can be pulled by hand or sprayed with a post-emergence weed control approved for use on your specific type of grass. Sprays are most effective when air temperatures are 60–80° and weeds are young and actively growing. Follow the directions on the product label.

☞ **Insects and Diseases:** It is still too cold for most insect and disease activity.

☞ **Reseeding:** September is the best time of year to reseed an established evergreen lawn. Spring reseeding is possible, but seedlings have trouble becoming established in uncultivated soil before summer arrives. Spend your money on pre-emergence weed control instead.

☞ **Other:** Evergreen lawns growing in acidic soil will benefit from an application of lime. Many Southern soils will need approximately 50 pounds of lime per 1000 square feet. Since lime moves slowly in the soil, one of the best times to apply it is immediately after core aerating.

*With all its top-growth mowed and removed, a
Zoysia lawn is ready to emerge from dormancy.*

III. MARCH ACTIVITIES

MARCH CAN BEGIN WITH ICE STORMS AND SNOW (REMEMBER THE GREAT BLIZZARD OF '93), but temperatures are usually mild by March 20 or 21, the official start of spring. On that day, the Vernal Equinox, night and day hours are equal. Springtime in the South usually begins earlier than the Vernal Equinox, but chilly nights and frost *do* stretch into April. Don't be fooled into buying your tomatoes and annuals.

A Southern spring is a sight to behold. I spent my college years in upstate New York and they are truly missing out. Spring in the North arrives May 1 and is over on May 15. In the South, springtime is a three-month parade of gorgeous plants, each trying to outshine the last. During March, the Star Magnolia, Bradford Pear, and 'Okame' Cherry Trees will be giving it their best shot. Meanwhile, the Carolina Jessamine bursts forth to show the trees a thing or two.

March is also a hectic month. The kids are out of school for Spring Break and if we're not packing the car for a vacation, we are desperately trying to find a very tiring activity for them. One of the best might be a little lawn raking. March is the perfect time to rake and remove last year's thatch. Lawns will thrive if you leave the soil surface fresh and clean for the coming growing season.

WARM-SEASON LAWN ACTIVITIES FOR MARCH:

(Bermuda Grass, Centipede, Saint Augustine, Zoysia)

☛ **Planting:** It is still too early to plug, seed, or sod a new warm-season lawn. Even though established lawns will begin to green later in the month, wait until soil temperatures reach 75–80° to begin planting a new lawn. This is usually in May. Warm-season lawns will grow rapidly and establish quickly once the ground is warm.

Green sod may be available at nurseries this month, but it is probably shipped from areas farther south. It will not be acclimated to our area and could be damaged in a late-season frost or freeze.

☛ **Mowing:** Warm-season lawns should be mowed this month to remove as much dead top-growth as possible. Mow after the danger of hard freezes has passed, but before the lawn begins to green. This is usually in mid-March when the Bradford Pear trees are in full-bloom. Do not mow below about .5 inches or you may damage roots, stolons, and rhizomes growing near the soil surface. Rake and remove all of the mowed debris so it will not accumulate as thatch.

Overseeded lawns should be mowed, as well, to slow the growth of the overseeded grass and prevent it from competing with the emerging warm-season grass.

☛ **Irrigation:** Dormant lawns should be irrigated this month during warm, dry periods. This will prevent roots, stolons, and rhizomes near the soil surface from drying during the critical spring green-up. On average, dormant lawns only need .25–.5 inches of water at a time.

☛ **Fertilizer:** Do not fertilize warm-season grasses this month. Wait until the danger of frost has passed and lawns are at least 50% green. This is usually next month, when the Dogwoods are in bloom. Fertilizing before the danger of frost has passed will encourage tender top-growth that will suffer in freezing temperatures.

If you apply pre-emergence weed control in early March, make sure it does not contain fertilizer.

Do not fertilize overseeded lawns this month, even if they are light green. Try to slow the overseeded grass's growth so that your permanent lawn can recover.

Centipede and Saint Augustine lawns may be yellow as they emerge. This happens when the soil is too cold for grass roots to absorb the needed nutrients. In most cases, your lawn will turn green in a couple of weeks. If it does not, check the soil pH.

☛ **Aerating:** The best time for a once-a-year lawn aeration is in the late spring when the soil temperature rises to 80°. This is usually in late May. Aerating this month will damage tender roots and shoots at a time when they are low on stored energy. Also, it will disrupt the chemical barrier of your pre-emergence weed control and open the soil to weed seed infiltration.

☛ **Dethatching:** One of the best ways to prevent thatch is to mow and remove dead top-growth before your lawn begins to green in the spring (see "Mowing" above). I prefer not to mechanically dethatch dormant lawns with a rented vertical mower because it will disrupt roots, rhizomes, and stolons when they are low on stored energy. If needed, warm-season lawns can be vertically mowed during the summer.

☞ **Topdressing:** Do not topdress dormant warm-season lawns this month. Wait until the active growing season when roots, stolons, and rhizomes will grow quickly into the new soil. Even then, there are very few situations when an entire lawn will need to be topdressed.

☞ **Weed Control:** Apply pre-emergence weed control to warm-season lawns when soil temperatures reach a consistent 50°, if you have not done so already. This is usually in early March when the Forsythia is in bloom. Use a pre-emergence weed control that does not contain fertilizer and is approved for use on your specific type of grass. Warm-season grasses do not need fertilizer until they are green and the danger of frost has passed.

Irrigate your lawn after broadcasting granular pre-emergence weed control in order to activate the chemical (unless otherwise stated on the bag).

Wait until late spring to begin spraying established weeds with a post-emergence weed control. Spraying now may slow, or even harm, the growth of your lawn as it is emerging from dormancy. It is usually safe to spray once you have mowed at least twice.

☞ **Insects and Diseases:** Fungal diseases may arrive on lawns as they begin to green this month. Be especially watchful when daytime air temperatures are 65–80°, nighttime air temperatures are 50–60°, and lawns are moist. Lawn diseases appear as off-color or dead areas with clearly defined edges. They can be controlled with a lawn fungicide approved for use on your specific type of grass.

It is still too early in the season for most insect pests.

☞ **Overseeding:** Mow overseeded lawns below 2 inches (see "Mowing") to stall their growth and allow your permanent warm-season lawn to recover.

☞ **Other:** Watch out for late-season cold snaps. If temperatures are to drop into the low 20s, water your lawn to increase soil moisture. Frozen ground will remain around the freezing point while dry soil will allow frigid air to penetrate the root zone.

Lawns can be limed at any time during the year to raise the pH. A soil test will determine the exact pH of your soil and recommend the amount of lime needed. Many lawns will need about 50 pounds per 1000 square feet. Do not lime Centipede lawns since they prefer an acid soil.

EVERGREEN LAWN ACTIVITIES FOR MARCH:

(Tall Fescue, Creeping Red Fescue, Chewing Fescue, Kentucky Bluegrass)

☞ **Planting:** March is the second best time of year to seed a new evergreen lawn. Begin seeding when soil temperatures rise to at least 55° and the danger of hard freezes has passed. This is usually when the Bradford Pear trees are in full bloom. Cultivate prior to seeding and keep the soil moist for two weeks to ensure even germination. Seedlings need to be prepared for the heat of summer as soon as possible. Mow frequently with a sharp blade at the recommended height. Also, wean seedlings off frequent light irrigation over a 4–6 week period. By May, you should be watering deeply and infrequently.

March is also a good time to lay fescue sod. Fescue roots grow best when soil temperatures are 50–65°. With proper care, fescue sod laid this month will become established before the heat of summer arrives.

☞ **Mowing:** Mow evergreen lawns consistently at the recommended height. This is very important in the spring. Proper mowing will encourage grass plants to spread and grow roots deep into the soil.

Recommended Mowing Heights (in inches)		
	Height:	Mow When:
Kentucky 31 Fescue	3–4	4.5–6
Turf-type Fescue	2.5–3	3.75–4.5
Creeping Red and		
Chewing Fescue	2–2.5	3–3.75
Kentucky Bluegrass	2.5–3	3.75–4.5

☞ **Irrigation:** Evergreen lawns may need water this month during warm, dry spells. Apply .5–1 inch of water per week if there has been no significant rainfall.

Newly seeded evergreen lawns should be watered frequently as they germinate. After two weeks, begin reducing the frequency but increasing the amount of each watering. By 4–6 weeks after seeding, you should be irrigating deeply and infrequently.

As temperatures warm later in the month, shift your watering schedule so that you irrigate during the day when water will evaporate more quickly from leaf blades. Fungal lawn diseases can develop when grass remains moist.

☛ **Fertilizer:** Fertilize established evergreen lawns early in the month when soil temperatures reach a consistent 50°, if you have not done so already. This is usually when the Forsythia is in bloom. Use a high-nitrogen, low-phosphorus fertilizer like 18-0-4 that includes a pre-emergence weed control. It is best if the nitrogen is NOT in a slow-release form. It should be in a soluble form like ammonium nitrate, ammonium sulfate, or potassium nitrate. Apply at the rate of 1 pound of actual nitrogen per 1000 square feet. This application will last 4–6 weeks.

Do not apply pre-emergence weed control if you plan to seed an evergreen lawn this spring.

☛ **Aerating:** The best time of year to aerate evergreen lawns is in early September, just prior to fertilizing and applying pre-emergence weed control. The second best time is in late February/early March, just prior to fertilizing and applying pre-emergence. Do not aerate this month if you have already applied a pre-emergence weed control. It will disrupt the chemical barrier and open the soil to weed seed infiltration.

☛ **Dethatching:** Evergreen lawns do not usually have thatch problems. If you have the energy, rake with a metal-tined leaf rake this month to remove thatch and other debris.

☛ **Weed Control:** Apply a granular pre-emergence weed control early in the month when soil temperatures reach a consistent 50°, if you have not done so already. This is usually when the Forsythia is in bloom. This application is usually combined with fertilizer (see "Fertilizer").

Do not apply pre-emergence weed control if you plan to seed an evergreen lawn this spring.

Irrigate your lawn after broadcasting granular pre-emergence weed control in order to activate the chemical (unless otherwise stated on the bag).

Winter annual weeds like chickweed, henbit, and wild onion continue to be a problem this month. They can be pulled by hand or sprayed with a post-emergence weed control approved for use on your specific types of grass. Sprays are most effective when air temperatures are 60–80° and weeds are actively growing. You may have to spray twice to kill mature weeds. Always read the product label for important information and directions.

☛ **Insects and Diseases:** As air temperatures begin to warm late in the month, fungal diseases may arrive on evergreen lawns. Be especially watchful when daytime air temperatures are 65–80°, nighttime air temperatures are 50–60°, and lawns are moist. Lawn diseases often appear as off-color or dead areas with clearly defined edges. They can be controlled with a lawn fungicide approved for use on your specific type of grass.

It is too early in the season for most insect pests.

☛ **Reseeding:** September is the best time of year to reseed an evergreen lawn. Reseeding in March is possible, but seedlings have trouble becoming established in uncultivated soil before summer arrives. Save your money for fertilizer.

☛ **Other:** Watch out for late cold snaps. If temperatures are to drop into the low 20s, water your lawn to increase soil moisture. Frozen ground will remain around the freezing point while dry soil will allow frigid air to penetrate the root zone.

Evergreen lawns prefer a soil pH of 6–6.5 and can be limed at any time during the year to raise the pH. A soil test will determine the exact pH of your soil and recommend the amount of lime needed. Many Southern soils will need about 50 pounds per 1000 square feet. Since lime moves slowly in the soil, one of the best times to apply it is immediately after core aerating.

Sharpen or replace your lawn mower blade if you have not done so already. A dull blade will rip the tips of grass blades and cause them to turn brown.

*Fescue lawns thrive in the cooler
temperatures of spring.*

IV. APRIL ACTIVITIES

APRIL MAY BE THE PERFECT MONTH OF THE YEAR IN THE SOUTH. IT IS COOL IN THE MORNings, mild in the afternoons, and the sky is azure. People are everywhere—walking, jogging, and gardening. Easter comes, the last frost passes, and an afternoon rocking on the porch by the Dogwood is pure pleasure. The bumblebees are jousting for the last Caroline Jessamine blooms and the Snowball Viburnum are nodding in a gentle breeze.

Azaleas are everywhere: Christmas Cheer, Coral Bell, Hino Crimson, George Taber, and Snow. The list goes on and the show continues. The Kurume azaleas will pass but will soon be followed by the Satsuki azaleas. Meanwhile, our Southern azaleas like the Piedmont, Florida Flame, and Flame almost shame those brought from exotic places.

April is also a month for lawns. Both evergreen and warm-season lawns are a verdant green this month and it is a joy to mow. The smell of a freshly cut lawn on a cool afternoon in April makes you realize how many scents we miss in the winter. And new spring grass just feels good underfoot. It is also wonderful that lawns seem to appreciate the attention. More than any other time of the year, mowing *does* make the lawn look manicured and fertilizing *does* improve its color.

WARM-SEASON LAWN ACTIVITIES FOR APRIL:

(Bermuda Grass, Centipede, Saint Augustine, Zoysia)

☞ **Planting:** You can begin planting warm-season grass lawns after the danger of frost has passed and the soil begins to warm. This is usually in mid-late April. Warm-season grasses prefer summer temperatures, however, and sod/plugs/seed will establish most quickly if planted next month when soil temperatures reach 75–80˚.

☞ **Mowing:** Begin mowing warm-season lawns as soon as they reach the recommended height. Do not mow lower than the recommended height during spring green-up or you may shock the grass.

Recommended Mowing Heights (in inches)		
	Height:	Mow When:
Common Bermuda	2	3
Hybrid Bermuda	1–1.5	1.5–2.25
Centipede	1.5–2	2.25–3
Saint Augustine	2–3	3–4.5
Zoysia	1–2	1.5–3

It is too late to mow lawns below the recommended height to remove last year's dead top-growth.

☞ **Irrigation:** Water warm-season lawns carefully during spring green-up. Even a short period of drought can stress a lawn as it emerges from dormancy. Apply 1 inch of water per week if there has been no significant rainfall.

Fungal diseases love cool weather and moist grass. At this time of year, it is best to water during the day when moisture will evaporate quickly from leaf blades.

☞ **Fertilizer:** Begin fertilizing warm-season lawns this month as soon as the danger of frost has passed and lawns are at least 50% green. This is usually in April when soil temperatures have reached a consistent 65–70˚. Use a complete lawn fertilizer that contains a slow-release form of nitrogen. Apply at the rate of 1.5 pounds of actual nitrogen per 1000 square feet. This application should last 2–3 months.

Fertilize Centipede lawns after the danger of frost has passed and they are mostly green. This is usually in mid-April. Use a slow-release fertilizer specifically designed for Centipede lawns. Apply at the rate of .75 pounds of actual nitrogen per 1000 square feet. If you cannot find a Centipede fertilizer, use a slow-release lawn fertilizer with as little phosphorus (the middle number of the N-P-K ratio) as possible.

If using a liquid fertilizer, or a soluble granular fertilizer, be careful not to apply more than 1 pound of actual nitrogen per 1000 square feet. High levels of nitrogen will cause excessive top growth, little root growth, and promote disease. Also, these types of fertilizer will last only 4–6 weeks. If you commit to using them, fertilize consistently so your lawn will not experience fluctuating levels of soil nutrients.

Centipede and Saint Augustine lawns may be yellow as they emerge. This happens when the soil is too cold for grass roots to absorb the needed nutrients. In most cases, your lawn will turn green in a couple of weeks as the soil warms. If it does not, check the soil pH.

☛ **Aerating:** Wait until May to begin core aerating. Aerating now will disrupt your pre-emergence weed control and open the soil to weed seed infiltration. Warm-season lawns will respond best to aeration once soil temperatures reach 80°.

☛ **Dethatching:** Once lawns have begun to green, it is too late to mow and remove dead top growth. If you suspect your lawn has a thatch problem, wait until next month when soil temperatures reach 80° to consider dethatching with a rented vertical mower.

☛ **Topdressing:** Wait until later in the growing season to topdress, if necessary. Topdressing is only appropriate in very specific situations.

☛ **Weed Control:** The pre-emergence weed control you applied in late February/early March is still effective this month. Do not disrupt the chemical barrier by aerating or mechanically dethatching.

Wait until next month to begin spraying established weeds with post-emergence weed control. Weed control sprays can damage new growth when a lawn is turning green in the spring. It is usually safe to spray once you have mowed at least twice.

☛ **Insects and Diseases:** Fungal diseases can be a problem this month. They develop quickly when daytime air temperatures are 65–80°, nighttime air temperatures are 50–60°, and lawns are moist. Lawn diseases appear as off-color or dead areas with clearly defined edges. These areas will grow concentrically as the disease spreads. Examine the edges for wilted, discolored, or spotted grass blades. They can be controlled with a lawn fungicide approved for use on your specific type of grass.

Now that the weather is warmer, insects may arrive to live and feed on your lawn. Keep watch for sod webworms and cutworms. Both feed on grass blades at night. Webworms will leave spidery webs on the lawn surface visible early in the morning. Cutworms will leave patches of cut grass blades. Both can be controlled with a soil insecticide approved for use on your specific type of grass.

Armyworms occasionally arrive this early in the season. They feed in masses and eat voraciously. Keep a careful watch and treat them as soon as possible with a soil insecticide approved for use on your specific type of grass.

Chinch bugs, a major concern on Saint Augustine and Centipede lawns, will begin arriving on lawns as the temperatures warm. Watch for patches of yellow or wilted grass in sunny areas of the lawn. To confirm their presence, cut the top and bottom from a coffee can and pound it several inches into the yellow grass. Fill the inside of the can with several inches of water and maintain the water level for five minutes. The chinch bugs will float to the surface. If you find them, treat the area with a soil insecticide approved for use on your specific type of grass.

Mole crickets are a horrible problem in the sandy soils of the lower South, and the adults may be seen flying this month when night air temperatures remain above 60°. Mole cricket damage usually looks like someone cultivated areas of your lawn. They can be controlled with a soil insecticide approved for use on your specific type of grass. Treatment may be more effective in mid-summer when mole crickets are more vulnerable.

Despite what the huge displays at the home store say, you should not apply a soil insecticide this month to control white grubs. Wait until late July/early August when it will be most effective.

☛ **Overseeding:** Mow your warm-season grass lawn consistently at the recommended height to promote its growth at the expense of the overseeded grass.

☛ **Other:** As trees begin to leaf-out, take a critical look at your lawn. Are some areas too shady for a lawn grass? Consider redefining the edges of your lawn to avoid dense shade and areas with shallow tree roots. See **ground cover** in the glossary for some alternative plants for shady areas.

EVERGREEN LAWN ACTIVITIES FOR APRIL:

(Tall Fescue, Creeping Red Fescue, Chewing Fescue, Kentucky Bluegrass)

☛ **Planting:** The best time of year to seed a new evergreen lawn is in September. If you want to seed this month, do so as soon as possible. Seedlings will need as much cool weather as possible to become established before the heat of summer arrives. Mow frequently with a sharp blade at the recommended height. Also, wean seedlings from frequent light irrigation over a 4–6 week period. By May, you should be watering deeply and infrequently.

Lay fescue sod as soon as possible. Fescue prefers soil temperatures of 50–65° for optimal root growth. Sod planted late in the spring will not grow roots into the soil below and will be susceptible to drought damage during the summer.

☛ **Mowing:** Mow evergreen lawns consistently at the recommended height. Never reduce the height of your lawn by more than one-third at a time. Proper mowing will encourage grass plants to spread and grow roots deep into the soil.

☞ **Irrigation:** Water carefully this month. Apply 1 inch of water per week if there has been no significant rainfall. Remember that fungal lawn diseases can develop quickly on moist lawns in cool weather. At this time of year, it is best to water during the day when moisture will evaporate quickly from leaf blades.

Newly planted lawns should be watered carefully, as well, since seedlings are especially susceptible to fungal diseases like pythium.

Recommended Mowing Heights (in inches)		
	Height:	**Mow When:**
Kentucky-31 Fescue	3–4	4.5–6
Turf-type Fescue	2.5–3	3.75–4.5
Creeping Red and		
Chewing Fescue	2–2.5	3–3.75
Kentucky Bluegrass	2.5–3	3.75–4.5

Remember that light, frequent irrigation encourages a shallow root system. Lawns need to develop a deep root system in advance of the coming summer season. Always water deeply and infrequently.

☞ **Fertilizer:** Fertilize established evergreen lawns 4–6 weeks after your late winter fertilizer application. This should be early in the month. Use a complete lawn fertilizer that contains a slow-release form of nitrogen. Apply at the rate of 1.5 pounds of actual nitrogen per 1000 square feet. This application should last through the summer.

Fertilize newly seeded evergreen lawns 4 weeks after sowing with a complete lawn fertilizer that contains a slow-release form of nitrogen. Apply at the rate of 1.5 pounds of actual nitrogen per 1000 square feet. This application should last through the summer.

☞ **Aerating:** The best time of year to aerate is in early September, just prior to fertilizing and applying pre-emergence weed control. Aerating now will disrupt your pre-emergence weed control and open the soil to weed seed infiltration.

☞ **Dethatching:** Evergreen lawns do not normally have thatch problems. It is always helpful, though, to rake them with a metal-tined leaf rake to remove thatch and other debris.

☞ **Weed Control:** The pre-emergence weed control you applied in late February/early March is still effective this month. Do not disrupt the chemical barrier by aerating or cultivating. If you have not applied pre-

emergence weed control this season, it would still be useful to apply it now. Pre-emergence weed control products are effective for about 3 months.

Spray established and emerging weeds with a post-emergence weed control approved for use on your specific type of grass. Young, actively growing weeds will die quickly with one application. Mature weeds may require two applications. Sprays are usually most effective when air temperatures are 60–80°. Never spray on a windy day and always follow directions on the label.

Do not apply pre-emergence or post-emergence weed control on newly seeded or sodded evergreen lawns until you have mowed at least two times. Check the product label for specific instructions.

Weed control sprays can damage ornamental plants, shrubs, and trees. Never spray underneath shallow-rooted plants like Dogwoods and Boxwoods because they will absorb the chemical through their root system.

☞ **Insects and Diseases:** Fungal diseases may arrive on lawns this month. Be especially watchful when daytime air temperatures are 65–80°, nighttime air temperatures are 50–60°, and lawns are moist. Lawn diseases often appear as off-color or dead areas with clearly defined edges. These areas will grow concentrically as the disease spreads. Examine the edges for wilted, discolored, or spotted grass blades. They can be controlled with a lawn fungicide approved for use on your specific type of grass.

Webworms and cutworms may be a problem this month. Both feed on grass blades at night. Webworms will leave spidery webs on the lawn surface visible early in the morning. Cutworms will leave patches of cut grass blades. Both can be controlled with a soil insecticide approved for use on your specific type of grass.

Armyworms occasionally bother evergreen lawns. They feed in masses and eat voraciously. Keep a careful watch and treat them with a soil insecticide as soon as you see them.

Do not apply a soil insecticide this month to control white grubs. Wait until late July/early August when it will be more effective.

☞ **Reseeding:** September is the best time of year to reseed an evergreen lawn. Reseeding this month will do little good. Seedlings will not have time to become established in uncultivated soil before the heat of summer arrives. Most will die in June.

☞ **Other:** Sharpen or replace your lawn mower blade if you have not done so already. A dull blade will rip the ends of grass blades and cause the tips to turn brown.

*A lawn is an essential component
of any landscape.*

V. MAY ACTIVITIES

IN THE SOUTH, MAY HAS TWO PERSONALITIES. IN THE EARLY PART OF THE MONTH, MAY IS truly a spring month with cool nights, rain showers, and vibrant green growth. It is the time to plant summer annuals on a pleasant Saturday afternoon and wave to the neighbors. The second half of May is different. We usually have our first dry spell and succulent plants like Blue/Pink Hydrangeas droop in the midday sun. It is also hot. By Memorial Day, temperatures may reach the mid-nineties and summer is certainly here to stay.

The majority of azaleas may have bloomed, but spring is still alive and well. Oakleaf Hydrangeas, Southern Magnolias, and Rhododendron will soon be in bloom and will rival the best azalea display. You can also count on the first crop of roses just in time for Mother's Day. Not to be forgotten, newly planted annuals like Geraniums, Begonia, and Salvia quickly fill the flower border and promise to keep us company throughout the summer.

As the soil warms throughout the month, our warm-season grass lawns will be hitting their stride. They love hot weather and will be growing furiously. Now is the perfect time to aerate and renovate troubled areas before the summer barbeque season arrives. With this added attention, your lawn may grow so well that a once-a-week mowing may not be enough. Meanwhile, evergreen lawns grow slowly as the soil warms and summer heat arrives. Their time has come and gone and the rest of the summer will be like treading water until fall.

WARM-SEASON LAWN ACTIVITIES FOR MAY:

(Bermuda Grass, Centipede, Saint Augustine, Zoysia)

☛ **Planting:** May is the best time of year to plant warm-season grass lawns from sod, plugs, or seed. Warm-season grasses will establish quickly as soil temperatures push toward 80° later in the month. Then, they will have the entire growing season to grow into a thick, lush lawn. Remember to cultivate, amend the soil, and fertilize before planting. These steps should be followed whether you sod, plug, or seed your new lawn.

☛ **Mowing:** Mow warm-season lawns consistently and at the correct height. There are few things worse for a lawn than mowing sporadically.

Recommended Mowing Heights (in inches)

	Height:	Mow When:
Common Bermuda	2	3
Hybrid Bermuda	1–1.5	1.5–2.25
Centipede	1.5–2	2.25–3
Saint Augustine	2–3	3–4.5
Zoysia	1–2	1.5–3

☛ **Irrigation:** May is often a dry month in the South. While it might not seem like summer, warm-season lawns can suffer this month if not watered correctly. A lawn will discolor and thin during even a short period of drought. Apply one inch of water per week if there has been no significant rainfall.

Check your automatic sprinkler system to make sure all the zones are working and that they are emitting enough water.

☛ **Fertilizer:** Fertilize warm-season lawns early in the month if you have not done so already. Use a complete lawn fertilizer that contains a slow-release form of nitrogen. Apply at the rate of 1.5 pounds of actual nitrogen per 1000 square feet. This application will last 2–3 months.

Fertilize Centipede lawns at the beginning of the month, if you have not done so already. Use a fertilizer specifically approved for use on Centipede and apply at the rate of .75 pounds of actual nitrogen per 1000 square feet. If you cannot find a Centipede fertilizer, use a complete lawn fertilizer with as little phosphorus (the middle number of the N-P-K ratio) as possible.

If using a liquid fertilizer, or a soluble granular fertilizer, be careful not to apply more than 1 pound of actual nitrogen per 1000 square feet. High levels of nitrogen will cause excessive top growth, little root growth, and promote diseases. These types of fertilizer will last only 4–6 weeks.

☛ **Aerating:** Begin aerating warm-season lawns with a rented core aerator as soil temperatures near 80°. This is usually in the second half of the month. Core aerators work best on slightly moist soil, so irrigate a couple of days before aerating. If the cores bother you, you can rake the lawn and most will break and drop below the level of the grass where they are not as visible. With time, this soil will fall to the soil surface and help thatch to decompose.

☛ **Dethatching:** Warm-season grasses with excessive accumulations of thatch (greater than .5 inches) can be mechanically dethatched this month using a rented vertical mower, or "dethatcher." Lawns will rebound quickest when soil temperatures are near 80°. Vertical mowers are tricky and can cause more harm than good if used improperly. Be careful!

☛ **Topdressing:** Once soil temperatures reach 80° late in the month, warm-season lawns can be topdressed with soil or sand to fill individual holes and gullies. Never spread more than .25 inch of topdressing at a time. Topdressing an entire lawn is only appropriate in very specific situations.

☛ **Weed Control:** The pre-emergence weed control you applied in late February/early March will be effective for most of the month. If necessary, apply pre-emergence weed control (without fertilizer) again in late May/early June. If your lawn is mostly weed-free, and weeds do not usually blow in from surrounding areas, you can skip this application.

Irrigate your lawn after broadcasting granular pre-emergence weed control in order to activate the chemical (unless otherwise stated on the bag).

Begin spraying established and emerging weeds with a post-emergence weed control approved for your specific type of grass. Liquid sprays are usually most effective when air temperatures are 60–80° and weeds are young and actively growing. Always follow the directions on the label. Spraying excessively will not provide better weed control and may damage your lawn.

Remember that weed control products like Round-Up are non-selective and will kill your lawn grass as well.

☛ **Insects and Diseases:** Fungal diseases may arrive on your lawn, especially in the first half of the month. They develop quickly when daytime air temperatures are 65–80°, nighttime air temperatures are 50–60°, and lawns are moist. Lawn diseases often appear as off-color or dead areas with clearly defined edges. These areas will grow concentrically as the disease spreads. Examine the edges for wilted, discolored, or spotted grass blades. Fungal diseases can be controlled with a lawn fungicide approved for use on your specific type of grass.

As temperatures continue to rise throughout the month, you will notice increased numbers of insects on your lawn. A few insects, like webworms and cutworms, have the potential to cause damage. Both feed on grass blades at night. Webworms will leave spidery webs on the lawn surface visible early in the morning. Cutworms will leave patches of cut grass blades. Both larval worms can be controlled with a soil insecticide approved for use on your specific type of grass.

Armyworms may arrive this month, depending on the weather. These horrible creatures feed in masses and eat voraciously. Keep a careful watch and listen for reports from neighbors and government agencies. If they arrive on your lawn, treat the area as soon as possible with a soil insecticide approved for use on your specific type of grass.

Chinch bugs also arrive with warmer weather and are a major concern on Saint Augustine and Centipede lawns. Watch for patches of discolored or wilted grass in sunny areas of the lawn. To confirm their presence, cut the top and bottom from a coffee can and pound it several inches into the yellow grass. Fill the inside of the can with several inches of water and maintain the water level for five minutes. The chinch bugs will float to the surface. Once you find them, treat the area with a soil insecticide approved for use on your specific type of grass.

Mole crickets are a horrible problem in the sandy soils of the lower South and they are especially damaging to Bermuda Grass. Adult mole crickets will be more active now that it is warm. Damage usually looks like someone cultivated areas of your lawn. They can be controlled with a soil insecticide labeled for control of mole crickets and approved for use on your specific type of grass.

Mature white grubs will be moving closer to the soil surface this month. They will feed briefly on grass roots before pupating. Unfortunately, soil insecticides are not very effective on mature white grubs. Wait until late July/early August to treat the next round of newly hatched white grubs.

☛ **Overseeding:** Continue to mow your warm-season grass lawn consistently at the recommended height to weaken your overseeded grass and force it to "burn out."

☛ **Other:** It is a good idea to lime Bermuda Grass, Zoysia, and Saint Augustine lawns immediately after aerating in May (if needed). These grasses prefer a soil pH of 6–6.5, and lime will raise the pH of acidic soils. A soil test will determine the exact pH of your soil and recommend the amount of lime needed for your specific type of grass. Many Southern soils will need about 50 pounds per 1000 square feet. Do not lime Centipede lawns, however, since they prefer a low pH.

EVERGREEN LAWN ACTIVITIES FOR MAY:

(Tall Fescue, Creeping Red Fescue, Chewing Fescue, Kentucky Bluegrass)

☞ **Planting:** It is too late to seed or reseed an evergreen lawn. Seedlings will suffer and probably die in the next couple of months. Wait until early September when soil temperatures cool into the 70s.

Plant fescue sod with extreme care. Sod laid this late in the spring will not grow roots into the soil below and will be highly susceptible to drought damage. Buyer beware!

☞ **Mowing:** Mow evergreen lawns consistently at the recommended height. Do not reduce the height of your lawn by more than one-third at a time. This is especially important toward the end of the month as the temperature rises and evergreen lawns begin to suffer.

Recommended Mowing Heights (in inches)		
	Height:	**Mow When:**
Kentucky 31 Fescue	3–4	4.5–6
Turf-type Fescue	2.5–3	3.75–4.5
Creeping Red and Chewing Fescue	2–2.5	3–3.75
Kentucky Bluegrass	2.5–3	3.75–4.5

☞ **Irrigation:** May is one of the driest months of the year. Be especially careful with your watering schedule since evergreen lawns will be feeling the effects of the heat. Apply 1 inch of water per week if there has been no significant rainfall.

Remember to water deeply and infrequently to encourage grass roots to grow deep into the soil where it is cooler.

☞ **Fertilizer:** Do not fertilize evergreen lawns this month. The slow-release fertilizer you applied in early April is still active. Over-fertilizing an evergreen lawn in the late spring can cause an imbalance between the roots and the shoots of the grass.

☞ **Aerating:** The best time of year to aerate an evergreen lawn is in early September, just prior to fertilizing and applying pre-emergence weed control. Aerating now will damage roots that will not re-grow before summer.

☞ **Dethatching:** Evergreen lawns do not usually have thatch problems. If you do have a thatch accumulation of more than .5 inches, do your best to remove it with a metal-tined leaf rake. If it is still a problem in late summer, mechanically dethatch with a rented vertical mower before reseeding in September.

☞ **Weed Control:** The pre-emergence weed control you applied in late February/early March will be effective for most of the month. If necessary, apply pre-emergence weed control (without fertilizer) again in late May/early June. If your lawn is mostly weed-free, and weeds do not usually blow in from surrounding areas, you can skip this application.

Spray established and emerging weeds as soon as you see them with a post-emergence weed control approved for use on your specific type of grass. Sprays are usually most effective when air temperatures are 60–80° and weeds are young and actively growing. Follow the directions on the label.

☞ **Insects and Diseases:** There is still a slight risk from fungal diseases early in the month. Beware when daytime air temperatures are 65–80°, nighttime air temperatures are 50–60°, and lawns are moist. Lawn diseases often appear as off-color or dead areas with clearly defined edges. These areas will grow concentrically as the disease spreads. Examine the edges for wilted, discolored, or spotted grass blades. Fungal diseases can be controlled with a lawn fungicide approved for use on your specific type of grass.

New and interesting insects will be arriving on your lawn all month. A few, like sod webworms and cutworms, have the potential to cause damage. Both feed on grass blades at night. Webworms will leave spidery webs on the lawn which are noticeable early in the morning. Cutworms will leave patches of cut grass blades. Both larval worms can be controlled with a soil insecticide approved for use on your specific type of grass.

Armyworms may arrive this month, depending on weather. These horrible creatures feed in masses and eat voraciously. Keep a careful watch and listen for reports from neighbors and government agencies. If they arrive on your lawn, treat the area as soon as possible with a soil insecticide approved for use on your specific type of grass.

Mature white grubs will be moving closer to the soil surface this month. They will feed briefly on grass roots before pupating. Unfortunately, soil insecticides are not very effective on mature white grubs. Wait until late July/early August to treat the next round of newly hatched white grubs.

While other garden plants thrive during June, fescue lawns need to be nursed.

VI. JUNE ACTIVITIES

JUNE IS HOT. TEMPERATURES ARE USUALLY IN THE MID-NINETIES AND IT REALLY TAKES superior discipline to drag yourself from an air-conditioned haven. I sometimes wonder how we managed, growing up without air-conditioning in the South. It didn't seem so bad for some reason. But then again, we seldom spent as much time in traffic jams waiting for interminable red lights.

June is often dry as well. There is usually some amount of rainfall, but it is sporadic and may come in intermittent floods. These are the times when gardeners rely on as much finesse as is humanly possible. People cope in different ways. Some monitor their rain gauges diligently. Others purchase all kinds of watering paraphernalia. I like to reach down through the mulch or grass and feel the soil. If there is moisture, I forgo watering. If the top layer is parched, I irrigate.

With the heat and sporadic drought, June always seems draining. Maybe it is because I haven't become acclimated to the heat, but I would rather be doing a thousand other chores than mowing the lawn. This is certainly the month when you rue the day you bought a push mower and not a rider. While it is hard to mow, it is hard on a lawn if we do not. Grass plants adjust their growth pattern to how high we mow and how frequently we mow. Changing either one can shock the lawn and cause it to thin. The only answer I have found is to mow in the early evening when you can listen to the baseball game on your headset and the temperatures have cooled.

WARM-SEASON LAWN ACTIVITIES FOR JUNE:

(Bermuda Grass, Centipede, Saint Augustine, Zoysia)

☛ **Planting:** Continue to plant warm-season grass lawns from sod, plugs, or seed. Warm-season grasses will establish quickly now that soil temperatures have warmed. Remember to cultivate, amend the soil, and fertilize before planting. These steps should be followed whether you sod, plug, or seed your new lawn. Do not forget to water new lawns during the heat of summer.

☛ **Mowing:** Mow warm-season lawns consistently, and at the correct height. In general, lawns will improve dramatically when mowed sooner rather than later.

Recommended Mowing Heights (in inches)

	Height:	Mow When:
Common Bermuda	2	3
Hybrid Bermuda	1–1.5	1.5–2.25
Centipede	1.5–2	2.25–3
Saint Augustine	2–3	3–4.5
Zoysia	1–2	1.5–3

☛ **Irrigation:** Rainfall can be torrential, sporadic, or non-existent during June. Be vigilant and responsive to changes in the weather. Even a short period of drought can stress a lawn and cause it to discolor. Worse yet, you can kill lawn areas that have poor drainage if you do not adjust your automatic sprinklers during wet periods. Apply 1 inch of water per week if there has been no significant rainfall.

☛ **Fertilizer:** The slow-release lawn fertilizer you applied in April/May will continue to be effective this month. Be prepared to fertilize again at the beginning of next month if needed.

Centipede lawns do not respond well to fertilizer. In fact, excess fertilizer can cause growth problems. Light green Centipede lawns (caused by improper pH) can be treated with iron to darken their color. Apply at the rate recommended on the bottle. Better yet, determine your soil pH with a soil test and lower the pH to the correct range using an elemental sulfur product.

If using a liquid fertilizer, or a soluble granular fertilizer, be careful not to apply more than 1 pound of actual nitrogen per 1000 square feet. High levels of nitrogen will cause excessive top growth, little root growth, and promote diseases. These types of fertilizer will last only 4–6 weeks.

☛ **Aerating:** Aerate warm-season lawns with a rented core aerator, if you have not done so already. Core aerators work best on slightly moist soil, so irrigate a couple of days before aerating. If the cores bother you, you can rake the lawn and most will break and drop below the level of the grass where they are not as noticeable.

161

This soil will eventually return to the soil surface where it will help thatch to decompose.

☞ **Dethatching:** Warm-season grasses with excessive accumulations of thatch (greater than .5 inch) can be mechanically dethatched this month using a rented vertical mower, or "dethatcher." Lawns will respond quickly now that soil temperatures are warm. Check the setting of the vertical mower and do not make more than one pass across your lawn. Vertical mowers are tricky and when used improperly will do more harm than good. Be careful!

☞ **Topdressing:** Topdressing an entire warm-season lawn is only appropriate in very specific situations. Ruts and dents in the lawn surface can be topdressed, however, to create a smoother surface. Take your time and apply no more than .25 inch of soil or sand at a time.

☞ **Weed Control:** The pre-emergence weed control you applied in late winter is no longer effective. If your lawn is mostly weed-free, and weeds do not usually blow in from surrounding areas, you will be okay until fall. Otherwise, apply a pre-emergence weed control (without fertilizer) to control annual and perennial weeds that continue to sprout during the summer months. Make sure the product is approved for use on your specific type of grass and follow the directions on the label.

Irrigate your lawn after broadcasting granular pre-emergence weed control in order to activate the chemical (unless otherwise stated on the bag).

Spray emerging and established weeds with a post-emergence weed control. Most sprays will be designed to treat either broadleaf or grassy weeds. Liquid sprays are usually most effective when air temperatures are 60–80° and weeds are young and actively growing. Make sure the product is approved for use on your specific type of grass. Also, avoid spraying newly seeded or sodded lawns until you have mowed at least twice.

Remember that weed control products like Round-Up are non-selective and will kill your lawn grass as well.

☞ **Insects and Diseases:** Fungal diseases are not usually as troublesome this month. Most prefer cooler daytime temperatures (65–80°) and cooler nights (50–60°). Beware, though, of off-color or dead areas with clearly defined edges. Examine the edges for wilted leaves or leaves with spots. If you find a fungal disease, treat the area with a lawn fungicide approved for use on your specific type of grass.

Watch out for webworms and cutworms, both of which feed on grass blades at night. Take an early morning stroll across the lawn to look for them. Webworms will leave spidery webs on the lawn surface. Cutworms will leave patches of cut grass blades. Both can be controlled with a soil insecticide approved for use on your specific type of grass.

Armyworms are another hazardous insect that feeds in masses during the day. They move quickly across a lawn and do incredible damage. They are so bad that you may hear reports of them from neighbors or government agencies before you see them yourself. Armyworms can be controlled with a soil insecticide approved for use on your specific type of grass.

Chinch bugs are a major concern on Saint Augustine and Centipede lawns. Watch for patches of discolored, yellow, or wilted grass in sunny areas of the lawn. To confirm their presence, cut the top and bottom from a coffee can and pound it several inches into the yellow grass. Fill the inside of the can with several inches of water and maintain the water level for five minutes. The chinch bugs will float to the surface. If you find some, treat the area with a soil insecticide approved for use on your specific type of grass.

Mole crickets are a horrible problem in the sandy soils of the lower South. Eggs may be hatching this month and the young nymphs will be active in droves. They can be controlled with a soil insecticide labeled for control of mole crickets and approved for use on your specific type of grass.

Wait until next month to begin treating lawns with a soil insecticide to control white grubs.

☞ **Other:** If you mow at the right height and at the right time, you will not need to bag Bermuda Grass, Centipede or Saint Augustine grass clippings. Small grass clippings fall easily to the soil surface and decompose quickly. Through this process, they return nitrogen to the soil.

Continue to bag Zoysia grass clippings to prevent thatch accumulations. This is especially important with Emerald Zoysia.

EVERGREEN LAWN ACTIVITIES FOR JUNE:

(Tall Fescue, Creeping Red Fescue, Chewing Fescue, Kentucky Bluegrass)

☞ **Planting:** It is too late to seed or sod an evergreen lawn. If absolutely necessary, plant sod and water frequently and diligently. Even then, expect widespread loss from heat and drought stress.

Fall-seeded evergreen lawns may be "burning-out" this month. If you still have the bag, read the seed label and see if you used a seed mixture that contained a grass unsuitable for the South. Never choose a mixture that contains Annual or Perennial Ryegrass. In the middle South, avoid fescue mixtures that contain Kentucky Bluegrass.

☛ **Mowing:** Mow evergreen lawns consistently at the recommended height. As a general rule, do not reduce the height of your lawn by more than one-third at a time.

Recommended Mowing Heights (in inches)		
	Height:	Mow When:
Kentucky 31 Fescue	3–4	4.5–6
Turf-type Fescue	2.5–3	3.75–4.5
Creeping Red and Chewing Fescue	2–2.5	3–3.75
Kentucky Bluegrass	2.5–3	3.75–4.5

Family vacations can cause havoc on lawns. Try to mow immediately before leaving and soon after you return. I know this is a tall order. If your lawn does grow out of control (6 or more inches), mow at the highest setting possible when you return. Then, mow at the recommended height a day or two later.

☛ **Irrigation:** Evergreen lawns need to be nursed through the summer. This is not easy since rainfall is haphazard during June. Be especially careful with your watering schedule when evergreen lawns are suffering in the heat. To add insult to injury, fescue produces seed this time of year, sapping even more of its energy. Apply 1 inch of water per week if there has been no significant rainfall. Remember to water deeply and infrequently.

☛ **Fertilizer:** Do not fertilize evergreen lawns this month. Fertilizing now will exacerbate your lawn's problems with hot weather.

If your lawn is light green or yellow, however, apply a complete lawn fertilizer at the moderate rate of .5 pounds of actual nitrogen per 1000 square feet.

☛ **Aerating:** Do not aerate evergreen lawns during the summer. The best time of year to aerate is in early September, just prior to fertilizing, liming, and applying pre-emergence weed control.

☛ **Dethatching:** Do not mechanically dethatch ever-

green lawns during the summer. If you are worried about thatch and grass clippings, rake your lawn with a metal-tined leaf rake.

☛ **Weed Control:** Apply granular pre-emergence weed control (without fertilizer) to evergreen lawns at the beginning of the month. Make sure the product is approved for use on your specific type of grass and apply at the recommended rate. Thinning, weak lawns will benefit most from this application since it will prevent weeds from germinating in bare ground. If your fescue is lush, weed-free, and weed seeds do not usually blow in from surrounding areas, you can skip this application.

Spray established and emerging weeds with a post-emergence weed control spray as soon as possible. Most sprays will be designed to treat either broadleaf or grassy weeds. Summer weeds rob the soil of water and nutrients at a time when fescue is already in a weakened state. Sprays are usually most effective when air temperatures are 60–80° and weeds are young and actively growing. Make sure the product is approved for use on your specific type of grass and apply at the recommended rate.

☛ **Insects and Diseases:** Evergreen lawns are usually disease-free over the hot summer months. Most fungal diseases prefer cooler daytime temperatures (65–80°) and cooler nights (50–60°). Beware, though, of any off-color or dead areas with clearly defined edges. Examine the edges for wilted or discolored leaves. Fungal diseases can be controlled with a lawn fungicide approved for use on your specific type of grass.

Evergreen lawns are the perfect haven for hundreds of different insects. The taller mowing height provides insects with a nice shelter from their natural predators. Do not apply soil insecticide unless insects are damaging your lawn. Damage will often appear as areas of brown or discolored turf with irregular outlines. Problem insects can be controlled with a granular soil insecticide approved for use on fescue.

Wait until late July to begin treating evergreen lawns with a soil insecticide to control white grubs.

☛ **Other:** If mowed at the right height and at the right time, you do not need to bag your grass clippings. Clippings a couple of inches long will fall easily to the soil surface and decompose.

Fescue is not very tolerant of foot traffic, especially during the summer heat. Be careful during your summer barbecue.

Evergreen grass lawns prefer the cooler temperatures in the mountains of the upper South.

VII. JULY ACTIVITIES

MOST OF US HAVE RETREATED FROM THE GARDEN BY JULY. THE WEATHER IS HOT AND muggy and even gardeners spend their afternoons inside looking out. There are those occasions, however, like the Fourth of July, when the entire neighborhood shuns the indoors for screened porches, patios, and the cool shade of an oak tree.

There is a lot going on in the garden in July. The Crape Myrtles are beginning to bloom, Butterfly Bushes continue to amaze us, and Purple Coneflowers last forever. Better yet, the blueberries and figs are ripe for picking and it's a race with the birds to see who is fed first. While it may be dry at times, the occasional thunderstorm always seems to arrive just in time to wash away the dust and revive everything that is green. There are few spectacles like giant "Peegee" Hydrangea blossoms bending low after a July thunderstorm.

While many gardening activities seem to have waned, lawns need constant attention. Warm-season lawns are having a field day with the heat and a little attention will help them grow into a thick, impenetrable shield against weeds. Evergreen lawns will begin to show signs of stress this month. The best thing to do is mow and irrigate consistently so they will only have to worry about the temperature.

WARM-SEASON LAWN ACTIVITIES FOR JULY:

(Bermuda Grass, Centipede, Saint Augustine, Zoysia)

☞ **Planting:** Plant new warm-season grass lawns as soon as possible. The more warm weather they have to become established, the better. Warm-season lawns are usually planted from sod, plugs, or seed. Remember to cultivate, amend the soil, and fertilize before planting. These steps should be followed whether you sod, plug, or seed your new lawn. Be especially attentive in watering new lawns during the summer.

☞ **Mowing:** Continue to mow warm-season lawns consistently and at the correct height. Warm-season lawns will grow quickly after you fertilize them early in the month. Remember not to reduce the height of your lawn by more than one-third at any single mowing.

Recommended Mowing Heights (in inches)		
	Height:	Mow When:
Common Bermuda	2	3
Hybrid Bermuda	1–1.5	1.5–2.25
Centipede	1.5–2	2.25–3
Saint Augustine	2–3	3–4.5
Zoysia	1–2	1.5–3

If you mow at the right height and at the right time, you will not need to bag Bermuda, Centipede or Saint Augustine grass clippings. Small grass clippings fall easily to the soil surface and decompose quickly. Through this process, they return nitrogen to the soil.

Continue to bag Zoysia grass clippings to prevent thatch accumulations.

☞ **Irrigation:** Apply 1 inch of water per week if there has been no significant rainfall. Whenever possible, water deeply and infrequently. For instance, it is better to apply 1 inch on a single day rather than .25 inches a day for four days. Stop irrigating, however, if water begins to run on the surface.

☞ **Fertilizer:** Fertilize Bermuda Grass and Saint Augustine lawns at the beginning of the month. Use a complete lawn fertilizer with a slow-release form of nitrogen. Apply at the rate of 1.5 pounds of actual nitrogen per 1000 square feet for Bermuda Grass and 1 pound of actual nitrogen per 1000 square feet for Saint Augustine. This application will last until you fertilize again in early September.

Fertilize Zoysia lawns at the beginning of the month if they are not lush and dark green. Avoid excess fertilizer because it can contribute to thatch build-up. Use a complete lawn fertilizer with a slow-release form of nitrogen. Apply at the rate of 1 pound of actual nitrogen per 1000 square feet. This application will last until you fertilize again in early September.

Fertilize Centipede lawns at the beginning of the month. Use a slow-release fertilizer specifically designed for Centipede lawns. Apply at the rate of .75 pounds of actual nitrogen per 1000 square feet. If you cannot find a Centipede fertilizer, use a slow-release lawn fertilizer with as little phosphorus (the middle number of the N-P-K ratio) as possible. This will be your second and final fertilizer application of the season.

If your Bermuda, Zoysia, or Saint Augustine lawn is overrun with weeds, consider using a fertilizer that contains a post-emergence weed control in granular form. Follow the labeled instructions explicitly for best results. Most products will need to be applied when your lawn is wet.

In most cases, applying extra fertilizer will not improve the color of your warm-season lawn. Instead, it will cause the grass to grow faster and you will have to mow more often.

If you are using a liquid fertilizer, or a soluble granular fertilizer, do not apply more than 1 pound of actual nitrogen per 1000 square feet. High levels of nitrogen can cause insect and disease problems. These products will last only 4–6 weeks.

☛ **Aerating:** There is still time to aerate warm-season lawns with a rented core aerator, if you have not done so already. Core aerators work best on slightly moist soil, so irrigate a couple of days before aerating. If the cores bother you, you can rake the lawn and most will break and drop below the level of the grass where they are not as noticeable. This soil will eventually drop to the soil surface and help thatch to decompose.

You can renovate steep, dry banks by core aerating followed by increased irrigation. Aerating will increase water penetration into the dry soil.

Do not aerate if you applied a pre-emergence weed control last month. You will disturb the chemical barrier of the control.

☛ **Dethatching:** Continue to watch warm-season grass lawns, especially Zoysia lawns, for excessive accumulations of thatch (greater than .5 inches). Heavy thatch accumulations can be removed, if needed, with a rented vertical mower (also known as a "dethatcher").

Do not use a vertical mower if you applied a pre-emergence weed control last month. You will disturb the chemical barrier of the control.

☛ **Topdressing:** Topdressing your entire lawn is appropriate only in very specific situations. Ruts and dents in the lawn surface can be topdressed, however, to create a smoother surface. Take your time and apply no more than .25 inches of soil or sand at a time.

☛ **Weed Control:** Spray established weeds with a post-emergence weed control as soon as you see them.

Most sprays will be designed to treat either broadleaf or grassy weeds. Liquid sprays are usually most effective when air temperatures are 60–80° and weeds are young and actively growing (check the product label).

Remember that weed control products like Round-Up are non-selective and will kill your lawn grass as well.

☛ **Insects and Diseases:** Fungal diseases are not usually as troublesome this month. Most prefer cooler daytime temperatures (65–80°) and cooler nights (50–60°). Beware of clearly defined off-color or dead patches of grass. Examine the edges for wilted leaves and leaves with spots. If found, spray with a lawn fungicide approved for use on your specific type of grass.

Watch for webworms and cutworms, both of which feed on grass blades at night. Take an early morning stroll across the lawn to look for them. Webworms will leave spidery webs on the lawn surface. Cutworms will leave patches of cut grass blades. Both can be controlled with a soil insecticide approved for use on your specific type of grass.

Armyworms are another hazardous insect that feeds in masses during the day. They move quickly across a lawn and do incredible damage. Armyworms can be treated with a soil insecticide approved for use on your specific type of grass.

Chinch bugs are a major concern on Saint Augustine and Centipede lawns. At first, damage will look much like your lawn is suffering from drought. Next, watch for patches of yellow, discolored, or wilted grass in sunny areas of the lawn. To confirm their presence, cut the top and bottom from a coffee can and pound it several inches into the yellow grass. Fill the inside of the can with several inches of water and maintain the water level for five minutes. The chinch bugs will float to the surface. If you find some, treat the area with a soil insecticide approved for use on your specific type of grass.

Mole crickets might be a problem in the sandy soils of the lower South. Damage usually appears as if someone loosened or cultivated areas of your lawn. Treat the areas with a soil insecticide labeled for control of mole crickets and approved for use on your specific type of grass.

Begin treating for white grub larvae at the end of the month. Newly hatched grubs will be feeding voraciously on grass roots. They can be controlled with a soil insecticide approved for use on your specific type of grass.

EVERGREEN LAWN ACTIVITIES FOR JULY:

(Tall Fescue, Creeping Red Fescue, Chewing Fescue, Kentucky Bluegrass)

☛ **Planting:** It is too late to seed or sod an evergreen lawn. If absolutely necessary, plant sod and water frequently and diligently. Even then, expect widespread loss from heat and drought stress.

☛ **Mowing:** Mow evergreen lawns consistently at the recommended height. As a general rule, do not reduce the height of your lawn by more than one-third at a time.

Recommended Mowing Heights (in inches)		
	Height:	Mow When:
Kentucky 31 Fescue	3–4	4.5–6
Turf-type Fescue	2.5–3	3.75–4.5
Creeping Red and Chewing Fescue	2–2.5	3–3.75
Kentucky Bluegrass	2.5–3	3.75–4.5

If you mow at the right height and at the right time, you do not need to bag your grass clippings. Clippings two inches long or less will fall easily to the soil surface and decompose.

Family vacations can be very troublesome for a lawn. Try to mow immediately before leaving and soon after you return. I know this is a tall order. If your lawn does grow out of control (6 or more inches), mow at the highest setting possible when you return. Then, mow at the recommended height a day or two later.

☛ **Irrigation:** Evergreen lawns need to be nursed through the summer. Even short periods of drought can cause your lawn to discolor and thin. Apply 1 inch of water per week if there has been no significant rainfall. Remember to water deeply and infrequently.

☛ **Fertilizer:** Do not fertilize evergreen lawns this month. Fertilizing will cause growth that the grass plants cannot sustain.

If your lawn is light green or yellow, however, fertilize with a complete lawn fertilizer that contains a slow-release form of nitrogen. Apply at a rate of .5 pounds of actual nitrogen per 1000 square feet. Irrigate immediately after you fertilize to prevent burning.

☛ **Aerating:** Do not aerate evergreen lawns during the summer. The best time of year to core aerate is in early September, just prior to fertilizing and applying pre-emergence weed control.

☛ **Dethatching:** Do not mechanically dethatch evergreen lawns during the summer when they are suffering in the heat.

☛ **Weed Control:** Spray established and emerging weeds as soon as possible with a post-emergence weed control approved for use on your specific type of grass. Most sprays will be designed to treat either broadleaf or grassy weeds. Summer weeds rob the soil of water and nutrients and can be particularly damaging to a thinning, weak lawn. Weed control sprays are usually most effective when air temperatures are 60–80° and weeds are young and actively growing. Make sure the product is approved for use on your specific type of grass and apply at the recommended rate.

☛ **Insects and Diseases:** Evergreen lawns are usually disease-free over the hot summer months. Most fungal diseases prefer cooler daytime temperatures (65–80°) and cooler nights (50–60°). Be on guard, however, for clearly defined off-color or dead patches of grass. Examine the edges for wilted or discolored leaves. Once found, spray with a lawn fungicide approved for use on your specific type of grass.

You may be seeing large numbers of June Beetles and Japanese Beetles. Both are adult forms of white grubs. Begin treating for white grub larvae at the end of the month. Newly hatched grubs will be feeding voraciously on evergreen grass roots. They can be controlled with a soil insecticide approved for use on your specific type of grass.

Evergreen lawns are a great place for insects to live. The tall grass blades provide them with wonderful shelter from their natural predators. But do not apply a soil insecticide unless you have identified an insect that is damaging your lawn.

☛ **Other:** Evergreen lawns are not very tolerant of foot traffic, especially during the summer heat. Be careful during your summer barbecue.

*Augustt is the month that determines whether
a plant is suitable for the South.*

VIII. AUGUST ACTIVITIES

AUGUST IS RIGHT IN THE MIDDLE OF THE "DOG DAYS" OF SUMMER. IF YOU ARE NEW TO the South, or have never heard the saying, it means that it is darned hot. It is amazing to think that next month temperatures will be cooling dramatically and that fall is just around the corner. You would never know it on the eighth day of August.

August is not only hot, it is a defining month in the Southern garden. It is really the summer month that most determines whether a plant will grow here or not. One of our family's favorite things to do is visit rose gardens during August. It is sad, but revealing, to see prize-winning roses defoliated and pitiful in the blazing sun. Most of the prizes were handed out far to the north of us where life is much gentler for a rose. Unfortunately, it is easier for companies to market and ship "prize-winning" roses into our climate than to award a separate prize for roses that deserve recognition in the South.

The same is true for evergreen lawns. Many evergreen lawns will simply burn away this month. The problem is that evergreen lawn seed mixtures suited for northern climates continue to be sold in the South. An evergreen lawn mixture with Perennial Rye and Kentucky Bluegrass might grow just fine in Pennsylvania, but it has no business being sold in the middle South. As homeowners, our best revenge is to simply read the label. If we stop buying northern grass mixtures, companies will have no choice but to ship them where they belong.

WARM-SEASON LAWN ACTIVITIES FOR AUGUST:

(Bermuda Grass, Centipede, Saint Augustine, Zoysia)

☛ **Planting:** It is almost too late to plant new warm-season grass lawns. If needed, plant as early in the month as possible. Warm-season lawns prefer hot weather and will need time to become established before fall weather arrives. Warm-season lawns are usually planted from sod, plugs, or seed. Remember to cultivate, amend the soil, and fertilize before planting. Be especially attentive in watering new lawns in August.

☛ **Mowing:** Continue to mow warm-season lawns consistently and at the correct height. Warm-season lawns will be growing quickly despite the hot muggy weather. Remember not to reduce the height of your lawn by more than one-third at any mowing.

Recommended Mowing Heights (in inches)		
	Height:	Mow When:
Common Bermuda	2	3
Hybrid Bermuda	1–1.5	1.5–2.25
Centipede	1.5–2	2.25–3
Saint Augustine	2–3	3–4.5
Zoysia	1–2	1.5–3

☛ **Irrigation:** Apply 1 inch of water per week if there has been no significant rainfall. It is better to apply 1 inch on a single day rather than .25 inches a day for four days. Stop irrigating, however, if water begins to run on the surface.

Don't be afraid to turn off your automatic sprinklers completely during a rainy spell.

☛ **Fertilizer:** Begin fertilizing Bermuda Grass, Zoysia, and Saint Augustine lawns in late August/early September. Use a complete lawn fertilizer with a slow-release form of nitrogen. If possible, use a fertilizer with a low phosphorus and higher potassium similar to 12-4-14 or 12-0-12. Apply at the rate of 1.5 pounds of actual nitrogen per 1000 square feet. This will be your final fertilizer application of the season.

Water approximately 1 inch after fertilizing to wash fertilizer from grass blades and move it into the soil.

☛ **Aerating:** There is still time to aerate warm-season lawns with a rented core aerator, if you have not done so already. It is best to finish aerating before you apply your fall pre-emergence weed control. Core aeration will improve the quality and consistency of your lawn's growth. If the cores bother you, you can rake the lawn and most will break and drop below the level of the grass where they are not as noticeable. This soil will eventually drop to the soil surface and help thatch to decompose.

☛ **Dethatching:** Continue to watch warm-season

169

grasses, especially Zoysia grass, for excessive accumulations of thatch (greater than .5 inches). Heavy thatch accumulations can be carefully removed with a rented vertical mower. It is best to finish this job before you apply your fall pre-emergence weed control.

☛ **Topdressing:** Topdressing your entire lawn is only appropriate in very specific situations. Continue to fill holes and depressions in the lawn surface, however, to create a smoother mowing surface. Take your time and apply no more than .25 inches of soil or sand at a time.

☛ **Weed Control:** Wait until next month when soil temperatures drop to 70° to apply fall pre-emergence weed control to warm-season lawns. This is usually September 15 in the upper South and October 15 in the lower South. If you think you will forget, you can apply pre-emergence in combination with fertilizer but you will be sacrificing some effectiveness. Make sure the weed control is approved for use on your specific type of lawn. This application will last 2–3 months.

Do not apply pre-emergence weed control if you are planning to overseed your warm-season grass lawn for a winter cover.

Continue to spray established weeds with a post-emergence weed control. Most sprays will be designed to treat either broadleaf or grassy weeds. Liquid sprays are usually most effective when air temperatures are 60–80°. In August, weeds are usually established and it will require several applications to kill them. Make sure the weed control is approved for use on your specific type of lawn.

Remember that weed control products like Round-Up are non-selective and will kill your lawn grass as well.

☛ **Insects and Diseases:** Fungal diseases may arrive on your lawn late in the month as night temperatures cool. Most prefer daytime air temperatures of 65–80° and nights air temperatures of 50–60°. Fungal diseases often appear as discolored or dead areas with clearly defined edges. Examine the edges for wilted leaves and leaves with spots. Once located, spray with a lawn fungicide approved for use on your specific type of grass.

White grub larvae will be feeding on grass roots this month. August is a good time to control them with a soil insecticide approved for use on your specific type of grass, if you have not done so already.

Continue to watch for webworms and cutworms feeding on grass blades at night. Take an early morning stroll across the lawn to look for them. Webworms will leave spidery webs on the lawn surface. Cutworms will leave patches of cut grass blades. If you find them, treat the area with a soil insecticide approved for use on your specific type of grass.

Beware of armyworms! These pests feed in masses during the day and can do incredible damage in a relatively short time. Listen carefully for reports from neighbors and government areas that they have been spotted in your area. Armyworms should be treated immediately with a soil insecticide approved for use on your specific type of grass.

Chinch bugs are a major concern on Saint Augustine and Centipede lawns. Watch for patches of yellow, discolored, or wilted grass in sunny areas of your lawn. To confirm their presence, cut the top and bottom from a coffee can and pound it several inches into the yellow grass. Fill the inside of the can with several inches of water and maintain the water level for five minutes. The chinch bugs will float to the surface. If you find some, treat the area with a soil insecticide approved for use on your specific type of grass.

Continue to watch for mole crickets in the sandy soils of the lower South. They are especially destructive to Bermuda Grass lawns. Damage usually looks like someone cultivated areas of your lawn. They can be controlled with a soil insecticide labeled for control of mole crickets and approved for use on your specific type of grass.

☛ **Other:** Do not cut your lawn lower, or higher, than recommended during August. Low mowing will shock the plant and raising your mower will disrupt the shoot-to-root ratio.

EVERGREEN LAWN ACTIVITIES FOR AUGUST:

(Tall Fescue, Creeping Red Fescue, Chewing Fescue, Kentucky Bluegrass)

☛ **Planting:** August is the worst time of the year to start an evergreen lawn from sod. Wait until September, which is the best time of the year to sod or seed an evergreen lawn.

☛ **Mowing:** Continue to mow evergreen lawns consistently at the recommended height. Do not reduce the height of your lawn by more than one-third at any single mowing.

Recommended Mowing Heights (in inches)		
	Height:	Mow When:
Kentucky 31 Fescue	3–4	4.5–6
Turf-type Fescue	2.5–3	3.75–4.5
Creeping Red and		
Chewing Fescue	2–2.5	3–3.75
Kentucky Bluegrass	2.5–3	3.75–4.5

If you return from the family vacation to find that your lawn is over 6 inches tall, mow at the highest setting possible on your lawn mower. Wait two days, then mow at the recommended height.

☛ **Irrigation:** Evergreen lawns will be weak and suffering in the muggy heat of August. Water consistently and accurately so that they do not experience drought as well. Apply 1 inch of water per week if there has been no significant rainfall. Remember to water deeply and infrequently.

☛ **Fertilizer:** Wait until next month to begin fertilizing evergreen lawns.

☛ **Aerating:** The best time of year to core aerate an evergreen lawn is in early September, just prior to fertilizing and applying pre-emergence weed control.

☛ **Dethatching:** Evergreen lawns seldom develop thatch problems and should not be mechanically dethatched this month. If you do have a major thatch accumulation, dethatch with a rented vertical mower in early September and then reseed your lawn.

☛ **Weed Control:** Wait until next month when soil temperatures drop to 70° to apply fall pre-emergence weed control to evergreen lawns. This is usually September 15 in the upper South and October 15 in the lower South. If you think you will forget, you can apply pre-emergence in combination with fertilizer but you will be sacrificing some effectiveness. Make sure the weed control is approved for use on your specific type of grass. This application will last 2–3 months.

Do not apply pre-emergence weed control if you are planning to seed or reseed an evergreen lawn. The pre-emergence control will prevent weeds and lawn seed from sprouting.

Continue to spray established and emerging weeds with a post-emergence weed control approved for use on your specific type of grass. Most sprays will be designed to treat either broadleaf or grassy weeds. Sprays are usually most effective when air temperatures are 60–80° and weeds are actively growing (not experiencing drought). It may take two applications to kill mature weeds. Always follow the directions on the product label.

☛ **Insects and Diseases:** Fungal diseases seldom appear on evergreen lawns during the hot, muggy dog days of August. They usually prefer cooler daytime temperatures (65–80°) and cooler nights (50–60°). If you notice a discolored or dead area of grass, examine the edges for wilted or discolored leaves. This is a sure sign of a fungal disease. Once located, spray with a lawn fungicide approved for use on your specific type of grass.

White grubs are the larval forms of Japanese Beetles and June Beetles. White grub larvae will be feeding on grass roots this month. August is a good time to control them with a soil insecticide approved for use on your specific type of grass, if you have not done so already.

Webworms and cutworms sometimes arrive to feed on grass blades at night. Webworms will leave spidery webs on the lawn surface as their calling card. Cutworms will leave patches of cut grass blades. Both larval worms can be controlled with a soil insecticide approved for use on your specific type of grass.

☛ **Other:** Your mower blade may need to be sharpened or replaced.

*Flower borders and evergreen
lawns rebound in September.*

IX. SEPTEMBER ACTIVITIES

SEPTEMBER IS A TRANSITION MONTH IN THE SOUTHERN GARDEN. IT BEGINS AS HOT AS the dog days of August, but it ends with cooler nights and the official beginning of fall on September 22 or 23 (the Fall Equinox). On that day the nighttime hours equal daytime hours.

September is also busy. The kids are back in school and it seems like we are constantly hauling them from one practice to another. Luckily, there is plenty to see as we commute. Summer perennials like Black-eyed Susan are packed in their borders, the Sweet Autumn Clematis is in bloom, and the Sourwood trees in the mountains are already a rusty red. One of my favorite sights is bright red Southern Magnolia seeds hanging precipitously from their cones as they wait for a pileated woodpecker to swoop down for dinner.

While it may be hard to make time in your hectic schedule, September is a critical month for the Southern lawn. It is the most important month of the year for evergreen lawns and a fairly important month for our warm-season lawns. What's more, some of the lawn activities like applying pre-emergence weed control are very dependent on good timing. Other activities like planting and fertilizing will also be much more successful if you complete them on time. My only advice is to do the best you can. If you're a little late, there is always next year.

WARM-SEASON LAWN ACTIVITIES FOR SEPTEMBER:

(Bermuda Grass, Centipede, Saint Augustine, Zoysia)

☛ **Planting:** Do not plant new warm-season grass lawns or patch old warm-season grass lawns this month. There is not enough time for grass roots to become established before cold weather. Soil temperatures are already dropping below the 80° that warm-season grass roots prefer. If you have no choice, lay sod as early in the month as possible. Remember to cultivate, amend the soil, and fertilize before planting.

☛ **Mowing:** Continue to mow warm-season lawns at the correct height in the beginning of the month. Remember not to reduce the height of your lawn by more than one-third at any mowing.

Recommended Mowing Heights (in inches)

	Height:	Mow When:
Common Bermuda	2	3
Hybrid Bermuda	1–1.5	1.5–2.25
Centipede	1.5–2	2.25–3
Saint Augustine	2–3	3–4.5
Zoysia	1–2	1.5–3

Once the soil temperature drops below 70°, allow your warm-season grass lawn to grow to three inches in preparation for the dormant season. This is usually in late September/early October. The added height will act as winter insulation for tender roots, rhizomes, and stolons growing near the soil surface. If you are planning to overseed, continue to mow at the regular height.

☛ **Irrigation:** September is one of our driest months in the South. The worst of the heat has passed, but there is still a chance for damaging drought. Apply 1 inch of water per week if there has been no significant rainfall. Whenever possible, water deeply and infrequently. Stop irrigating, however, if water begins to run on the surface.

☛ **Fertilizer:** Fertilize Bermuda Grass, Zoysia, and Saint Augustine lawns at the beginning of the month, if you have not done so already. Use a complete lawn fertilizer with a slow-release form of nitrogen. If possible, use a fertilizer with a low phosphorus and higher potassium similar to 12-4-14 or 12-0-12. Apply at the rate of 1.5 pounds of actual nitrogen per 1000 square feet. This will be your final fertilizer application of the season.

Do not fertilize Centipede lawns this month.

Water approximately 1 inch after fertilizing to wash fertilizer from grass blades and move it into the soil.

☛ **Aerating:** Do not aerate warm-season lawns this month. Root growth is slowing and your lawn will not have time to recover before going dormant. Also, aerating will disrupt your pre-emergence weed control and open the soil to weed seed infiltration.

☛ **Dethatching:** Wait until next year to dethatch warm-season lawns, if necessary.

☞ **Topdressing:** It is too late in the growing season to topdress effectively. Warm-season grass lawns will not have enough time to grow into the new soil before cold weather arrives. Wait until next year.

☞ **Weed Control:** Wait until soil temperatures drop to 70° to apply pre-emergence weed control (without fertilizer) to warm-season lawns. This is usually September 15 in the upper South and October 15 in the lower South. If you think you will forget, you can apply pre-emergence in combination with fertilizer but you will be sacrificing some effectiveness. Make sure the weed control is approved for use on your specific type of lawn. This application will last 2–3 months.

Do not apply pre-emergence weed control if you are planning to overseed your warm-season grass lawn for a winter cover.

Continue to spray established weeds with a post-emergence weed control. Liquid sprays are usually most effective when air temperatures are 60–80° and weeds are actively growing. It may take two applications to kill an established weed.

Remember that weed control products like Round-Up are non-selective and will kill your lawn grass as well.

☞ **Insects and Diseases:** September is a dangerous time for warm-season lawns. Fungal diseases may arrive as daytime air temperatures drop to 65–80° and night air temperatures drop to 50–60°. Fungal diseases often appear as clearly defined discolored or dead areas of grass. These areas will grow concentrically as the disease spreads. Examine the edges for wilted leaves and leaves with spots. Fungal diseases can be controlled with a lawn fungicide approved for use on your specific type of grass.

Continue to watch for webworms and cutworms feeding on grass blades at night. Webworms will leave spidery webs on the lawn surface. Cutworms will leave patches of cut grass blades. Both can be controlled with a soil insecticide approved for use on your specific type of grass.

Beware of fall armyworms! These hideous pests feed in masses during the day and can do incredible damage in a relatively short time. Listen for reported sightings from your neighbors and government agencies. Armyworms should be treated immediately with a soil insecticide approved for use on your specific type of grass.

Chinch bugs are a major concern, especially on Saint Augustine and Centipede lawns. Watch for patches of yellow, discolored, or wilted grass in sunny areas of the lawn. To confirm their presence, cut the top and bottom from a coffee can and pound it several inches into the yellow grass. Fill the inside of the can with several inches of water and maintain the water level for five minutes. The chinch bugs will float to the surface. Once you find some, treat the area with a soil insecticide approved for use on your specific type of grass.

Mole crickets may still be a problem this month in the sandy soils of the lower South. They are especially destructive to Bermuda Grass. Damaged areas usually look like someone cultivated your lawn. They can be controlled with a soil insecticide labeled for control of mole crickets and approved for use on your specific type of grass.

It is too late to treat lawns for white grubs. Grubs will be moving deeper into the soil this month in preparation for winter.

☞ **Overseeding:** Begin overseeding Bermuda, Centipede, and Saint Augustine lawns when soil temperatures drop to 70°. This is usually around September 15 in the upper South and October 15 in the lower South. A good, generic grass for overseeding is Annual Ryegrass (a.k.a. Italian Ryegrass). If you want to get fancy, call your local golf course superintendent and see what he/she recommends. Mow and prepare the soil surface as recommended before seeding.

EVERGREEN LAWN ACTIVITIES FOR SEPTEMBER:

(Tall Fescue, Creeping Red Fescue, Chewing Fescue, Kentucky Bluegrass)

☞ **Planting:** Begin seeding and sodding new evergreen lawns at the beginning of the month. Evergreen lawns will establish quickly as soil temperatures drop into the 70s. Remember to cultivate, amend the soil, and fertilize before planting. These steps should be followed whether you sod or seed your new lawn.

Early September is the best time of year to reseed a thinning evergreen lawn.

Do not apply pre-emergence weed control if you plan on seeding, sodding, or reseeding an evergreen lawn.

☞ **Mowing:** Continue to mow evergreen lawns consistently at the recommended height. Do not reduce the height of your lawn by more than one-third at any single mowing.

Recommended Mowing Heights (in inches)		
	Height:	Mow When:
Kentucky 31 Fescue	3–4	4.5–6
Turf-type Fescue	2.5–3	3.75–4.5
Creeping Red and		
Chewing Fescue	2–2.5	3–3.75
Kentucky Bluegrass	2.5–3	3.75–4.5

Mow newly seeded evergreen lawns with a sharp blade as soon as they reach the recommended mowing height. Do not allow them to grow tall and flop over.

Consider bagging your grass clippings when mowing a newly seeded lawn. Succulent young grass clippings mat easily and can damage your new lawn.

☛ **Irrigation:** September is typically a dry month in the South. Continue to water your evergreen lawn with about 1 inch of water per week if there has been no significant rainfall. Recently fertilized lawns will respond quickly and dramatically if watered properly.

Water newly seeded, sodded, or reseeded lawns carefully. Begin reducing the frequency of your irrigation after about two weeks. By 4–6 weeks, you should be watering deeply and infrequently.

☛ **Fertilizer:** Fertilize evergreen lawns at the beginning of the month, if you have not done so already. Use a complete lawn fertilizer with a slow-release form of nitrogen. Apply at the rate of 1.5 pounds of actual nitrogen per 1000 square feet. This will be your final fertilizer application of the season.

☛ **Aerating:** September is the best time of year to aerate an evergreen lawn using a rented core aerator. Lawns will respond quickly to the added oxygen in the soil and initiate new root and top growth. Try to core aerate in early September, just prior to fertilizing, liming, and applying pre-emergence weed control. Aerating afterwards will disrupt the chemical barrier of your pre-emergence weed control. If the cores bother you, you can rake the lawn and most will break and drop below the level of the grass where they are not as noticeable. This soil will eventually drop to the soil surface and help thatch to decompose.

☛ **Dethatching:** Evergreen lawns rarely develop thatch problems. If your lawn has thatch accumulations greater than .5 inches, you can mechanically dethatch with a rented vertical mower immediately before you reseed. Rake and remove all of the debris it dredges to the surface.

☛ **Weed Control:** Wait until soil temperatures drop to 70° to apply fall pre-emergence weed control (without fertilizer) to evergreen lawns. This is usually around September 15 in the upper South and October 15 in the lower South. If you think you will forget, you can apply pre-emergence in combination with fertilizer but you will be sacrificing some effectiveness. Make sure the weed control is approved for use on evergreen lawns. This application will last 2–3 months. Remember: do not apply pre-emergence weed control if you plan to seed, reseed, or sod your evergreen lawn.

Continue to spray established and emerging weeds with a post-emergence weed control spray approved for use on evergreen. Sprays are usually most effective when air temperatures are 60°–80° and weeds are actively growing. Always follow the directions on the product label. Do not, however, spray newly seeded, reseeded, or sodded lawns.

☛ **Insects and Diseases:** Fungal diseases may arrive this month on established and newly seeded evergreen lawns. They love cool daytime temperatures of 65–80°, and cool nighttime temperatures of 50–60°. It's a good idea to schedule your watering time for the middle of the day when excess moisture will evaporate quickly from leaf blades. Fungal diseases often appear as discolored or dead areas of grass with regular outlines. Examine the edges of the dead areas for wilted or discolored leaves. Once identified, spray with a lawn fungicide approved for use on your specific type of grass.

Webworms and cutworms may be a problem this month. Both feed on leaf blades at night. Webworms will leave spidery webs on the lawn surface visible early in the morning. Cutworms will leave patches of cut grass blades. Both larval worms can be controlled with a soil insecticide approved for use on your specific type of grass.

Fall armyworms occasionally bother evergreen lawns. They feed in masses and eat voraciously. Treat them with a soil insecticide as soon as you see them.

White grub larvae may still be feeding on grass roots this month but will be maturing and moving deeper in the soil. It is too late to treat for them effectively.

☛ **Other:** Early September is a good time to sharpen or replace your mower blade. This is especially important if you have seeded or reseeded your lawn. A dull mower blade will drag tender grass seedlings from the soil.

Overseeded Annual Ryegrass grows quickly and should be mowed frequently.

X. OCTOBER ACTIVITIES

OCTOBER IS THE LAST MONTH OF THE GROWING SEASON FOR MUCH OF THE SOUTH, with cold weather arriving in the lower South next month. Nights are chilly and days are sunny and cool. Everywhere you look, plants are slowly preparing for winter. Perennials are almost spent, annuals are making one last courageous stand, and roses are sending up the final bloom of the season.

I will concede that a Southern fall may play second fiddle to New England, but there is still plenty to admire. By the end of the month, September's rusty red Sourwoods will disappear in a mélange of orange Sugar Maples, bright Red Maples, and yellow Hickories. And don't forget the fall displays of Oakleaf Hydrangea, Nandina, and Pyracantha. My favorite these days are common Blueberries. Some years they rival even the Burning Bush with their fire-engine-red fall color.

Warm-season lawns are also preparing for winter this month. Most will not enter dormancy with as much flair as a Sugar Maple, but a Bermuda Grass lawn's random discoloration does hold a strange attraction. The unique patchwork of tan and green is oddly mesmerizing.

With the first frost, your fescue lawn will hopefully not be a unique patchwork of tan and green.

WARM-SEASON LAWN ACTIVITIES FOR OCTOBER:

(Bermuda Grass, Centipede, Saint Augustine, Zoysia)

☛ **Planting:** Do not plant warm-season grass lawns this month. Grass seed will not germinate well and sod will not become established before winter temperatures arrive. Sod sitting on the soil surface through the winter is susceptible to cold damage and heaving. Save your time and money for the spring.

☛ **Mowing:** Warm-season grass lawns will be growing very slowly this month. Allow your lawn to grow to approximately 3 inches in preparation for the dormant season. This added height will act as winter insulation for tender roots, rhizomes, and stolons growing near the soil surface. If you are still planning to overseed, continue to mow at the regular height.

Recommended Mowing Heights (in inches)		
	Height:	Mow When:
Common Bermuda	2	3
Hybrid Bermuda	1–1.5	1.5–2.25
Centipede	1.5–2	2.25–3
Saint Augustine	2–3	3–4.5
Zoysia	1–2	1.5–3

Mow warm-season grass lawns overseeded with Annual Ryegrass at 2–2.5 inches whenever the Annual Ryegrass reaches 3 inches. This will help the Annual Ryegrass to toughen and prevent it from clumping and flopping over.

☛ **Irrigation:** As temperatures cool in October, there is usually a fair amount of rainfall. Watch out for dry spells, though. Apply .5–1 inch of water per week if there has been no significant rainfall. Whenever possible, water deeply and infrequently. Stop irrigating, however, if water begins to run on the surface.

The middle and upper South will have their first frost this month. Remember to winterize your irrigation system and outside hose bibs (if necessary).

☛ **Fertilizer:** It is too late to fertilize warm-season lawns. If you forgot to fertilize last month, you might as well wait until the spring.

Do not believe fertilizer salesmen who try to convince you to "winterize" your warm-season grass lawn with a special fertilizer application in late fall. Research shows the benefits to be negligible and the detriments to be potentially damaging. Save your money for next season.

☛ **Aerating:** Do not aerate warm-season lawns this month. Aerating will disrupt your pre-emergence weed control, open the soil to weed seed infiltration, and allow cold temperatures to penetrate the root zone.

☛ **Dethatching:** Wait until next year to dethatch warm-season lawns, if necessary.

☛ **Topdressing:** Do not topdress warm-season lawns this month. Warm-season grasses are not growing actively. If you topdress now, you might smother your lawn.

☛ **Weed Control:** Once soil temperatures drop to 70°,

apply pre-emergence weed control (without fertilizer) to warm-season lawns, if you have not done so already. This is usually around September 15 in the upper South and October 15 in the lower South. Make sure the weed control is approved for use on your specific type of lawn. This application will last 2–3 months.

Do not apply pre-emergence weed control if you are still planning to overseed your warm-season grass lawn for a winter cover.

Spray established weeds with a post-emergence weed control approved for use on your specific type of grass. Liquid sprays are usually most effective when air temperatures are 60–80° and weeds are actively growing. It may take two applications to kill an established weed during the winter. Do not use weed control sprays, however, on lawns in which overseeded grass is germinating.

Remember that weed control products like Round-Up are non-selective and will kill your lawn grass as well. You can use Round-Up on dormant Bermuda Grass, but wait a month or two to make sure the grass is fully dormant.

☛ **Insects and Diseases:** Continue to watch diligently for fungal diseases, especially in early October. Most fungal diseases prefer daytime air temperatures of 65–80° and night air temperatures of 50–60°. They often appear on lawns as clearly defined discolored or dead areas of grass. These areas will grow concentrically as the disease spreads. Examine the edges for wilted leaves or leaves with spots. Fungal diseases can be controlled with a lawn fungicide approved for use on your specific type of grass.

Webworms and cutworms may be a problem early in the month. Both feed on grass blades at night. Webworms will leave spidery webs on the lawn surface that are noticeable early the next morning. Cutworms will leave patches of cut grass blades. Both can be controlled with a soil insecticide approved for use on your specific type of grass.

Fall armyworms can still be a nuisance this month. These horrible creatures feed in large numbers during the day and can do incredible damage in a relatively short time. Armyworms should be treated immediately with a soil insecticide approved for use on your specific type of grass.

Continue to watch for chinch bugs, especially on Saint Augustine and Centipede lawns. Inspect any abnormal patch of grass with yellow, discolored, or wilted grass. To confirm their presence, cut the top and bottom from a coffee can and pound it several inches into the yellow grass. Fill the inside of the can with several inches of water and maintain the water level for five minutes. The chinch bugs will float to the surface. If you find any, treat the area with a soil insecticide approved for use on your specific type of grass.

It is too late to treat lawns for white grubs. Grubs will be deep in the soil this month.

☛ **Overseeding:** Continue to overseed Bermuda Grass, Centipede, and Saint Augustine lawns once soil temperatures drop to 70°. This is usually early in the month in the upper South and the middle of the month in the lower South. A good generic choice is Annual Ryegrass (a.k.a. Italian Ryegrass). Mow and prepare the soil surface as recommended before seeding.

☛ **Other:** Rake or blow leaves from lawn areas as soon as possible. A layer of leaves can smother and damage even a dormant lawn. Besides, rain is on the way and dry leaves are much easier to blow than wet leaves.

EVERGREEN LAWN ACTIVITIES FOR OCTOBER:

(Tall Fescue, Creeping Red Fescue, Chewing Fescue, Kentucky Bluegrass)

☛ **Planting:** Plant and reseed evergreen lawns as soon as possible. Fescue and Kentucky Bluegrass seed will germinate as long as the soil temperature is above 55°, but germination becomes spotty with colder weather. It is best to allow seedlings 3–4 weeks (at very least) to become established before the first frost. Remember to cultivate, amend the soil, and fertilize.

Lay sod as soon as possible. Sod roots will grow quickly into the soil when soil temperatures are around 60–65° but no less than 50°. The longer you wait to lay sod, the more potential there is for cold damage. Sod should not be laid on unprepared soil. Cultivate, amend the soil, and fertilize before planting.

Do not apply pre-emergence weed control if you plan on seeding, sodding, or reseeding an evergreen lawn. Wait until you have mowed at least 2 times at the recommended height. In most cases, you may as well wait until your late winter pre-emergence weed control application.

☛ **Mowing:** Continue to mow evergreen lawns consistently at the recommended height. Do not reduce the height of your lawn by more than one-third at any single mowing.

Recommended Mowing Heights (in inches)		
	Height:	Mow When:
Kentucky 31 Fescue	3–4	4.5–6
Turf-type Fescue	2.5–3	3.75–4.5
Creeping Red and		
Chewing Fescue	2–2.5	3–3.75
Kentucky Bluegrass	2.5–3	3.75–4.5

Mow newly seeded evergreen lawns with a sharp blade as soon as they reach the recommended mowing height. Do not allow them to grow beyond 4 inches. Mowing causes the grass to toughen and spread.

It is helpful to bag your grass clippings when mowing a newly seeded lawn. Succulent young grass clippings mat easily on the lawn surface and can damage your new lawn.

☛ **Irrigation:** Moisture does not evaporate from grass or from soil as quickly during cooler weather. Continue to water during dry spells, however, with .5 inches of water at a time.

Water newly seeded, sodded, or reseeded lawns carefully. Begin reducing the frequency of your irrigation two weeks after planting. By 4–6 weeks after planting, you should be watering deeply and infrequently.

The middle and upper South will have their first frost this month. Remember to winterize your irrigation system and outside hose bibs (if necessary).

☛ **Fertilizer:** Evergreen lawns should have been fertilized last month. If you have not done so, fertilize as soon as possible. Use a fertilizer like 10-10-10 that does not contain slow-release form of nitrogen. Slow-release fertilizers are not as effective when soil temperatures are cold. Apply at the rate of 1 pound of actual nitrogen per 1000 square feet. This translates to 10 pounds of 10-10-10 per 1000 square feet.

☛ **Aerating:** There is still time to aerate evergreen lawns using a rented core aerator. Evergreen grass roots are actively growing and lawns will appreciate the added oxygen in the soil. Do not aerate, however, if you have already applied pre-emergence weed control. Aerating will disrupt the chemical barrier of you pre-emergence weed control and open the soil to weed seed infiltration.

The best sequence is to apply pre-emergence weed control immediately after core aerating.

☛ **Dethatching:** Evergreen lawns rarely develop thatch problems. If your lawn has thatch accumulations greater than .5 inches, begin by raking it vigorously with a metal-tined leaf rake. A vertical mower will damage an established evergreen lawn and it is too late to reseed.

☛ **Weed Control:** Once soil temperatures drop to 70°, apply pre-emergence weed control (without fertilizer) to evergreen lawns, if you have not done so already. This is usually around September 15 in the upper South and October 15 in the lower South. Make sure the weed control is approved for use on your specific type of lawn. This application will last 2–3 months. Do not apply pre-emergence, however, if you are seeding, reseeding, or sodding your evergreen lawn.

Continue to spray established and emerging weeds with a post-emergence weed control spray approved for use on your specific type of grass. Sprays are usually most effective when air temperatures are 60–80° and weeds are actively growing. Do not, however, spray newly seeded, reseeded, or sodded lawns. Always follow the directions on the product label.

☛ **Insects and Diseases:** Fungal diseases may arrive early in the month on established and newly seeded evergreen lawns. They prefer daytime temperatures of 65–80°, and night temperatures around 50–60°. Fungal diseases often appear as discolored or dead areas of grass with regular outlines. These areas will grow concentrically. Examine the edges of the dead areas for wilted or discolored leaves. Fungal diseases can be controlled with a lawn fungicide approved for use on your specific type of grass.

Webworms and cutworms may still be active early in the month. Both feed on grass blades at night. Webworms will leave spidery webs on the lawn surface visible early in the morning. Cutworms will leave patches of cut grass blades. Both larval worms can be controlled with a soil insecticide approved for use on your specific type of grass.

Fall armyworms occasionally bother evergreen lawns. They feed in masses and eat voraciously. Treat them with a soil insecticide as soon as you see them.

Do not apply soil insecticides to control white grubs this late in the season. It will not be effective.

☛ **Other:** Rake or blow leaves from lawn areas as soon as possible. Heavy leaf fall can smother and damage an evergreen lawn. This is especially important with newly seeded grass. Besides, rain is on the way and dry leaves are much easier to rake than wet leaves.

*A Tall Fescue lawn loses some color
in November but remains green.*

XI. NOVEMBER ACTIVITIES

NOVEMBER IN THE SOUTH BEGINS WITH COOL NIGHTS, MILD DAYS, AND AN OCCASIONAL frost on the windshield. By Thanksgiving, winter has truly arrived with freezing temperatures and a little ice on lakes and ponds. Most of the plants that can survive light frosts will usually succumb by the end of the month.

Thanksgiving is a magical time in the plant world with special events to mark the holiday. Some years the Ginkgo trees will be such a clear yellow they almost glow. Other years, every last leaf will have dropped almost simultaneously into a giant heap below. Just about the same time, the fragrant Tea Olive and mid-season Camellia begin to bloom in the middle and lower South.

When it comes to lawns in the South, November is our first real month to rest. Evergreen and warm-season lawns are growing very slowly, if at all, and are essentially dormant. It's been a long growing season and a lot has happened—drought, insects, moles, broken sprinklers, busted hoses, cracked lawn mower wheels, spilled fertilizer, drainage problems, and weeds. Thinking back, it sounds exhausting. But then again, there were barbeques, children's birthday parties, soccer, baseball, kite flying, and kids wrestling dogs. Somehow, despite all the work, a good lawn is always worth the time and effort.

WARM-SEASON LAWN ACTIVITIES FOR NOVEMBER:

(Bermuda Grass, Centipede, Saint Augustine, Zoysia)

☞ **Planting:** It is too late to plant new warm-season grass lawns this year. Wait until late spring when soil temperatures have warmed and grass is actively growing.

☞ **Mowing:** Most warm-season grass lawns will be dormant by now or will be growing extremely slowly. It is a good idea to leave grass at about 3 inches to provide winter insulation for tender roots, rhizomes, and stolons growing near the soil surface. Uneven lawn surfaces can be mowed when dormant, however, to provide a more kempt appearance. You will need to remove only about .25 inches.

Centipede, Bermuda Grass, and Saint Augustine lawns overseeded with a temporary cool-season grass like Annual Ryegrass should be mowed at 2–2.5 inches whenever the grass reaches 3 inches. Do not allow the overseeded grass to grow over 3 inches at any one time. It will begin to clump and be ugly.

☞ **Irrigation:** There is usually no need to water dormant lawns this month. Occasionally, we will have a warm, dry spell that may cause shallow roots, rhizomes, and stolons to desiccate. Apply about .5 inches of water if the top .25 inches of soil is dry to the touch.

If possible, water dormant lawns when temperatures are expected to drop below 20°. Wet soil will freeze and keep soil temperatures close to 32°, while dry soil allows damaging sub-20° air to penetrate the root zone.

Remember to winterize your irrigation system and outside hose bibs if you have not done so already.

☞ **Fertilizer:** There is no need to fertilize warm-season lawns this month. Wait until the late spring, after the danger of frost has passed.

Advertisements and fertilizer salesmen will be trying to convince you to winterize your lawn with a special fertilizer application this month. Research shows the benefits to be negligible and the detriments to be potentially damaging. Save your money!

Warm-season lawns overseeded with a cool-season grass like Annual Ryegrass may need to be fertilized if the Annual Ryegrass is light green or growing slowly. Use a fertilizer like 10-10-10 that does not contain a slow-release form of nitrogen. Slow-release fertilizers are not as effective when soil temperatures are cold. Apply about .5 pounds of actual nitrogen per 1000 square feet at a time. This translates to 5 pounds of 10-10-10 per 1000 square feet. Fertilizing more than this will cause outrageous growth that requires frequent mowing.

☞ **Aerating:** The best time to aerate warm-season lawns is in late spring/early summer. If you aerate now, it will disrupt your pre-emergence weed control, open the soil to weed seed infiltration, and allow damaging cold temperatures to penetrate the root zone.

☞ **Dethatching:** Do not worry about thatch this month. If you dethatch with a vertical mower, it will only expose stolons, roots, and rhizomes to colder temperatures. Wait until next spring.

☞ **Topdressing:** Do not topdress warm-season lawns this month. Warm-season grasses are not growing actively and topdressing could smother your lawn.

☞ **Weed Control:** Winter weeds are germinating! If you have not done so already, apply granular pre-emergence weed control to warm-season lawns as early in the month as possible. Look for a product that does not contain fertilizer and is approved for use on your specific type of grass. This application should last 2–3 months.

Do not apply pre-emergence weed control if you still plan to overseed your warm-season grass lawn for a winter cover.

Spray newly emerging annual weeds like henbit and chickweed that have escaped your pre-emergence weed control. Use a post-emergence weed control approved for use on your specific type of grass. Liquid sprays are usually most effective when daytime air temperatures are 60–80° and weeds are actively growing. Young tender weeds are more susceptible to spray, so spray them before they mature and start to flower. This is no small matter since each weed has the potential to produce hundreds of weed seeds that will plague you in the future. You may have to spray twice (over a week or so) to kill mature weeds.

Remember that weed control products like Round-Up are non-selective and will kill your lawn grass as well. You can use Round-Up on dormant Bermuda Grass, but wait another month or so to make sure the grass is fully dormant.

☞ **Insects and Diseases:** With the advent of cold weather and freezing temperatures, insects and diseases will be as dormant as your warm-season grass. We can finally relax.

Do not use soil insecticides during the late fall and winter months.

☞ **Overseeding:** In the lower South, Bermuda Grass, Centipede, and Saint Augustine lawns can still be overseeded with a temporary cool-season grass, but hurry. A good choice is Annual Ryegrass (a.k.a. Italian Ryegrass). Mow and prepare the soil surface as recommended before seeding. Be patient in areas that have already experienced a frost because germination may be slow and spotty.

☞ **Other:** Continue to rake or blow leaves from lawn areas. Heavy piles of leaves can smother and damage even a dormant lawn.

EVERGREEN LAWN ACTIVITIES FOR NOVEMBER:

(Tall Fescue, Creeping Red Fescue, Chewing Fescue, Kentucky Bluegrass)

☞ **Planting:** The best time of year to plant and reseed an evergreen lawn is in early September. The second best time is in the spring when the danger of hard freezes has passed and soil temperatures rise to 55° (approximately mid-March). If possible, wait until spring.

Evergreen lawn seed will germinate as long as the soil temperature is above 55°, but germination becomes erratic with colder weather. In addition, seedlings are tender and susceptible to freezing temperatures. If you are dying to seed this month, remember to cultivate, amend the soil, and fertilize so that seedlings will have a better chance to survive.

Wait until mid-spring to lay fescue sod. Fescue sod roots will grow quickly into the soil when soil temperatures reach 55–60°. This is usually in March.

☞ **Mowing:** Continue to mow evergreen lawns consistently at the recommended height. Do not reduce the height of your lawn by more than one-third at any single mowing.

Recommended Mowing Heights (in inches)		
	Height:	Mow When:
Kentucky 31 Fescue	3–4	4.5–6
Turf-type Fescue	2.5–3	3.75–4.5
Creeping Red and		
Chewing Fescue	2–2.5	3–3.75
Kentucky Bluegrass	2.5–3	3.75–4.5

Mow newly seeded lawns with a sharp blade as soon as they reach the recommended mowing height. Do not allow them to grow beyond 4 inches. Mowing will help the grass to toughen and spread.

Continue to bag your grass clippings when mowing a newly seeded lawn. Succulent young grass clippings mat easily on the lawn surface and can damage your new lawn.

☞ **Irrigation:** Established evergreen lawns seldom need to be irrigated in November. Beware of the rare warm, dry spell. Apply .5 inches of water if the top .25 inches of soil is dry to the touch.

Water newly seeded, sodded, or reseeded lawns carefully. You should be reducing the frequency of your irrigation by now. Lawns will only need .5–1 inch of water if there has been no significant rainfall, and the soil surface is dry to the touch.

Remember to winterize your irrigation system and outside hose bibs if you have not done so already.

☛ **Fertilizer:** It is normal for even the healthiest evergreen lawn to lose a little of its dark green color during the winter months. Fertilizer is not the answer. When soil temperatures are below 45–50°, grass roots will not absorb the fertilizer and the nitrogen may leach into nearby streams and waterways. Hold off!

☛ **Aerating:** Do not aerate evergreen lawns this month. Wait until late February/early March, immediately before you apply pre-emergence weed control. Evergreen grass roots grow best when soil temperatures are 50–65°. This usually occurs in March.

☛ **Dethatching:** Evergreen lawns rarely develop thatch problems. If your lawn has thatch accumulations greater than .5 inches, rake it vigorously with a metal-tined leaf rake. November is not a good month to mechanically dethatch with a rented vertical mower.

☛ **Weed Control:** Winter annual weeds will be germinating this month. If you have not done so already, apply a granular pre-emergence weed control as soon as possible. Look for a product that does not contain fertilizer and is approved for use on your specific type of grass. This application should last 2–3 months.

This is your last chance to apply pre-emergence weed control to evergreen lawns you are planning to seed or reseed in the spring. Pre-emergence weed control applied in the next several months will prevent your lawn seed from germinating.

Spray newly emerging winter annual weeds like henbit and chickweed as soon as you notice them. Use a post-emergence weed control approved for use on your specific type of grass. Spray on a warm afternoon when air temperatures are 60–80° and weeds are actively growing. Young tender weeds are more susceptible to spray, so spray them before they mature and start to flower. This is no small matter since each weed has the potential to produce hundreds of weed seeds that will plague you in the future.

Established weeds like ground ivy can also be sprayed now. You may have to spray twice (over a week or so) to kill a tough, established patch of weeds.

☛ **Insects and Diseases:** Do not worry about insects and diseases now that the weather is cold.

Do not apply soil insecticides to control white grubs or other soil-inhabiting insects. It will not be effective.

☛ **Other:** Continue to rake or blow leaves from lawn areas. Heavy piles of leaves can smother and damage an evergreen lawn.

*A dormant Zoysia lawn is
almost as dreary as the weather.*

XII. DECEMBER ACTIVITIES

DECEMBER IS SUCH A BUSY MONTH THAT WE SELDOM EVEN THINK ABOUT GARDENING. Even worse, December 21 is the shortest day of the year (the Winter Solstice) and there isn't a daylight hour to spare. Amid the dreary cold of December, a dormant warm-season lawn is not much encouragement to leave the house. Evergreen lawns aren't much better. At least they can be cut every now and then, if they have grown during a winter warm spell.

There are plenty of reasons to leave the house in December, if not to mess with the lawn. Holly and Magnolia branches can be harvested and placed as greenery along the mantle. You can shoot mistletoe from a high Oak branch, or collect some Turkey Foot for a homemade wreath. If you haven't had a chance, remember to start Giant Flowering Amaryllis and Paperwhite Narcissus as early in the month as possible. Paperwhites seem to bloom sooner and sooner with each passing year, but you should still count on at least four weeks to force the blossoms.

WARM-SEASON LAWN ACTIVITIES FOR DECEMBER:

(Bermuda Grass, Centipede, Saint Augustine, Zoysia)

☛ **Planting:** Do not plant new warm-season grass lawns this month. Wait until late spring when lawns are growing actively and will establish quickly.

☛ **Mowing:** Warm-season grass lawns are dormant this month. It is a good idea to leave your lawn at about 3 inches to provide winter insulation for tender roots, rhizomes, and stolons growing near the soil surface. Uneven or weedy lawn surfaces can be mowed when dormant, however, to provide a more kempt appearance. You will need to remove only about .25 inches.

Mow Centipede, Bermuda Grass, and Saint Augustine lawns that are overseeded with a temporary cool-season grass like Annual Ryegrass at 2–2.5 inches whenever the grass reaches 3 inches. Do not allow the overseeded grass to grow above 3 inches at any one time. It will begin to clump and become ugly.

☛ **Irrigation:** Dormant lawns will need to be irrigated only if the weather is unseasonably warm and dry. Apply about a .5 inches of water if the top .25 inches of soil is dry to the touch to prevent shallow roots, rhizomes, and stolons from desiccating.

If possible, water dormant lawns when temperatures are expected to drop below 20°. Wet soil will freeze and keep soil temperatures close to 32°, while dry soil allows damaging sub-20° air to penetrate the root zone.

Remember to winterize your irrigation system and outside hose bibs, if you have not done so already.

☛ **Fertilizer:** There is no need to fertilize warm-season lawns this month. Wait until late spring, after the danger of frost has passed.

Warm-season lawns overseeded with a cool-season grass like Annual Ryegrass may need fertilizing if the Annual Ryegrass is light green or growing slowly. Use a fertilizer like 10-10-10 that does not contain a slow-release form of nitrogen. Slow-release fertilizers are not as effective when soil temperatures are cold. Apply about .5 pounds of actual nitrogen per 1000 square feet at a time. This translates to 5 pounds of 10-10-10 per 1000 square feet. Fertilizing more than this will cause outrageous growth that requires frequent mowing.

☛ **Aerating:** Do not aerate warm-season lawns this month. Aerating now will disrupt your pre-emergence weed control, open the soil to weed seed infiltration, and will allow damaging cold temperatures to enter the root zone. The best time to aerate warm-season lawns is in late spring/early summer.

☛ **Dethatching:** Do not dethatch warm-season lawns this month. If you dethatch with a rented vertical mower, you will expose stolons, roots, and rhizomes to colder temperatures. Wait until next summer.

☛ **Topdressing:** Do not topdress warm-season lawns this month. Warm-season grasses are not growing actively. If you topdress, you might smother your lawn.

☛ **Weed Control:** The pre-emergence weed control you applied in early fall will be losing its effectiveness. If your lawn is mostly weed-free, and weeds do not usually blow in from surrounding areas, you can wait until late winter (February/early March) to re-apply. Otherwise, apply a pre-emergence weed control approved for use on your specific type of grass. Look for a product that does not contain fertilizer and follow the labeled directions. This application should last 2–3 months.

It is easy to locate weeds on a tan, dormant warm-season lawn. Spray newly emerging annual weeds (henbit, chickweed) and established perennial weeds (ground ivy, pennywort) with a post-emerge weed control approved for use on your specific type of grass. These sprays are usually designed to control either broadleaf weeds or grassy weeds. Spray on a warm afternoon when air temperatures are between 60–80° and follow the labeled directions. You may have to spray twice (over a week or so) to kill tough, mature weeds.

Remember that weed control products like Round-Up are non-selective and will kill your lawn grass as well. You can use Round-Up on dormant Bermuda Grass, but check to make sure leaves and stolons have not emerged from dormancy in a winter warm spell. Even then, expect some Bermuda Grass around the weed to die.

☛ **Insects and Diseases:** Insects and diseases are not a problem this month. Relax!

☛ **Overseeding:** It is too late to effectively overseed Bermuda Grass, Centipede, and Saint Augustine lawns with a temporary cool-season grass like Annual Ryegrass (a.k.a. Italian Ryegrass). Cool-season grass seed may germinate, but will look more like a weed than a winter grass cover.

☛ **Other:** Finish raking or blowing leaves from lawn areas. Heavy piles of leaves can smother and damage even a dormant lawn.

EVERGREEN LAWN ACTIVITIES FOR DECEMBER:

(Tall Fescue, Creeping Red Fescue, Chewing Fescue, Kentucky Bluegrass)

☛ **Planting:** Do not plant new evergreen lawns from seed or sod this month. The best time of year to plant an evergreen lawn is in early September. The second best time is after the danger of hard freezes has passed and the soil warms to 55° (approximately mid-March). Wait until spring.

☛ **Mowing:** Mow evergreen lawns at the recommended height. Try not to let your lawn grow beyond these heights, even in the winter. Otherwise, you will shock the plant by reducing the height of your lawn by more than one-third in a single mowing.

Mow newly seeded evergreen lawns with a sharp blade as soon as they reach the recommended mowing height. Do not allow them to grow above 4 inches. Mowing causes the grass plants to toughen and spread.

Continue to bag your grass clippings when mowing a newly seeded lawn. Succulent young grass clippings mat easily on the lawn surface and can damage your new lawn.

Recommended Mowing Heights (in inches)		
	Height:	Mow When:
Kentucky 31 Fescue	3–4	4.5–6
Turf-type Fescue	2.5–3	3.75–4.5
Creeping Red and		
Chewing Fescue	2–2.5	3–3.75
Kentucky Bluegrass	2.5–3	3.75–4.5

☛ **Irrigation:** Established, as well as fall-seeded, evergreen lawns seldom need to be irrigated this month. Occasionally, they may need water during a warm, dry spell. Apply .5 inches of water if the top .25 inches of soil is dry to the touch.

☛ **Fertilizer:** It is normal for even the healthiest evergreen lawn to lose a little of its dark green color during the winter months. Fertilizer is not the answer. When soil temperatures are below 45–50°, grass roots will not absorb the fertilizer and the nitrogen may leach into nearby streams and waterways. Wait until February.

☛ **Aerating:** Do not aerate evergreen lawns this month. Wait until soil temperatures reach 50° in late February/early March and aerate immediately before you apply pre-emergence weed control. Evergreen grass roots grow best when soil temperatures are 50–65°.

☛ **Dethatching:** Evergreen lawns rarely develop thatch problems. If your lawn has thatch accumulations greater than .5 inches during the winter, rake it vigorously with a metal-tined leaf rake.

☛ **Weed Control:** The pre-emergence weed control you applied in early fall will be losing its effectiveness. If your lawn is mostly weed-free, and weeds do not usually blow in from surrounding areas, you can wait until February/early March to re-apply. Otherwise, apply a pre-emergence weed control approved for use on your specific type of grass. Look for a product that does not contain fertilizer and follow the labeled directions. This application should last 2–3 months.

Do not apply pre-emergence weed control this month if you are planning to seed or reseed in the spring. It may prevent lawn seed from germinating.

Spray established and newly emerging weeds as soon as you notice them in your evergreen lawn. Use a post-emergence weed control approved for use on your specific type of grass. Spray on a warm afternoon when air temperatures are 60–80° and weeds are actively growing. Young tender weeds are more susceptible to herbicides, so spray them before they mature and start to flower. Established weeds may require more than one application. Always follow the directions on the label.

You can begin using weed control products on newly seeded or sodded evergreen lawns once you have mowed them two or three times.

☛ **Insects and Diseases:** Insects and diseases will not be a problem now that the weather is cold.

☛ **Other:** Finish raking or blowing leaves from lawn areas. Heavy piles of leaves will smother and damage an evergreen lawn.

Southern Lawn Pests and Problems

A BEAUTIFUL LAWN BEGINS WITH GOOD PLANTING AND LASTS WITH GOOD MAINTENANCE. In the meantime, you will probably have your share of lawn problems. Some of these problems will pass without notice; others will overwhelm you in a single season. In general, though, lawn problems are easily recognized and can be cured with a reasonable amount of time and energy.

Lawn problems often evolve. A blocked drain may not be noticeable during a dry month. You increase your irrigation frequency and the lawn flourishes. Then, the rain returns and the soggy corner of your lawn floods. When the water dissipates in a week or so, the grass is thin, weak, and choked with silt. Soon after, nutsedge begins to sprout in the remaining thin turf. It spreads quickly, and before you know it, the whole corner of the lawn is more nutsedge than turfgrass. When it comes to a lawn, a small problem like a blocked drained can avalanche and cause your entire lawn to decline.

Lawn problems do not fix themselves. We have to be alert for small changes so we can act quickly before the problem spreads too far. The reason for this is that a lawn is all about repetition. Mowing, fertilizing, watering, and aerating are all repetitious activities. If your push mower is set higher on one side than the other, you will scalp the low side as you mow across the lawn. The scalping continues, pass after pass, until your lawn looks like a zebra.

Insect and disease problems start small as well. You would never even notice a single white grub eating grass roots. Two white grubs are hardly noticeable, either. It is not until the white grub population reaches about two per square foot that you wake up to a major problem.

The best way to avoid problems is to get to know your lawn. Take a walk around and keep your eyes open for anything abnormal. Then, come back a week later and see if anything has changed. Is the ground ivy patch growing? Is the dry corner under the pine tree thinning? Is it still soggy down by the swing set? The problems that cause a lawn to fail will be there day after day and week after week. Consequently, the person who mows the lawn is usually the most likely one to notice and identify problems.

The following section contains some of the most common lawn problems. Hopefully, it will help you recognize a problem in your own lawn before it takes a heavy toll. It may also help you narrow the list of suspects. Either way, remember that each lawn, and each lawn problem, is slightly different. A fertilizer burn may be brown on your lawn and orange-brown on your neighbor's lawn. Begin with these photographs to compile a list of suspects, but look for first-hand clues to apprehend the problem.

LEFT: *Dull Mower Blade: A dull mower blade will rip the end of a grass blade and cause the tip to turn gray. You may not realize it, but the cumulative effect of thousands of gray tips in a lawn is noticeable. Mowing with a sharp blade may actually cause your lawn to appear several shades darker green. You may want to check the price of a new blade because it is sometimes cheaper than sharpening the old one.*

BILLBUG

Billbugs are a class of hard-shelled insects known for their short, curved snout. They mate in mid to late spring and lay their eggs in lawn areas. The eggs hatch into legless white grubs that feed on grass roots during the late spring and summer. Your lawn may look like it is suffering from drought with irregular areas of brown or yellowing grass. If you tug on the discolored turf, it will easily pull from the soil. Billbug beetles and larvae can be controlled with a soil insecticide.

COMPACTION

About 50% of a soil's volume is made up of pore space. The pore space is filled with varying amounts of water and air, both of which are critical to healthy root growth. Cars, foot traffic, and construction work will compact the soil and cause the pore space to collapse. Without the pores, air and water have difficulty entering the root zone and grass plants die. In addition, compacted soils dry quickly and will often cause water to puddle on the surface. Compacted soil can be renovated by rototilling before you plant or core aerating afterwards. Also, soils will naturally loosen during the winter freeze/thaw processes.

DOG URINE

Dog urine contains urea, a source of nitrogen. Dog urine can cause two different problems. First, it can cause areas of dark green growth if the lawn has not been fertilized. Second, dog urine can burn a lawn in the week or so immediately after you fertilize. The effect is the same as if you had spilled fertilizer and looks like an orange, tan, or bleached patch of grass. A lawn that has been fertilized, but not recently, will show no sign that a dog has visited. As an aside, this problem is often worse with female dogs because they urinate heavily in one spot.

DROUGHT

Anyone who has grown a lawn knows that there is no such thing as a drought-tolerant lawn. Sure, Bermuda Grass plants go into a "drought dormancy" and will slowly turn green again when rainfall returns. BUT, the Bermuda Grass lawn will be thin and infested with weeds. Let's face it, we all want a lawn that is healthy, green, and beautiful. The only way to have one is to water during dry spells. If you cannot irrigate during a drought, prepare yourself for the job of controlling weeds and nursing the remaining grass plants back to life when rainfall returns.

FERTILIZER BURN

Fertilizer can burn a lawn if spilled or applied heavily in a single area. The fertilizer dissolves in extremely high concentrations and becomes toxic to the grass. The central area of the spill will die while the outer edges of the area will be "well-fertilized" and dark green. Fertilizer spills usually happen when loading a spreader or when making tight turns without turning off the spreader. If this happens, pick up as much of the spilled fertilizer as possible. Next, flush the area with several inches of water to dilute the remaining fertilizer. Even then, grass plants in the immediate vicinity may die.

GRADING

It is common these days for an entire lot to be graded before a new home is built. During the process, the top layers of soil are stripped, buried, or hauled away. Unfortunately, these top layers contain the majority of organic matter, known as humus, found in soil. Humus improves soil drainage, soil nutrition, and soil water retention. Whether you are growing a lawn in clay soil or sandy soil, one of the best ways to improve graded soil is to add humus before you plant.

IMPROPER OVERSEEDING

It may seem like a good idea to overseed a warm-season grass with a permanent evergreen grass like Tall Fescue. The evergreen grass would make the lawn look green in the winter while the warm-season grass would compensate for the weakened fescue in the summer. No! Instead, the evergreen grass makes the warm-season grass look weedy, or at best, funny during the summer. In the winter, your lawn will look half-dead, not half-dormant.

JAPANESE BEETLES/WHITE GRUBS

Japanese Beetles begin to emerge from grass and lawn areas in June to feed voraciously on all kinds of plants, shrubs, and trees. In midsummer, they mate and lay their eggs in lawn and grassy areas. The eggs hatch and develop into soil-inhabiting white grubs that feed heavily on grass roots. Infested lawns usually appear as if they were suffering from drought. Treat infested lawns with a soil insecticide beginning in early August when the white grubs are tender and easily killed.

LACK OF HUMUS

The majority of Southern soils are clay-based soils. Clay-based soils are wonderful because they hold nutrients and water very well. Unfortunately, years of cotton farming and development have depleted our soils of organic matter. Without organic matter, also known as humus, clay-based soils suffer tremendously. They compact easily, become impenetrable to rain water, and dry quickly. The best solution is to amend the soil with humus before you plant your lawn. My favorite soil amendment is sphagnum peat moss.

MOSS IN LAWNS

Moss growing on the surface of your lawn is often an indication of acidic soil. While most lawn grasses perform well in mildly acidic soil with a pH levels between 6 and 7, essential nutrients like nitrogen become less available at soil pH levels below 6. The soil pH can be raised fairly easily by broadcasting pelletized lime. Many lawns will need 50 pounds of lime per 1000 square feet. As the pH rises over 2–3 months, the moss will die and your lawn grass will thicken. Do not apply lime to Centipede lawns, however, because they grow best in acidic soils.

NUTSEDGE

Nutsedge is a horrible weed that will spread by underground rhizomes to plague areas of your lawn. It is so notorious that it has prompted the saying: "The only way to control nutsedge is to move." It often arrives in damp or soggy areas of the lawn, although it knows no bounds. The problem is that many of our most common and effective weed killers do not control nutsedge. If you find it in your lawn, look for a weed control spray that is specifically recommended for control of nutsedge.

PATCHED LAWNS

By the end of a long summer, a warm-season lawn may be speckled with fertilizer burns, scalped areas, weeds, and holes dug by your neighbor's dog. Your immediate reaction might be to run out to the nursery in September to buy several blocks of sod to patch these areas. Sod planted in the fall will not grow roots into the soil below and will be more susceptible to winter injury. In the spring, the patches may remain brown or light green while the rest of your lawn turns green.

POOR DRAINAGE

There are few things worse for a lawn than standing puddles of water or soggy soil. They are usually caused by bad grading, poor soil structure, or a constant source of water. In most situations, a poorly drained lawn will thin and will be quickly invaded by weeds. Begin by correcting the drainage problem. This may be as simple as unclogging a drain. Next, spray the weeds that have invaded. If you act quickly, the thinning turf may revive. Otherwise, you may need to re-plant the area.

SODDING ON UNCULTIVATED SOIL

Time and time again, I see people lay sod on top of rubble, existing grass, uneven soil, or uncultivated soil. This method might be easier than planting the correct way, but will be disastrous in the end. Sure, you can usually keep one of these lawns alive for several months with constant water, but it will be half-dead by next year because of drought, compaction, or poor drainage. Then you will be ordering in another couple of pallets and starting over.

SPRING DEAD SPOT

Spring Dead Spot is a major fungal disease on Bermuda Grass lawns across the South. As the lawn turns green in the spring, circular dead areas appear that may be several feet across. Once you notice the spot, the disease has passed and the dead area will not expand. Bermuda Grass stolons and roots in the circle will be rotted. During the summer, the surrounding grass plants slowly grow to cover the dead area. Spray the area with lawn fungicide in late summer/fall to help prevent it from returning the next spring.

SPRINKLER HEAD PROBLEMS

An automatic sprinkler system can save a lawn, but they are not always in perfect running order. Check your sprinkler heads once or twice a season. Make sure they are distributing water and not blowing a powerful stream of water into nearby shrubs, banks, or grass. Most sprinklers patterns can be adjusted easily by turning a screw on top of the sprinkler head. This sprinkler head is set too low in the ground. It should be replaced with a sprinkler head that pops up higher.

STEEP BANKS

There are few things as frustrating as trying to grow a beautiful lawn on a steep bank. They are hard to plant, difficult to water deeply, and almost impossible to mow evenly. Here are a few hints. First, spend extra time cultivating and amending the soil before planting. This will help grass plants to become established quickly. Second, understand that steep banks will need special irrigation since they need more water applied in lower amounts (to avoid run-off). Finally, consider core aerating on a regular basis because the holes become "water reservoirs" in the soil surface.

TREE ROOTS

Tree roots extend well beyond the reaches of tree limbs and gravitate toward lawn areas because of the extra water and nutrient levels in the soil. As the roots enlarge, they may appear on the surface of the soil. It is no fun bouncing across Red Maple roots on a riding lawn mower. The best answer is to redefine the lawn area to avoid exposed tree roots. Underground roots at the edge of a lawn may compete dramatically with your grass for water and nutrients. If possible, increase your irrigation in those areas to accommodate for both the tree and the grass roots.

ANNUAL BLUEGRASS

An annual grassy weed that germinates during the fall, grows during the winter, produces seed, and dies in early summer. It can be controlled with a pre-emergence weed control applied in early fall.

CHICKWEED

An annual broadleaf weed that germinates during the fall, grows during the winter, produces seed, and dies by early summer. It can be controlled with a pre-emergence weed control applied in early fall.

CLOVER

A perennial broadleaf weed that usually sprouts in the fall. Established patches can be controlled with a post-emergence broadleaf weed control spray applied whenever the clover is actively growing.

CRABGRASS

An annual grassy weed that begins to germinate in early spring and grows throughout the summer. It can be controlled with a pre-emergence weed control applied in late winter.

Dandelion

A perennial broadleaf weed that flowers from early spring through summer. Established plants can be controlled with a post-emergence broadleaf weed control applied whenever the dandelion is actively growing.

Ground Ivy

A perennial broadleaf weed that spreads quickly during the growing season. It can be controlled with a post-emergence broadleaf weed control spray applied whenever the ground ivy is actively growing.

Henbit

An annual broadleaf weed that sprouts in the fall and grows through the winter and early spring. It can be controlled with a pre-emergence weed control applied in early fall.

Wild Onion

A perennial broadleaf weed that grows during the cooler months of the year. It can be controlled with a post-emergence broadleaf weed control spray applied on a warm winter day.

Using Chemical
Insect and Weed Controls

MOST OF THE INSECT AND WEED CONTROL PRODUCTS AVAILABLE IN THE SOUTH CONTAIN chemicals. These chemicals may be natural or synthetic. In addition, some may be synthetic versions of a natural chemical. All will have been tested extensively and approved for their specified uses. Whenever using chemical insect and weed controls, protect your family, pets, neighbors, plants, and wildlife. Begin by reading the product label for specific cautions and warnings. This is your best source of information on how to apply a chemical and how to apply it safely. Following are some other tips.

SAFETY

1. Wear long sleeves, long pants, rubber gloves, eye protection, and a mask or respirator.
2. Wear safety equipment when you are mixing the chemical since this is a common time for splashes.
3. Do not mix different chemicals.
4. Mix concentrates at the recommended rate. Do not mix more or less.
5. Do not spray on a windy day. Chemical sprays can drift easily.
6. Read the product label for directions on when you can re-enter a sprayed area. Keep your children, pets, and neighbors away from the area for the designated time.
7. Use a different sprayer for herbicides and insecticides/fungicides. Herbicide residue can damage your other plants.
8. Do not spray herbicides near ornamental plantings.
9. Do not spray herbicides on lawn areas near shallow-rooted trees and shrubs like Dogwoods, Boxwoods, and Magnolias. The herbicide can be absorbed through the root system and harm the plant.

EFFECTIVENESS

1. Spray weeds when they are young and actively growing so that they absorb the material quickly and die.
2. Weed controls are not as effective during cold weather or during a drought because the weed may be in a dormant condition.
3. Do not spray weed control when the air temperature is over 90°.
4. Do not mow your lawn before you spray weed control. Weeds are harder to find after you mow and you will have removed weed leaves that you could have sprayed.
5. Do not mow immediately after spraying weed control. You may remove weed leaves that have absorbed the herbicide before it moves into the plant. Wait at least two days.
6. Do not spray newly seeded or sodded lawns with weed controls until you have mowed at least two times.
7. Do not spray weed controls if rain is forecasted in the next 24 hours.
8. Do not irrigate for 24 hours after you spray a weed control. Remember to turn off your automatic sprinkler system.

GLOSSARY

Acidic Soil: A soil with a pH level less than 7, characterized by a relatively high number of hydrogen ions.

Aerating: A method of stimulating grass growth by opening passages for air, water, and nutrients into the root zone. Aerating is best accomplished with a core aerator. Core aerating should not be confused with spiking.

Alkaline Soil: A soil with a pH level above 7, characterized by a relatively low number of hydrogen ions; a basic soil.

Backpack Blower: A gas-powered machine, worn on the back like a backpack, used for blowing leaves and other debris.

Basic Soil: A soil with a pH level above 7, characterized by a relatively low number of hydrogen ions; an alkaline soil.

Broadcast: To sow evenly over an area rather than in rows.

Broadleaf Weed: In general, a weed like pennywort that has wide, flat leaves situated on a stem.

Chlorosis: A yellowing of plant leaves due to an underproduction of chlorophyll, a green pigment essential for photosynthesis.

Compacted Soil: Soil that has been compressed by weight or foot traffic to the point where it has lost pore space in between its solid components. Soil pore space allows air and water to move through the soil. Compacted soil is usually low in oxygen and moisture.

Complete Lawn Fertilizer: A fertilizer that contains a percentage of all three major nutrients as depicted in the N-P-K ratio.

Cool-Season Grass: A lawn grass that performs the majority of its growth during the cooler months of the year; another name for an evergreen grass.

Core Aerator: A machine that removes cores of soil from a lawn and deposits them on top of the grass. Most people rent a core aerator from a tool rental store or hire someone to core aerate their lawn.

Cultivar: A horticultural term derived from "cultivated variety." A cultivar is horticulturally but not taxonomically different from the botanical species within which it falls. Cultivars are usually chosen for a particular attribute and are given a name.

Dethatch: To manually or mechanically remove accumulations of thatch from a lawn.

Dethatcher: Another name for a vertical mower.

Disease: A damaging condition caused by fungi or viruses that affects the health and appearance of a lawn.

Dogwood: A flowering tree, *Cornus florida*, that blooms in the spring around the time of the last frost.

Dormant: A condition occurring when a plant stops its growth, usually indicated in a grass plant by the browning of its grass blades, which are replaced when growth starts again.

Edging: To create a line or border by cutting grass along the sides of driveways, paths, and landscape beds.

Evapotranspiration: The total amount of water that is lost from the soil through evaporation and lost from plants through transpiration (the loss of water from leaves).

Evergreen Grass: A grass that does not go dormant but remains green throughout the year.

Fertilize: The act of applying nutrients of any type to a plant.

Fertilizer: A mixture of nutrients used by plants to produce food through photosynthesis, and also required for growth. Nitrogen, phosphorus, and potassium are the nutrients used in largest quantities. Two cups of granular fertilizer usually weigh one pound.

Fertilizer Spreader: A device used to distribute fertilizer evenly onto a lawn. Fertilizer spreaders are often hand-held or rolling. "Drop-type" fertilizer spreaders allow  the fertilizer to drop from the container onto the lawn. "Broadcast" fertilizer spreaders distribute fertilizer from a rotating plate in a wide pattern.

Forsythia: A deciduous shrub with bright yellow flowers. Forsythia blooms in late winter when the soil temperature rises to approximately 50° (just before  crabgrass seed begin to germinate) and can be used as an indication of when to apply pre-emergence weed control.

Glyphosate: The main chemical ingredient of the popular herbicide "Round-Up."

Grass Blend: Several cultivars of the same grass species sold together in a single bag. An example would be a single bag containing several named cultivars of Tall Fescue.

Grass Mixture: Several different grass species sold together in a single bag. An example would be a single bag containing Kentucky Bluegrass, Perennial Ryegrass, and Creeping Red Fescue.

Grassy Weed: In general, a weed that looks similar to a lawn grass in that it has narrow grass blades.

Ground Cover: Lawn grasses are often replaced with ground covers in areas with dense shade or shallow roots. Some popular and proven ground covers for the South include Mondo Grass (*Ophiopogon japonicus*), English Ivy  (*Hedera Helix*), Periwinkle (*Vinca minor*), and Pachysandra (*Pachysandra terminalis*).

Hard Freeze: Temperatures below 28–32 degrees Fahrenheit that last for many hours.

Herbicide: A substance used to kill weeds or other plants.

Humus: Decomposed plant material which is useful in improving soils. Sphagnum peat moss is a type of humus commonly available.

Insect Pest: Any type of insect that inhabits a lawn in populations large enough to directly or indirectly cause damage.

Iron Chlorosis: A yellowing of plant leaves caused by an underproduction of chlorophyll due to deficient levels of iron in the soil; often caused indirectly by high soil pH levels.

Irrigation: To artificially supply water to a lawn so that soil moisture levels remain at approximately 25% of the total soil volume.

Lime: A substance derived from calcium carbonate that is used to raise soil pH. Most commonly used to neutralize acid soils.

Lower South: The areas of the South that include the Coastal Plain from Virginia south to Georgia and west through Alabama to Texas.

Meristem: A type of plant tissue that contains actively dividing cells. Meristems are the regions of plant growth and are located at the base of a grass plant as opposed to the outer extremities of shrubs and trees.

Metabolic Activity: The chemical and physical processes occurring within a living plant.

Metal-Tined Rake: A rake with metal tines. This may be a leaf rake which has flexible metal tines, or a garden rake which has rigid metal tines.

Middle South: The areas of the South that include the Piedmont regions extending south from Virginia to Georgia and west through Alabama to Texas.

Mowing Pattern: An alternating pattern visible in a lawn caused by mowing consistently in one direction one week, and mowing consistently in a perpendicular direction  the following week. Diamond patterns are created the same way except the second week's mowing is at a 45-degree angle rather than a perpendicular direction. Mowing patterns are most easily created when using a reel mower.

N-P-K Ratio: The three-number sequence on all fertilizer products that describes the percentages of nitrogen (N), phosphorus (P), and potassium (K) contained in the bag. Percentages are determined using the bag's net weight.

Overseed: To sow a temporary cool-season grass into a permanent warm-season grass lawn during the fall. The temporary grass will sprout and provide a green cover over the dormant brown warm-season grass during the winter months. Subsequently, the temporary, overseeded grass dies during hot weather in late spring, allowing the warm-season grass to recover completely.

Pan Evaporation Rate: The amount of water that evaporates from an open pan of water, usually measured in shade.

Peat Moss: Decomposed sphagnum mosses that are usually found in bogs. It is the stage before complete decomposition into muck. Peat moss is usually sold in dry, compacted bales.

pH: see Soil pH.

Plug: A small piece of grass sod usually 4 inches in diameter. Plugs are planted at intervals so that grass can grow into the bare soil.

Poor Drainage: A soil condition in which water occupies the majority of soil pore space for an extended period of time and excludes needed oxygen from the root zone.

Post-Emergence Weed Control: A herbicide designed to kill weeds once they have sprouted and they are growing in a lawn. These herbicides usually kill either grassy weeds or broadleaf weeds. They are most commonly sold as a liquid spray.

Pre-Emergence Weed Control: A herbicide designed to kill weeds as they germinate in a lawn. These herbicides are usually applied in a dry, granular form.

Quick-Release Fertilizer: Fertilizer that becomes available to plants soon after it is applied. It usually lasts 4–6 weeks, depending on environmental conditions.

Reel Mower: A lawn mower with a set of blades that rotates around an axle set between two wheels. The grass is cut with a scissor action as the grass is caught between a rotating blade and a stationary bar.

Reseed: To sow additional seed of the same species or cultivar into an existing lawn to thicken the grass stand.

Rhizome: A modified stem that grows horizontally on, or just below, the soil surface and sends up stems or leaves from the tip.

Rotary Mower: A lawn mower in which a blade rotates in a plane parallel to the soil surface. The grass is cut as the mowing blade slashes the grass leaves at a high speed.  Rotary mowers are further categorized as "riding mowers" or "push mowers" depending on whether you ride or walk behind the machine.

To adjust the blade height on your rotary mower, first move it to a flat surface like your driveway and turn it off. Next, cut a piece of stiff cardboard to the desired mowing height (1.5 inches, for instance). Sit on the driveway and rotate the mower blade with your hand so that it is easily visible through the vent in the mower deck. Slide the piece of cardboard under the blade so it measures the height from the driveway to the blade. Then, lower the blade until it is resting gently on the top of the cardboard. With a riding mower, you will probably need someone to sit on the mower to lower the blade for you. With a push mower, make sure the height of the blade is the same in the front of the mowing deck as in the rear.

Rototiller: A machine used for cultivating that has a set of blades or tines that rotate perpendicular to the soil surface.  On a "front-tine" rototiller, the blades are situated under the engine. On a "rear-tine" rototiller, the blades are located behind the tires and away from the engine. Rear-tine rototillers are easier to operate and cultivate to deeper depths.

Scalp: To mow below the recommended height. Or, to wait so long to mow that you remove a majority of the green grass blades.

Seed Label: A label attached or printed on a bag of grass seed that describes the percentages of seed contained in the bag, the origin of the seed, the net weight of the bag, the germination test date, and the percentage of seed expected to germinate.

Slow-Release Fertilizer: Fertilizer that is specifically formulated to become available to grass plants slowly over an extended period of time.

Sod: A piece of turf that includes grass plants, roots, and soil matted together into one solid block. Sod blocks are sold individually at a nursery or on a pallet delivered to your house.

Soil Insecticide: An insecticide broadcast on a lawn or soil that kills insects near or below the soil surface; often sold in granular form.

Soil pH: A measurement of the relative concentration of hydrogen ions in a soil. The pH scale runs from 0–14 with 7 being neutral. Soil pH below 7 is acidic while soil pH above 7 is alkaline. The concentration of hydrogen ions in the soil is directly linked to the availability and toxicity of chemical elements used by plants.

Soil Temperature: The temperature of the soil, usually measured at approximately 4 inches deep. Soil temperatures are usually averaged over a 24-hour period and referred to as a single number.

Soil Thermometer: A thermometer with a metal probe that is used to measure the temperature of the soil. A meat thermometer that has temperature readings can be substituted for a specialized soil thermometer to achieve the same results.

Soluble Fertilizer: Fertilizer that easily dissolves in water and is quickly available to grass plants.

Spiking: An alternative method to aerate a lawn in which solid spikes are pressed into the soil. The surrounding soil is compacted as the spike penetrates the root zone. Spiking does not remove cores of soil and is less effective than core aerating.

Sprigging: A method of planting a new lawn in which you plant single grass plants at set intervals so that the grass can grow into the bare soil.

Sprinkler: A device that distributes water in a distinct pattern. Sprinklers are designed and sold according to the pattern of water they distribute. Of all the different types

of sprinklers, impulse sprinklers are the most consistent in distributing the same amount of water over a large area.

Stolon: A shoot that grows horizontally near the soil surface, rooting at the nodes to form new plants.

Street Blower: A gas-powered machine used for blowing leaves and other debris. It has wheels and is pushed by hand.

String Trimmer: A machine that cuts grass and weeds with a high-speed rotating plastic string.

Syringing: A technique used to alleviate hot temperatures on golf greens by misting them with water. It is often the only way to grow cool-season grasses like Creeping Bentgrass in regions where the grass would normally not survive.

Thatch: A collection of dead plant parts like stems and grass clippings that collect on the soil surface. Thatch is not a problem unless it accumulates to a depth of more than .5 inches.

Topdressing: A thin layer of soil or sand distributed across the grass surface. Topdressing is applied to smooth the playing surface of golf greens, not to modify soil or correct lawn growth problems.

Transition Zone: An alternative term used to describe the area of the upper South where some species of northern evergreen grasses can be grown in addition to the normal palette of Southern lawn grasses.

Upper South: The area of the South that includes the western Piedmont and mountain regions from Virginia and North Carolina west through northern Tennessee and Arkansas.

Vertical Mower: A machine with numerous blades that rotate vertically, not horizontally like a lawn mower. The blades cut into the soil surface, severing  roots, rhizomes, and stolons while churning debris to the surface. Vertical mowers are often used to remove thatch. They are also known as dethatchers.

Warm-Season Grass: Lawn grasses that turn brown with frosts and hard freezes in fall. They are dormant through the winter and start new growth in the spring.

INDEX